BREAKTHROUGH
SPANISH 1

FOURTH EDITION

ndra María Truscott
ordinator, The Languagewise Programme,
versity of Manchester

.h

osé Escribano

rian Hill
neral Editor
ad of the School of Languages
niversity of Brighton

2008

}

09

palgrave
macmillan

First published 1982 by Pan Books Ltd
First Palgrave Macmillan edition published 1988
Reprinted five times
Second edition published 1992
Reprinted five times
Third edition 1996
Reprinted seven times
Fourth edition 2003

Published by
PALGRAVE MACMILLAN
Houndmills, Basingstoke, Hampshire RG21 6XS and 175 Fifth Avenue, New York, N.Y. 10010
Companies and representatives throughout the world

PALGRAVE MACMILLAN is the global academic imprint of the Palgrave Macmillan division of St. Martin's Press, LLC and of Palgrave Macmillan Ltd. Macmillan® is a registered trademark in the United States, United Kingdom and other contries. Palgrave is a registered trademark in the European Union and other countries.

ISBN 1–4039–1559–8 book
ISBN 0–4039–1558–X book and cassette pack
ISBN 0–4039–1560–1 cassettes
ISBN 1–4039–1562–8 CDs

A catalogue record for this book is available from the British Library.

Audio producer for location recordings: Gerald Ramshaw, Max II
Audio producer for studio recordings for the first to third editions: Lynne Brackley, Prolingua
Audio producer for studio recordings for the fourth edition: Brian Hill
Actors: Eliud Porras, Marisa Julián, Carlos Fernández, Maika Gil, Rosa Hernández, Janette Grabham, Angel García Rodríguez, Jesús Colom Bataller, Roberto Martin Arrabal, Diana Bejarano Coca.

Design and typesetting design@djhunter

10	9	8	7	6	5	4	3	2	1
12	11	10	09	08	07	06	05	04	03

Printed in China

Acknowledgements

The author would like to thank the following people: the Guitián family for their support and help in recording the location dialogues, Harriet Truscott, and all those in Spain and in England who have contributed to the book in any way.

The following illustration sources are acknowledged: Frances Arnold p. 183; AVE p. 86; Pili Batley-Matías pp. 69, 87 top; Helen Beasley pp. 178, 181, 190, 193; Helen Bugler p. 124; Camera Press p. 199; J. Allan Cash Ltd pp. 1, 39, 91, 118, 123, 141, 171 foot, 185, 186, 203, 205; El Corté Inglés pp. 84, 116; D&J Hunter pp. 164, 202, 222; Popperfoto p. 171 top; RENFE pp. 80, 88; Daniel Rodriguez San José p. 165; Pilar San José Villacorta p. 204; Telefónica de España p. 88; Sandra Truscott pp. i, 3, 5, 12, 17, 31, 32, 34, 35, 36, 50, 53, 56, 59, 64, 65, 70, 75, 76, 77, 87 foot, 93, 95, 104, 105,109, 111, 113, 125, 126, 129, 131, 135, 136, 146, 153, 157, 159, 162, 166, 169, 170, 172, 173, 174, 195 top, 201, 206, 208, 229, 230; Sue Tyson-Ward p. 219; Robin Vowles p. 195 foot; Zefa pp. 29, 167.

Every effort has been made to trace all copyright holders, but if any have been inadvertently overlooked the publishers will be pleased to make the necessary arrangements at the first opportunity.

Contents

HOW TO USE THIS COURSE

Since the Breakthrough series was introduced in 1982, several million people world-wide have used the courses to learn a variety of languages. This is a completely revised edition: there are new recordings, new activities and new ways of presenting the material. We have talked to hundreds of learners about their 'Breakthrough' experiences and we have acted on what we were told to ensure the new course is even more enjoyable and useful.

Following this course will help you understand, speak and read most of the Spanish you are likely to need on holiday or on business trips. The course is based on recordings made in Spain of ordinary Spanish people in everyday situations. Step by step you will learn first to understand what they are saying and then to speak in similar situations yourself.

General hints to help you use the course

- Have confidence in us! Real language is complex and you will find certain things in every unit which are not explained in detail. Don't worry about this. We will build up your knowledge slowly, selecting only what is most important at each stage.

- Try to study regularly, but in short periods: 20–30 minutes each day is usually better than $3\frac{1}{2}$ hours once a week.

- To help you learn to speak, say the words and phrases out loud whenever possible.

- If you don't understand something, leave it for a while. Learning a language is a bit like doing a jigsaw or a crossword: there are many ways to tackle it and it all falls into place eventually.

- Don't be afraid to write in the book and add your own notes.

- Do review your work frequently. It helps to get somebody to test you – and they don't need to know Spanish.

- If you can possibly learn with somebody else you will be able to help each other and practise the language together.

- Learning Spanish may take more time than you thought. Just be patient and above all don't get angry with yourself.

Suggested study pattern

Each unit of the course consists of approximately sixteen pages in the book and fifteen minutes of recording. The first page of each unit will tell you what you are going to learn and will give some hints on language learning. You should follow the material at first in the order in which it is presented. As you progress with the course you may find that you evolve a method of study which suits you better – that's fine, but we suggest you keep to our pattern at least for the first two or three units or you may find you are not taking full advantage of all the possibilities offered by the material.

The book contains step-by-step instructions for working through the course: when to use the book on its own, when to use the recording on its own, when to use them both together and how to use them. On the recording our presenters will guide you through the various sections. Here is an outline of the pattern proposed:

Pronunciation notes

At the start of each unit there are some tips on pronunciation. One or two points are explained in the book, which are then picked up and practised on the recording. Remember that while good pronunciation of a foreign language is desirable, you will usually still be understood even if your accent is not quite accurate.

Conversations

Listen to each conversation, first without stopping the recording, and get a feel for the task ahead. Then go over it bit by bit in conjunction with the vocabulary and the notes. You should get into the habit of using the pause/stop and rewind buttons on your machine to give yourself time to think and to go over the conversation a number of times. Don't leave a conversation until you are confident that you have at least understood it. (The symbol ♫ means listen to the recording.) There are usually two or three conversations in each section, and three sets of conversations in a unit.

Practice

This section contains a selection of listening, reading and speaking activities which focus your attention on the most important language in the unit. To do them you will need to work closely with the book and often use your machine – sometimes you are asked to write the answers to an exercise and then check them on the recording, at others to listen first and then fill in answers in the book. Again, use your pause/stop and rewind buttons to give yourself time to think and to answer questions.

You will also find practice exercises for speaking the main words and phrases which you have already heard and had explained. The book gives only an outline of the exercises, so you are just listening to the recordings and responding. Usually you will be asked to take part in a conversation where you hear a question or statement in Spanish, followed by a suggestion in English as to what to say. You then give your reply in Spanish and listen to see if you were right. You will probably have to go over these spoken exercises a few times before you get them absolutely correct.

Grammar

At this stage in a unit things should begin to fall into place and you are ready for the Grammar section. If you really don't like grammar, you will still learn a lot without studying this part, but most people quite enjoy finding out how the language they are using actually works and how it is put together. In each unit we have selected just one or two important things. At the end of the book is a straightforward summary of the main grammar points.

Key words and phrases

This is a list of the most important words and phrases used in the unit. Pause at this section to see how much you can remember. Look first at the Spanish and find the English equivalent. Then try it the other way round, from English into Spanish. If you find there are some groups of words you have forgotten (don't worry – it happens to everybody!), turn back and have another look at the conversations and notes. These Key words and phrases are likely to crop up later in the course so it's worth getting to grips with them before you leave a unit.

Did you know?

In this section you will be given some practical background information on customs, culture and life in Spanish-speaking countries.

Answers

The answers to all the exercises can be found on the last page of each unit, if they have not already been given on the recording.

If you haven't learned languages using a recording before, just spend five minutes on Unit 1 getting used to the mechanics: try pausing the recording and see how long the rewind button needs to be pressed to recap on different length phrases and sections. Don't be shy – take every opportunity you can to speak Spanish to Spanish people and to listen to real Spanish. Try listening to Spanish broadcasts on the radio or watch satellite television. It's even a good idea to talk to yourself in Spanish as much as possible. Try describing what you see as you are travelling around, for instance. *¡Buena suerte!*　*Good luck!*

At the back of the book

At the back of the book is a reference section which contains:

1 MAKING NEW FRIENDS

WHAT YOU WILL LEARN

▶ Everyday courtesies
▶ How to ...
introduce yourself and others
say where you are from
say what job you do
say what languages you speak

BEFORE YOU BEGIN

The conversations you will hear in this course have mostly been recorded on location in Spain – that is, they are authentic and contain the sort of language you will hear and need to understand when travelling or working in Spanish-speaking countries. Obviously, the language has been kept simple and easy to follow in the early stages, but nevertheless there will be conversations you will find difficult when you listen to them for the first time. Persevere! Spanish as spoken in Spain is fast and you may need to listen to each conversation quite a few times. You will find that this will soon pay off and a few units into the course, you will be wondering why you found the first ones difficult.

Practise listening in different ways. Some learners listen to the conversations first, several times, and then look at the written version in the book. Others prefer to listen and read at the same time. Do whichever you find more effective for you personally – but remember that eventually you have to wean yourself off the written word. Make sure that you have read the 'How to use this course' section at the beginning of the book so you know how the course works and what is expected of you.

Pronunciation notes

Pronouncing Spanish vowels (**a**, **e**, **i**, **o** and **u**) is very simple. All the sounds are short and very open. The main error which English speakers make is to introduce a 'y' sound into the word – for example, pronouncing pa-e-ll-a as payella or ma-e-stro as maystro. Listen to Carlos giving examples of the vowel system on your recording.

hablo   es   día   hola   tú

▶ Saying hello

hola	hello
¿qué tal?	how are you?
¿qué hay?	how are things?/what's new?
buenos días	good morning, good day

Luis	Hola, ¿qué tal?
Eloisa	Hola, buenos días
Eme	Hola, ¿qué hay?
Pilar	Hola, buenos días

▶ **hola**   hello
▶ **¿qué tal?**   how are you, how are things?
▶ **buenos días**   good day, good morning
▶ **¿qué hay?**   what's new?

¿Qué tal? and **¿qué hay?** are greetings used in informal situations; use **buenos días** and **buenas tardes** (good afternoon) in a more formal setting. **Buenas tardes** is used after lunch (which can start as late as 3.00 pm in Spain) and continues through to dinner (around 9.00 or 10.00 pm) so it can mean both 'good afternoon' and 'good evening'. **Buenas noches** (good night) is used very late at night, especially just before going to bed. By the way, Spanish questions are always preceded by an upside down question mark. An inverted exclamation mark indicates that an exclamation is coming up.

▶ Introducing yourself

soy	I am

Carlos	Hola, buenos días, soy Carlos
Marisa	Hola, buenas tardes, soy Marisa

Soy means 'I am' (literally, just 'am'). Use it for introducing yourself. **Soy Marcus** I am Marcus. There is a separate word for I (**yo**) but you don't need to use it except for emphasis or contrast. There's more about this on page 12 in the grammar section.

▶ *Introducing other people*

LISTEN FOR...

éste es Pepe	this is Pepe
encantado	delighted

Luisa	Hola, Pepe, ¿qué tal? Pedro, éste es Pepe; Pepe, Pedro
Pedro	Hola, ¿qué tal?
Pepe	Muy bien. Encantado

▶ **éste** this person, this one
▶ **es** is
▶ **muy** very
▶ **bien** well
▶ **encantado** delighted

Pedro, éste es Pepe Pedro, this is Pepe. Use this formula for introducing one person to another. Then you only need to reverse the names the second time around: Pepe, Pedro. If you're introducing a woman you need to say **ésta: ésta es Marta** this is Marta.

Encantado means 'delighted'. If you are a woman, you will need to change the ending to **encantada**. You'll find out more about this on page 12.

1 How often are the words or phrases below used? Listen to the recording and place a cross next to each phrase each time you hear it. You'll have to rewind and listen a number of times.

ANSWERS P. 16

hola	☐
¿qué tal?	☐
¿qué hay?	☐
buenos días	☐
buenas noches	☐
buenas tardes	☐
soy	☐
encantado	☐
encantada	☐

Teresa José

Juan

2 Look at the drawing above, in which different people are being introduced. Write in the conversation in the space provided.

Juan Sánchez: Teresa, _____ es José; José, _____

Teresa Gómez: _____

José Pérez: _____

Listen to the recording for the correct version.

3 Now you try. You're at a cocktail party, being introduced to a number of different people. Eliud will prompt you with your replies.

4   Making new friends *Unit* 1

◗ Where are you from?

LISTEN FOR...	
¿eres de Santiago?	are you from Santiago?
soy de Santiago	I am from Santiago
eres gallega	you are from Galicia

María	¿Eres de Santiago?
Dependienta	
(shop-assistant)	Sí, soy de Santiago
María	O sea, que eres gallega
Dependienta	Sí

▶ **eres** you are
▶ **sí** yes
▶ **o sea** that is to say
▶ **que** that

¿Eres de Santiago? Are you from Santiago? **De** means 'of' or 'from'.
Use **eres** to mean 'you are' or, in a question, 'are you?' Each has a different sound
pattern. Listen out for it on the recording.
que eres gallega that you are from Galicia (Galicia is an area in north-west
Spain). If María had been talking to a man, she would have said **gallego**. Use
the **-o** ending for men and the **-a** ending for women when describing them. **Soy
gallego** I am from Galicia.

◗ Ángeles and Juan tell us where they are from

LISTEN FOR...	
¿y tú?	and you?
y usted, ¿de dónde es?	and you, where are you from?

Pepe	Y tú, ¿de dónde eres?
Ángeles	De Sevilla
Pepe	Y usted, ¿de dónde es?
Juan	De Corella, provincia de Navarra

▶ **y** and
▶ **tú** you (informal)
▶ **¿dónde?** where?

▶ **usted**   you (formal)

▶ **(la) provincia**   province

Y tú, ¿de dónde eres?   And you, where are you from? You may have noticed earlier that Spanish doesn't always use the word for 'you' because it is contained in the verb **eres** you are. But it is used sometimes if you wish to compare that person with another, as in this conversation.

Y usted, ¿de dónde es?   And you, where are you from? There are two new things to note here. **Usted** also means 'you' and is used in formal situations only. Use **tú** for friends, children and animals. However, you will find that more and more people are opting for **tú**, where a few years ago they would have used **usted**. It is best to stick to '**usted**' with people you don't know. In this conversation, Pepe uses **tú** to the girl and **usted** to her father. In writing, **usted** is usually abbreviated to **Vd.** or **Ud.**

(La) provincia de Navarra. In Spanish, all nouns or names of things are divided into two categories, masculine or feminine. **La** is the feminine form of 'the'. **El** is the masculine form: **el vino** the wine. Each noun will be preceded by **el** or **la** in your vocabulary lists, so that you know whether it is masculine or feminine. See the Grammar section on page 13.

Beatriz says she's from Manchester

LISTEN FOR...

¿es usted inglesa?   are you English?

Enrique	¿Es usted inglesa?
Beatriz	Sí, soy de Manchester

inglés/inglesa   English

¿Es usted inglesa?   Are you English. If Enrique had been speaking to a man, he would have said **¿Es usted inglés?** You may also need to know: **norteamericano/norteamericana** (American), **galés/galesa** (Welsh), **irlandés/irlandesa** (Irish), **escocés/escocesa** (Scottish), **español/española** (Spanish), **francés/francesa** (French), **alemán/alemana** (German) and **canadiense** (Canadian), which doesn't change: **soy canadiense, de Ottawa.**

PRACTICE

4 Try linking up the words in each column to make new phrases.

i.   y tú   a. Zamora

ii. y usted   b. provincia de Navarra

iii. de Corella   c. de Santiago

iv. de Sevilla   d. ¿de dónde eres?

v.   eres   e. en Andalucía

vi. soy de   f. ¿de dónde es?

5 Now listen to a short conversation which is similar to those you've heard earlier.
Then answer the following questions in English:

a.   What question does María ask?

b.   Where is the woman *not* from?

ANSWERS P. 16

6 On the recording you'll hear six people telling you where they are from. Insert the information they give you below. You may have to listen to the recording more than once.

i.   _____ Miguel. _____

ii. _____ Laura. _____

iii. _____ John. _____

iv. _____ Isabel. _____

v.   _____ Roger. _____

vi. _____ Sandra. _____

Now replay the recording and check that you have the correct replies. The written version is on p. 16.

Unit 1   Making new friends
7

Giving personal information to a hotel receptionist

LISTEN FOR...

su nombre	your name
por favor	please
¿cómo se escribe?	how is it written?
nacionalidad	nationality
muchas gracias	thank you very much

Recepcionista	Buenos días, su nombre, ¿cuál es por favor?
María	María Sandra Truscott
Recepcionista	Sería tan amable – ¿cómo se escribe?
María	T R U S C O T T
Recepcionista	¿Señora o señorita?
María	Señora
Recepcionista	¿Nacionalidad?
María	Británica
Recepcionista	Muchas gracias

HOTEL
NUEVO CHINCHON
RESTAURANTE - CAFETERIA
PISCINA - PUB
ABIERTO TODO EL AÑO
Urbanización
NUEVO CHINCHON
TELF. 893 51 28 · 894 05 44 · 893 50 58
28370 CHINCHON (MADRID)

▶ **(el/la) recepcionista**   receptionist
▶ **(el) nombre**   name
▶ **por favor**   please
▶ **(la) señora**   Mrs
▶ **(la) señorita**   Miss
Note also ▶ **(el) señor**   Mr
▶ **(la) nacionalidad**   nationality
▶ **británico/a**   British
▶ **muchas gracias**   thank you very much
Note also ▶ **gracias**   thank you

Recepcionista   receptionist. This is not necessarily a woman! Some professions end in **a** for both the masculine and feminine forms. **Dentista** is another example.

¿Nacionalidad? Británica.
Nationality? British. Earlier you saw how word endings need to change to agree with the person speaking (**inglés, inglesa**) and that each Spanish noun is either feminine or masculine. Words which describe the noun (adjectives) must also be masculine or feminine. María did not say **británica** because she is a woman, but because the word which describes **(la) nacionalidad** must also be feminine.

María asks Ana if she is a student or if she has a job

LISTEN FOR...

¿eres estudiante?	are you a student?
¿trabajas?	do you work?

María	¿Eres estudiante?
Ana	No
María	¿Trabajas?
Ana	Sí

¿Eres estudiante? Are you a student?
When you are talking about professions,
you don't need to say *a* student or *a*
doctor – simply say the equivalent of 'I am student' or 'I am doctor'. **Estudiante** has
the same form for both masculine and feminine.
¿Trabajas? Do you work? This is from the verb **trabajar** to work. Notice the
ending when you use the **tú** form.

 María asks Reme if she is a lawyer

LISTEN FOR...

es usted abogada, ¿no?	you're a lawyer, aren't you?
soy profesora	I'm a teacher
¿trabaja aquí?	do you work here?

María	Es usted abogada, ¿no?
Reme	No, soy profesora
María	Y¿ trabaja aquí en Santiago?
Reme	No, trabajo en Lugo

▶ **abogado/a** lawyer
▶ **profesor/a** teacher
▶ **aquí** here
▶ **en** in

Es usted abogada, ¿no? You're a lawyer, aren't you? This time, the formal **usted**
is used. As you would expect, a male lawyer is an **abogado**.
Soy profesora I am a teacher. The masculine form is **profesor**.
Other jobs and professions that you will be learning are: **camarero/a** waiter,
peluquero/a hairdresser and **azafata** air hostess.

¿Trabaja aquí en Santiago? Do you work here in Santiago? Again, the verb **trabajar** to work. Notice the **-a** ending when you use it with '**usted**'.
Trabajo en Lugo I work in Lugo. **Trabajar** now ends in **-o**, to go with 'I'.

María asks Pilar if she speaks the language of Galicia

LISTEN FOR...

¿hablas gallego?	do you speak the language of Galicia?
¿hablas castellano?	do you speak Spanish?
son mis dos lenguas	they are my two languages

María	¿Hablas gallego?
Pilar	Un poco, pero normalmente hablo en castellano
María	Y ¿hablas inglés?
Pilar	Muy poquito
María	¿Hablas francés?
Pilar	No
María	O sea, que hablas gallego y castellano
Pilar	Gallego y castellano ... son mis dos lenguas

▶ **(el) gallego**   the language of Galicia (in north-west Spain)
▶ **un poco**   a bit
▶ **pero**   but
▶ **normalmente**   normally
▶ **muy**   very
▶ **(un) poquito**   a little bit
▶ **(la) lengua**   language

¿Hablas gallego/inglés?   Do you speak the language of Galicia/English? Note the **-as** ending again to indicate that the informal **tú** form is being used.
Un poco   a little. **Un** means 'a' for masculine words. Use **una** for feminine ones: **una provincia** a province.
Hablo en castellano   I speak (in) Spanish. Note the **-o** ending again for 'I'. Both '**castellano**' (Castilian) and '**español**' (Spanish) are used for the Spanish language.
Mis dos lenguas.   My two languages. To form the plural in Spanish, add **s** to the end of the word or **es** if it ends in a consonant.
Gallego y castellano son mis dos lenguas.   The language of Galicia and Spanish are my two languages. You'll also hear the word **el idioma** for language. This word is masculine despite its ending (words ending in **-a** are usually feminine). **Lengua** follows the usual pattern and is feminine.
Note the word for 'are': **son**.

7

ANSWERS P. 16

Suzanne, Marcus and Elena are checking into a hotel. Fill in each form with their details in Spanish.

Suzanne Touvier – French, lawyer, lives in Paris

Marcus Jones – American, dentist, lives in New (Nueva) York

Elena Vázquez – Spanish, student, lives in Barcelona

Nombre _____
Nacionalidad _____
Profesión _____
Residencia _____

Nombre _____
Nacionalidad _____
Profesión _____
Residencia _____

Nombre _____
Nacionalidad _____
Profesión _____
Residencia _____

8

Link up the details with the correct person.

i. Jean-Paul   a. es francesa, es recepcionista

ii. Carmen   b. es alemana, es abogada

iii. Sean   c. es francés, es peluquero

iv. Ulrika   d. es dentista, es español

v. José   e. es azafata, es española

ANSWERS P. 16   vi. Marianne   f. es irlandés, es camarero

9

Now switch on and you will be asked what languages *you* speak.
Use full sentences including **hablo** I speak, or **no hablo** I don't speak.

GRAMMAR AND EXERCISES

The verb *ser* to be

So far in Unit 1, you have been introduced to the following parts:

singular	
(yo) soy	I am
(tú) eres	you are (informal)
(él) es	he is
(ella) es	she is
(usted) es	you are (formal)

In subsequent chapters you will be meeting the plural forms too.

plural	
(nosotros) somos	we are
(vosotros) sois	you are
(ellos) son	they are (masculine)
(ellas) son	they are (feminine)
(ustedes) son	you are (formal)

Spanish verbs fall into three main categories, recognizable by their endings: **-ar**, **-er** and **-ir**. (The full form is called the infinitive and is equivalent in English to 'to speak', 'to work' and so on.) Opposite is the full form for all Spanish verbs ending in **-ar**.

Hablar to speak

(yo) hablo	I speak
(tú) hablas	you speak (informal)
(él) habla	he speaks
(ella) habla	she speaks
(usted) habla	you speak (formal)
(nosotros) hablamos	we speak
(vosotros) habláis	you speak (informal plural)
(ellos) hablan	they speak (masculine plural)
(ellas) hablan	they speak (feminine plural)
(ustedes) hablan	you speak (formal plural)

Gender (Masculine/feminine)

In Spanish, nouns are divided into two categories which are called masculine and feminine. (A noun is the name of a person or thing: Juan, hotel.) Words which describe abstract ideas like profession or nationality are also nouns.

- The endings of words sometimes tell us which word is masculine and which is feminine. Masculine words often end in **-o** and feminine words in **-a**: **vino** (wine) is masculine and **paella** feminine. Other common feminine endings are **-dad** and **-ión**: **la ciudad** (city), **la nacionalidad**, **la profesión**.
- With some nouns (e.g. the names of professions) you can make the masculine form feminine, either by changing the final **-o** to an **-a**, or adding an **-a** if the word ends in a consonant:

abogado,	abogada
profesor,	profesora

If the profession ends in **-e** or **-ista**, do nothing – a single word covers both: **estudiante**, **dentista**.

- If the noun is masculine, the word for 'the' which accompanies it is **el**. If it's feminine, the word for 'the' is **la**:

el vino	the wine
la paella	the paella

Plurals

- To make nouns plural (more than one), add **s** if the noun ends in a vowel (a, e, i, o, u): **señora**, **señoras**; **estudiante**, **estudiantes**.
- If the word ends in a consonant (all the other letters) add **es**: **señor**, **señores**.
- If the word is masculine and plural, use **los** for 'the'; if it's feminine, use **las**:

los señores	the gentlemen/men
las señoras	the ladies/women

Adjectives

Adjectives are words which describe nouns (big, green, bouncy). In Spanish they have to agree with the noun they describe – that is, if the noun is singular and masculine the adjective must be too. If it's feminine and plural, so is the adjective.

las lenguas extranjeras	foreign languages
el señor norteamericano	the American man

- Masculine adjectives ending in **-o** change their ending to **-a** in the feminine:
  americano, **americana**
  s is added to make the adjective plural:
  americanos, **americanas**

Adjectives of nationality with other endings (like **escocés**) also add an **a** (**escocesa**) for the feminine form, **es** for the masculine plural form (**escoceses**) and **as** for the feminine plural (**escocesas**).

Most adjectives ending in a consonant or **-e** don't have a separate feminine form. Add **-es** or **-s** to form the plural:
verde (green), **verdes**.

10 Can you work out whether these words are masculine or feminine?
Write in the appropriate word for 'the' in each case:
a. ⎯ historia
b. ⎯ economía
c. ⎯ mundo (world)
d. ⎯ canción (song)
e. ⎯ diccionario
f. ⎯ pueblo (people, town)
g. ⎯ libro (book)

ANSWERS P. 16

11 Write in the correct form of **ser**, to be, in this short conversation.
Yo ⎯ Carmen y tú ⎯ Marta, ¿no?
Sí, ⎯ Marta Blasco ⎯ de Ecuador. Y éste ⎯ Tomás.
Él ⎯ de Bolivia.
¡Ah! ¿⎯ americanos?
Sí, ⎯ latinoamericanos.

ANSWERS P. 16

12 Now you know **hablar**, to speak, you also know the forms for **trabajar** (to work), **estudiar** (to study), **contestar** (to reply), etc. Complete this extract from a letter with the correct part of the verb:

New vocabulary
la pregunta question

Yo soy Marta Herranz y soy estudiante. (Estudiar) en Londres. (Hablar) inglés, español y francés. ¿Y tú? ¿(estudiar) o (trabajar)? ¿Qué lenguas (hablar)? ¡Muchas preguntas!, ¿no?

ANSWERS P. 16

KEY WORDS
AND PHRASES

hola	hello
¿Qué hay?/¿qué tal?	How are things?/what's new?
muy bien	fine, very good
buenos días	good day, good morning
buenas tardes	good afternoon, good evening
buenas noches	good night
Soy gallego/gallega	I am from Galicia
Soy norteamericano/norteamericana	I am American
Soy inglés/inglesa	I am English
Soy galés/galesa	I am Welsh
Soy escocés/escocesa	I am Scottish
Soy español/española	I am Spanish
Soy francés/francesa	I am French
Soy canadiense	I am Canadian (m. or f.)
Eres de Manchester	You are from Manchester
¿Eres de Santiago?	Are you from Santiago?
¿De dónde eres?	Where are you from? (informal)
Usted, ¿de dónde es?	Where are you from? (formal)
sí	yes
no	no
y	and
¿dónde?	where?
de	of, from
Éste es Pepe	This is Pepe
Ésta es Marta	This is Martha
encantado/encantada	delighted
(el) señor	Mr
(la) señora	Mrs
(la) señorita	Miss
(el) nombre	name
(la) nacionalidad	nationality
soy abogado/a	I am a lawyer
profesor/a	teacher
estudiante	student (m. or f.)
camarero/a	waiter/waitress
azafata	air hostess (f.)
dentista	dentist (m. or f.)
¿Eres (recepcionista)?	Are you a (receptionist)? (informal)
¿Es usted (secretaria)?	Are you a (secretary)? (formal)
Hablo inglés	I speak English
francés	French
castellano/español	Spanish
¿Hablas otros idiomas?	Do you speak other languages? (informal)
¿Habla usted gallego?	Do you speak the language of Galicia? (formal)
Trabajo en Manchester	I work in Manchester
¿Trabajas en Chester?	Do you work in Chester? (informal)
¿Trabaja usted en Salford?	Do you work in Salford? (formal)
Estudio en Madrid	I study in Madrid
¿Estudias en Santiago?	Do you study in Santiago? (informal)
¿Estudia usted en Santiago?	Do you study in Santiago? (formal)

The languages of Spain

SPAIN has four languages: Castilian (the language you are now learning), Basque, Catalan and the language of Galicia (**gallego**). These are all separate languages and not simply dialects. Forty per cent of Spaniards are bilingual in Spanish and another local language.

Castilian

Castilian (or Spanish) is the first language of nearly 300 million people and is spoken in over twenty countries. Besides Spain and Latin America, Spanish is also spoken in the Philippines, Morocco and the United States. Castilian is the form of Spanish originally spoken in Old Castille (hence its name), which became the standard language of the Castilian and later Spanish state. Spanish is derived from spoken Latin, like French, Italian, Catalan and the language of Galicia. Arabic has also been an enormous influence on the language as the Arabs occupied Spain for seven hundred years. Words like *alcohol* and *algebra* have Arab roots as do the names of many places you will recognize if you have visited Spain (Albacete, Guadarrama, Gibraltar, Medina and Benidorm). Because Spanish is so widely spoken, you're bound to hear many different accents when travelling through the Spanish-speaking world. Most foreigners find Northern accents easiest to follow, but the Andalusian accent is important too, because it is so similar to Latin American Spanish. This course includes a number of different accents to help you understand most native Spanish speakers.

Catalan

Catalan is spoken by about 9 million people living in Catalonia, Andorra, the Pyrénées Orientales in France, some parts of Aragón, Valencia, the Balearic Islands and the city of Alghieri in Sardinia. To place this in an international perspective, Catalan has more speakers than either Norwegian or Danish. Don't make the mistake of saying that Catalan is a variant of Spanish – Catalan speakers will be rightly angry. Their language is very precious to them as, throughout their history, other Spaniards have attempted to destroy it. All attempts have however failed, and Catalan is a healthy and buoyant language spoken by representatives of all social classes.

Basque

Basque is the only language in Spain which is not derived from Latin. Indeed, no one is quite sure from where it emerged, although current thinking is that it was the original language of the Iberian peninsula. It has no affinity with other European languages and is therefore very difficult: there is a legend which says that the Devil spent seven years trying to learn Basque and only managed to say yes and no. When he discovered that he had got these words the wrong way round, he gave up in disgust!

The language of Galicia

(known as '**gallego**') is the language of the north-west corner of Spain, bordering on Portugal. The language itself closely resembles Portuguese and is understood by almost all the two and three-quarter million Galicians who live there. It is, however, spoken mainly by country people and until recently, therefore, has enjoyed little status either inside or outside Galicia. Much effort is now being applied to teaching the language and raising its cultural and economic status.

AND FINALLY...

13 Now you are going to practise speaking some of the language you have learned in the conversations. Try not to look at the book – unless you want to check a point.

You're in a park in Mallorca and a teenager and her friend want to interview you for a school project.

You'll be practising:

introductions
soy (inglés/inglesa, escocés/escocesa, dentista)
hablo
trabajo

ANSWERS

EXERCISE 1
hola 2, ¿qué tal? 2, ¿qué hay? 1, buenos días 2, buenas noches 2, buenas tardes 2, soy 2, encantado 1, encantada 1.

EXERCISE 4
i d **ii** f **iii** b **iv** e **v** c **vi** a

EXERCISE 5
(a) where does the woman come from? **(b)** she is not from Galicia

EXERCISE 6
i. Soy Miguel. Soy de Sevilla. **ii.** Soy Laura. Soy de Valencia
iii. Soy John. Soy canadiense **iv.** Soy Isabel. Soy española
v. Soy Roger. Soy francés **vi.** Soy Sandra. Soy inglesa.

EXERCISE 7
Suzanne Touvier, francesa, abogada, París. Marcus Jones, norteamericana, dentista, Nueva York. Elena Vázquez, española, estudiante, Barcelona.

EXERCISE 8
i c **ii** e **iii** f **iv** b **v** d **vi** a

EXERCISE 10
(a) la historia **(b)** la economía **(c)** el mundo **(d)** la canción
(e) el diccionario **(f)** el pueblo **(g)** el libro

EXERCISE 11
Yo soy Carmen y tú eres Marta, ¿no?
Sí, soy Marta Blasco. Soy de Ecuador. Y éste es Tomás. Él es de Bolivia.
¡Ah! ¿sois americanos?
Sí, somos latinoamericanos.

EXERCISE 12
Estudio/hablo/estudias/trabajas/hablas

WHAT YOU WILL LEARN

▶ How to ...
give and understand directions
talk about your family
say where places are
count to 29

BEFORE YOU BEGIN

At this stage it is a good idea for you to invest in a folder and to begin to make and organize your study notes. Spanish, in common with many other languages, is a language where the endings of words constantly change according to who is speaking and when. You need to keep track of these changes as you go along. The Grammar section will help sort this out for you, but the more you can work out patterns and structures yourself, the more likely those are to stick in your memory.

It is also very important for you to say everything out loud, not only in the spoken exercises, but in the written ones too. And don't just give a one-word answer – saying a whole phrase is another way of ensuring that you retain what you learn and that you know how to combine isolated words into real sentences.

Madrid Puerta de Atocha

Pronunciation notes

Double **ll** (and **y**) is pronounced in several ways. Many people make a sound like the English 'y' in yes: this is simple for an English speaker. Some Spanish speakers still use what is considered the correct form – a sound like 'dy', with the tongue flat upon the palate. Yet others make a sound like the English 'l+y'. You will hear all forms in this course.

paella llamar caballeros gallego yo

In two separate conversations, María asks two young people if they are married and whether they have a girlfriend/boyfriend

LISTEN FOR...

soltero	a bachelor
soltera	an unmarried woman
¿tienes novio?	do you have a boyfriend?
¿tienes novia?	do you have a girlfriend?

María	¿Eres soltera?
Young woman	Sí, soltera
María	Y ¿tienes novio?
Young woman	Sí
María	¿Eres soltero?
Young man	Sí
María	Y ¿tienes novia?
Young man	Sí

- ▶ **(la) soltera** unmarried woman
- ▶ **(el) novio** boyfriend
- ▶ **(el) soltero** unmarried man
- ▶ **(la) novia** girlfriend

¿Tienes novio/novia? Do you have a boy/girlfriend? Here you have a new verb **tener**, meaning 'to have'. **Tienes** is the **tú** form.

María asks a young woman if she is married and whether she has any children

LISTEN FOR...

¿estás casada?	are you married?
¿tienes hijos?	do you have any children?
¿cuántos?	how many?

María	¿Estás casada?
Woman in the street	Sí
María	Y ¿tienes hijos?
Woman in the street	Sí
María	¿Cuántos?
Woman in the street	Dos
María	¿Hijos o hijas?
Woman in the street	Hijas

- ▶ **casado/a** married
- ▶ **(los) hijos** children, sons
- ▶ **(el) hijo** son
- ▶ **(la) hija** daughter

Note also ▶	▶

¿cuántos?   how many?
¿cuánto?   how much ?

¿Estás casada? In certain circumstances, you can use either the verb **estar**, also meaning 'to be', or the verb **ser. Estar casado/a** is one of these occasions. There is more about this on page 28.

¿Cuántos?   How many? María uses the plural here because she is asking how many children the woman has.

PRACTICE

1 It's St. Valentine's day (**el día de los enamorados**) and Carlos is out and about asking questions for a survey about marital status. Select the correct words from the list below to complete the gaps in the conversations.

Carlos: ¿Estás casado?

Juan: No, soy _____

Carlos: ¿_____ novia?

Juan: _____ , tengo novia.

Carlos: ¿_____ casada?

María: Sí, estoy _____

Carlos: ¿Tienes _____ ?

María: Sí.

Carlos: ¿_____ ?

María: Tengo uno.

¿cuántos? soltero sí casada hijos estás tienes

Now switch on the recording to check what you have written.

2 Fill in this grid with the opposite (that is, the masculine or feminine version) of each word. The first one has been done for you.

ANSWERS P. 32

M	F
señores	señoras
cuántos	_____
hijos	_____
_____	novia
casado	_____
_____	soltera

3 This time Carlos is asking you questions in the street. In this exercise, you're a woman, you're married and you have two sons. As in Unit 1, you will be prompted and then given the correct answer.

🔊 *María asks Reme how many pupils she has in her class*

LISTEN FOR...

alumnos	pupils
veintiuno	twenty-one
veintiséis	twenty-six
doce	twelve
catorce	fourteen

María	¿Cuántos alumnos tienes en tu clase, Reme?
Reme	En ésta tengo veintiuno
María	Y ¿en las otras?
Reme	En otra tengo veintiséis, en otra doce y en otra catorce

▶ **alumno/a**   pupil
▶ **(la) clase**   class
▶ **veintiuno**   twenty-one
▶ **doce**   twelve
▶ **catorce**   fourteen

en tu clase   in your class. María and Reme are now on familiar terms so María says **tu clase**, 'your class' (informal), rather than **su clase** (formal).

en ésta (clase)   in this one

Tengo veintiuno   I have twenty-one. (**Tengo** is the 'I' form of **tener** to have.)

en las otras (clases)   in the other ones. Notice how it's not necessary to keep repeating the word '**clase**'. (Remember that **las** is the feminine plural of 'the' and **los** the masculine plural: **los alumnos** the pupils.)

en otra (clase)   in another one

María asks Martiñu about his family

LISTEN FOR...

¿cómo te llamas?	what are you called?
es un nombre gallego	it is a name from Galicia
¿cuántos años tienes?	how old are you?
dieciséis	sixteen
¿cómo se llama?	what is she called?
hermanos	brothers and sisters

María	¿Cómo te llamas?
Martiñu	Martiñu
María	¿Martiñu? No es un nombre español, ¿verdad?
Martiñu	No, es un nombre gallego
María	Ah, y ¿cuántos años tienes, Martiñu?
Martiñu	Dieciséis
María	Dieciséis. Y ¿tienes hermanos?
Martiñu	Sí. Tengo una hermana mayor que yo
María	Y ¿cómo se llama?
Martiñu	Se llama Delia
María	Delia

▶ **(el) año**   year
▶ **(los) hermanos**   brothers and sisters
▶ **(la) hermana**   sister

Note also ▶   **(el) hermano**   brother

¿Cómo te llamas?   What are you called? (informal: literally, 'how yourself do you call?'). Reply by saying **me llamo** I am called.

No es un nombre español, ¿verdad?   It isn't a Spanish name, is it? Two new points here. Firstly, we meet **es** again, but this time meaning 'it is'. Remember it also means 'you are' (with **usted**) and 's/he is'. Also, **¿verdad?**, tagged on to a phrase means 'isn't it?', 'aren't you?', 'don't you?' etc., as appropriate.

¿Cuántos años tienes?   How old are you? (literally, 'how many years do you have?'). Notice again how **cuántos** has to agree with **años**: that is, it must have the masculine plural ending **-os** so that it matches **años**.

Tengo una hermana mayor que yo   I have a sister older than I (am).

¿Cómo se llama?   What is she called? (literally, 'how herself does she call?'). Martiñu replies by saying '**se llama ...**', she is called (literally, 'herself she calls ...'). If you say **¿Cómo se llama usted?** it means 'What are you called?': say this when you're addressing someone formally.

In this conversation, Jordi asks Marta, who's from Ecuador, where certain places are in Latin America

LISTEN FOR...

¿dónde está?	where is?
hacia el norte	towards the north
el sur	the south
la selva	the jungle
el este	the east
el oeste	the west

Jordi	¿Dónde está Quito?
Marta	Eh, Quito está hacia el norte del Ecuador
Jordi	¿Y Perú?
Marta	Eh, Perú está hacia el sur
Jordi	¿Y dónde está la selva?
Marta	Eh, la selva está hacia el este, cerca del Amazonas
Jordi	¿Y dónde están las islas Galápagos?
Marta	Las islas Galápagos están a unas seiscientas millas desde el oeste de la costa ecuatoriana

▶ **la selva**   the forest, the jungle
▶ **el Amazonas**   the Amazon
▶ **la isla**   the island
▶ **seiscientos/as**   six hundred
▶ **(la) milla**   mile
▶ **la costa**   the coast
▶ **ecuatoriano/a**   Ecuadorian, of or from Ecuador

¿Dónde está?   Where is? When talking about where things are, use the verb **estar** to be. (You've already come across this verb in the phrase **¿estás casada?**) Use the plural **están** for 'where are?' **¿Dónde están las islas Galápagos?** Where are the Galapagos islands?
hacia el norte   towards the north. Say **en** (**el norte**) to translate the English 'in' (the north). If the word you are using is masculine (like **norte**), use the masculine form for 'the' (**el**). If it's feminine (**selva**), use the feminine form (**la**).

A unas seiscientas millas desde el oeste de la costa ecuatoriana about 600 miles from the west of the Ecuador coast. **Desde ... hasta ...**   is a good pair to know. **Desde París hasta Londres** from Paris to London.

Now that you know the names of two Latin American countries, it's a good idea to learn some of the European ones. **España** (Spain), **Inglaterra** (England), **Escocia** (Scotland), **Gales** (Wales), **Irlanda** (Ireland), and **Alemania** (Germany). In North America, you'll need **Estados Unidos** (United States) and **Canadá** (Canada).

4 You will hear Marisa say the numbers from 0 to 10. Repeat them until you feel you really know them. (The numbers are set out for you on page 29.)

5 Listen to Carlos saying six numbers. Circle the ones you hear on the recording.

ANSWERS P. 32

6 Now listen to the numbers from 11 to 22. Carlos will be reading them out this time. Again, repeat this exercise until you feel confident.

7 Match up the number with its written form.

a.	diez	f.	cuatro	i.	14	vi.	10
b.	quince	g.	diecisiete	ii.	17	vii	23
c.	dieciséis	h.	veinte	iii.	15	viii.	16
d.	veintitrés	i.	catorce	iv.	4	ix.	29
e.	veintinueve	j.	veinticinco	v.	25	x.	20

ANSWERS P. 32

8 Look at the number card below and mark off the numbers as they are called out. You should be left with one number. Eliud will tell you which it is at the end of the exercise.

9 Switch on your recording to play another number game. Carlos says one number – and you have to give the number after it. Marisa will repeat the second number just to make sure you were correct.

10 In this exercise Marisa will be asking you about yourself. Reply according to the prompts.

▶ *María asks how to get to the children's department*

LISTEN FOR...

en la planta sótano	in the basement
bajando las escaleras	going down the stairs
a la derecha	to the right

María	¿Dónde está la sección niño, por favor?
Jefa *(manageress)*	En la planta sótano, bajando las escaleras a la derecha

▶ **bajar** to go down

la sección niño the children's department. You will also need **la sección caballero** the menswear department and **la sección señora** ladies' wear.

en la planta sótano in the basement.

bajando las escaleras going down the stairs. The '-ando' ending is equivalent to the English '-ing'.

a la derecha to the right. You will also need to know **a la izquierda** to the left.

sexta Planta

quinta planta

cuarta planta

tercera planta

segunda planta

primera planta

planta baja

planta sótano

◗ María asks for the toilets

LISTEN FOR...

los servicios	the toilets
al fondo	at the end
¿hay en todas las plantas?	are there some on all floors?

María	Señorita, ¿dónde están los servicios por favor?
Jefa	Pues al fondo a la derecha
María	¿Hay en todas las plantas?
Jefa	No, ¡qué va!, sólo en la planta baja
María	Bien

▶ **por favor**   please
▶ **pues**   well, then
▶ **sólo**   only
▶ **la planta baja**   the ground floor
▶ **bien**   fine

¿Dónde están los servicios?   Where are the toilets? Notice how **está** (is) becomes **están** (are) because **servicios** is plural.

al fondo   at the end. You can combine this with **de** to mean 'at the end of' or 'at the bottom of'. **Al fondo del pasillo** at the end of the corridor.

¿Hay en todas las plantas?   Are there (some) on all the floors? **Hay** is a useful word which means either 'there is' or 'there are', or 'is there?' or 'are there?'.

¡Qué va!   Certainly not! A useful phrase which expresses surprise or disbelief.

LISTEN FOR...

¿venden ustedes cremas para la piel?	do you sell skin creams?
en la tercera planta	on the third floor
juguetes para niños	children's toys

Pepe	Por favor, ¿venden ustedes cremas para la piel?
Dependienta	En la sección de perfumería
Pepe	¿Dónde está?
Dependienta	En la planta baja
Pepe	¿En la planta baja?
Dependienta	Planta baja
Pepe	¿Y dónde venden los juguetes para niños?
Dependienta	Eso está todo en la tercera planta

▶ **para**   for
▶ **(la) dependienta**   shop assistant
▶ **(la) perfumería**   cosmetics
▶ **(el) juguete**   toy
▶ **(los) niños**   children
Note also ▶ **(el) niño**   boy
and ▶ **(la) niña**   girl
▶ **eso**   that
▶ **todo**   all

¿Venden ustedes cremas para la piel?   Do you sell skin creams? (literally, 'sell you creams for the skin?'). **Vender** (to sell) is an **-er** verb. You'll find the full form on page 28. Notice the plural form of **usted**. Use **ustedes** when talking formally to more than one person. When written, **ustedes** is usually abbreviated to **Uds.** or **Vds**.

En la planta baja   On the ground floor. **La primera planta** the first floor, **la segunda planta** the second floor and **la tercera planta** the third floor. **Primera**, **segunda** and **tercera** can come before or after the word **planta**. In conversation they usually come before.

11 Look at each of these symbols and then choose the phrase which best describes it. Write it in the space provided.

a. _____

b. _____

c. _____

d. _____

e. _____

f. _____

i. a la derecha

ii. al fondo

iii. bajando las escaleras

iv. ¿dónde están los servicios?

v. en la tercera planta

vi. la sección de perfumería está en la planta baja

ANSWERS P. 32

12   You are in a large department store in Spain. Listen to the description of which items are to be found where and then answer the questions below in English. You'll learn three new items of clothes: **pantalones** trousers, **sombreros** hats and the general word for clothes **ropa**.

a. Where is the ladies' department?

_____

b. Where can you buy toys?

_____

c. How do you get to the basement?

_____

d. Where are men's trousers and hats to be found?

_____

e. Are the toilets to the right or left of the stairs?

ANSWERS P. 32

_____

13 You are at INFORMACIÓN in a large store. Switch on to ask the assistant where various departments are to be found.

GRAMMAR AND EXERCISES

Estar to be

In Spanish there are two verbs for to be: **ser** (which you looked at in Unit 1) and **estar**. Here is the present tense of **estar**:

estoy	I am
estás	you are (informal)
está	s/he is
está	you are (formal)
estamos	we are
estáis	you are (informal plural)
están	they are
están	you are (formal plural)

Use **ser** for:

i. identifying who or what things are
   es Juan   it's Juan
   soy Ana   I'm Ana

ii. talking about your nationality
   soy francés   I'm French

iii. saying what you do for a living
   soy médico   I'm a doctor

iv. saying where you are from
   soy de Chicago   I'm from Chicago

Use **estar** for:

i. describing where things and people are
   está en España   it's in Spain
   estoy en casa   I'm at home

ii. discussing temporary states, moods or reactions
   ¿qué tal estás?   how are you?
   estoy bien, gracias   I'm fine, thanks.

(with **soltero** and **casado** you can use either **ser** or **estar**)

Tener to have

tengo	I have
tienes	you have (informal)
tiene	s/he has
tiene	you have (formal)
tenemos	we have
tenéis	you have (informal plural)
tienen	they have
tienen	you have (formal plural)

Use **tener** to talk about possession:

tengo una casa en el campo
   I have a house in the country
tengo cinco hijos
   I have five children
no tengo novio
   I don't have a boyfriend

and use it also for talking about age:
tiene veintinueve años
   he's twenty-nine (literally, 'he has twenty-nine years')

Vender to sell

Verbs ending in **-er** usually follow the same pattern. **Vender** is a good example. Have a look at how it works.

vendo	I sell
vendes	you sell (informal)
vende	s/he sells
vende	you sell (formal)
vendemos	we sell
vendéis	you sell (informal plural)
venden	they sell
venden	you sell (formal plural)

Go back to Unit 1 and compare the endings with those of **hablar**.

14

Complete these sentences with the correct form of either **ser** or **estar**:

a. ¿Cómo _____ ? Muy bien, gracias.

b. _____ Juan, _____ de Venezuela.

c. ¿Le Mans? ¿Dónde _____?
   En el norte de Francia.

d. ¿Nacionalidad?
   _____ irlandés, de Dublín.

ANSWERS P. 32

15

Match up both columns to make correct sentences:

a. ¿Cuántas   i.   un hermano mayor que yo

b. ¿Cuántos   ii. hermanas tienes?

c. ¿Tienes   iii. años tienes?

d. ¿Tiene usted iv. hijos o hijas?

e. Tengo   v.   crema para la piel?

ANSWERS P. 32

16

Other **-er** verbs, such as **comer** (to eat) and **beber** (to drink), work like **vender**. So how do you say:

a. I eat paella

_____

b. He drinks beer (**cerveza**)

_____

c. We eat squid (**calamares**)

_____

d. Do you drink wine?

_____

e. They eat fruit (**fruta**)

_____

ANSWERS P. 32

cero	0		
uno	1	seis	6
dos	2	siete	7
tres	3	ocho	8
cuatro	4	nueve	9
cinco	5	diez	10
once	11	veintiuno/a	21
doce	12	veintidós	22
trece	13	veintitrés	23
catorce	14	veinticuatro	24
quince	15	veinticinco	25
dieciséis	16	veintiséis	26
diecisiete	17	veintisiete	27
dieciocho	18	veintiocho	28
diecinueve	19	veintinueve	29
veinte	20		

Madrid

KEY WORDS
AND PHRASES

¿Eres soltero/a?	Are you unmarried? (informal)
¿Es usted soltero/a?	Are you unmarried? (formal)
¿Tienes novio/a?	Do you have a boy/girlfriend? (informal)
¿Tiene novio/a?	Do you have a boy/girlfriend? (formal)
¿Eres/estás casado/a?	Are you married? (informal)
¿Es/está usted casado/a?	Are you married? (formal)
¿Tienes hijos?	Do you have any children? (informal)
¿Tiene usted hijos?	Do you have any children? (formal)
¿cuántos	how many
hijos	children
hermanos	brothers and sisters
años?	years?
¿Cómo te llamas?	What are you called? (informal)
¿Cómo se llama usted?	What are you called? (formal)
Se llama ...	He/she is called ...
¿Cuántos años tienes?	How old are you?
hijo/a	son/daughter
hermano/a	brother/sister
¿Dónde está ...?	Where is ...?
en el sur	in the south
en el norte	in the north
en el este	in the east
en el oeste	in the west
(la) Inglaterra	England
(la) Escocia	Scotland
(el) Gales	Wales
(la) Irlanda	Ireland
(los) Estados Unidos	America
(el) Canadá	Canada
(la) Alemania	Germany

¿Venden ustedes ...	Do you sell ...
sandalias	sandals
sombreros	hats
juguetes	toys
cremas para la piel	skin cream
perfume?	perfume?
¿Dónde venden ...?	Where do you sell ...?
la planta sótano	the basement
la planta baja	the ground floor
la primera planta	the first floor
la segunda planta	the second floor
la tercera planta	the third floor
al fondo	at the end, at the bottom
a la derecha	on the right
a la izquierda	on the left
bajando las escaleras	going down the stairs
hay (servicios)	there is/there are (toilets)
en todas las plantas	on each floor
la sección niño	the children's department
la sección caballero	the men's department
la sección señora	the ladies' department

The Spanish-speaking world

SPAIN is the third largest country in Europe and the second most mountainous (after Switzerland). The Canary Islands and the Balearic Islands (Mallorca, Menorca and Ibiza) also belong to Spain, as do the two North African enclaves, Ceuta and Melilla. The country is really a number of quite different geographical regions, each, as we have seen, with its own language and culture.

South and Central America formed part of the vast Spanish empire of the 16th and 17th centuries. The inhabitants of these countries are known as **sudamericanos** and people from the United States are known as **estadounidenses,** or **norteamericanos. Americanos** are people from both South and North America. Anyone who is not an **americano** is a **gringo** – not a very polite term for a foreigner. Latin America is a fascinating continent because of its different languages, cultures and peoples. Countries in the north-east (Venezuela and Brazil) have been radically influenced by African and Caribbean cultures. (The language of Brazil is of course Portuguese, itself the fifth most widely spoken language in the world.)

Argentina and the Southern Cone (**el Cono Sur**) are very Europeanized, with a variant of Spanish which is heavily Italianized, due to the large number of Italians who emigrated to Buenos Aires. The Andean countries (Peru, Bolivia and Ecuador) are very Indian in character, with Quechua and Aymara widely spoken in the highlands.

One of the interesting things about studying the Spanish language is the difference between peninsular (Spain) and Latin American Spanish. The most obvious difference is the pronunciation of **c** and **z**: as a lisped 'th' in Spain but as a strong 's' in America. The vocabulary changes too. In Spain the expression 'to drive a car' is **conducir un coche** but in Latin American Spanish it is **manejar un carro**. The **cena** (dinner in Spain) becomes **la comida** in Chile: and **un autobús** is a **guagua** – pronounced **wawa** – in the Caribbean as well as in the Canary Islands. Don't worry about these differences however – basic Spanish is understood the world over.

17 Now Carlos will be asking you more about your family and where you live. You'll be using:

soy/estoy casada/soltera
tengo/no tengo hijos
tengo/no tengo hermanos
se llama(n)
tiene(n)

ANSWERS

EXERCISE 2

cuántos/cuántas, hijos/hijas, novio/novia, casado/casada soltero/soltera

EXERCISE 5

You should have circled 5, 8, 0, 2, 4, 9.

EXERCISE 7

(a) vi   **(b)** iii   **(c)** viii   **(d)** vii   **(e)** ix   **(f)** iv   **(g)** ii
(h) x   **(i)** i   **(j)** v

EXERCISE 11

(a) iv   **(b)** i   **(c)** iii   **(d)** vi   **(e)** v   **(f)** ii

EXERCISE 12

(a) on the ground floor   **(b)** in the basement
(c) down the stairs   **(d)** on the third floor to the right
(e) to the left

EXERCISE 14

(a) estás   **(b)** soy, soy   **(c)** está   **(d)** soy

EXERCISE 15

(a) ii   **(b)** iii   **(c)** iv   **(d)** v   **(e)** i

EXERCISE 16

(a) Como paella   **(b)** Bebe cerveza   **(c)** Comemos calamares
(d) ¿Bebe usted vino?   **(e)** Comen fruta

WHAT YOU WILL LEARN

▶ How to say ...
something about where you live
more about your family

▶ And how to ...
book a room at a hotel
use numbers from 30 to 100

BEFORE YOU BEGIN

One of the important things about being a successful language learner is to be able to filter out surplus information and go for the essentials. This is why you are asked to watch out for certain words and phrases before you listen. You need to be able to recognize these amongst a barrage of language which may be too fast or complicated for you to understand – especially the first time. So don't panic when faced with a new conversation and don't feel that you have to understand every single word. It just isn't necessary.

Remember too that there will be language which you will want to be able to produce yourself and a great deal more which you will want to understand, but not necessarily to use. It's a good idea at this stage to distinguish between what you want to *say* (active language) and what you simply want to *understand* (passive). Why not mark new vocabulary either 'a' for active or 'p' for passive?

Pronunciation notes

There are two ways of pronouncing **r**. A single **r** is produced by a tap of the tongue against the palate. Use a rolled **r** (several taps of the tongue) for double **rr** or an **r** at the beginning of a word. It helps to remember that the word for 'to roll' in Spanish is **vibrar** to vibrate: this is exactly what the tongue does. Listen to Carlos and Marisa demonstrating the difference between the single and double **r** on your recording. You'll hear three pairs of words where the meaning changes according to whether they contain a single or double r.
pero (but), **perro** (dog)
caro (expensive), **carro** (a cart or car)
foro (forum), **forro** (lining).

Reme asks Raquel about where she lives

LISTEN FOR...	
¿dónde vives?	where do you live?
un piso	a flat
una casa	a house
¿cuántas habitaciones tiene?	how many rooms does it have?

Reme	¿Dónde vives, en un piso, una casa o un apartamento?
Raquel	En una casa
Reme	¿Una casa de varias plantas?
Raquel	De dos plantas
Reme	¿Cuántas habitaciones tiene?
Raquel	Tenemos tres dormitorios, una cocina, un salón-comedor, una sala de estar, tres cuartos de baño y nada más

▶ **el piso**   flat (or floor)
▶ **la casa**   house
▶ **el apartamento**   flat (generally smaller and more modern than **piso**)
▶ **varios** (m.), **varias** (f.)   several, a number of
▶ **la habitación**   room, bedroom
▶ **la cocina**   kitchen
▶ **el salón-comedor**   sitting/dining room

Note also ▶ **el comedor**   dining room

▶ **la sala de estar**   sitting room
▶ **el cuarto de baño**   bathroom

¿Dónde vives?   Where do you live?
Vivir (to live) is an example of the third type of verb in Spanish, those ending in **-ir**. More about this in the Grammar section.

¿Cuántas habitaciones tiene?   How many rooms/bedrooms does it have?
Habitación can either mean 'room' in general or 'bedroom' in particular.

Tiene is the he/she/Vd./it form of **tener**.

Tenemos tres dormitorios   We have three bedrooms. The 'we' form of **tener**.

nada más   nothing else (literally, nothing more).

And now Eme asks Adelaida about her home

LISTEN FOR...

es muy grande, ¿no?	it's very big, isn't it?
vivimos toda la familia juntos	all the family lives together
somos también bastantes	there's quite a lot of us

Eme	Adelaida, ¿tú dónde vives?
Adelaida	Vivo en un piso, está en la calle de la Reina
Eme	¿Es muy grande?
Adelaida	Bueno, sí, vivimos toda la familia juntos y es un dúplex
Eme	¿Es un dúplex? ¿Cuántos dormitorios tiene en total?
Adelaida	Tiene cinco dormitorios
Eme	¿Y salas de estar?
Adelaida	Una y un salón
Eme	Caray, pues es muy grande, ¿no?
Adelaida	Somos también bastantes
Eme	¡Estupendo!

- **muy** very
- **grande** big
- **el dúplex** a two-storied flat/apartment
- **en total** in all
- **caray** really! goodness! (expresses surprise)
- **bastante** enough, quite a lot

la calle de la Reina Queen Street (literally, the street of the queen).
Vivimos toda la familia juntos All the family lives together (literally, we live all the family together). **Vivimos** is the 'we' form of **vivir** to live. Adelaida uses this form because she includes herself within the family.
Somos también bastantes There are quite a lot of us (literally, we are also quite a lot). **Somos** is the 'we' form of **ser** to be.

 ## Eme talks to Adelaida about her family

LISTEN FOR...

¿cuántos sois?	how many are there of you?
mis padres	my parents
¡qué familia tan numerosa!	what a big family!

Eme	¿Cuántos sois en total?
Adelaida	Somos, bueno, mis padres, yo y otros tres hermanos. Tengo dos hermanos mayores, una hermana que se llama Sandra y un hermano Moncho y queda uno pequeño, que es Andrés.
Eme	Pero entonces sois seis en total, ¿no?
Adelaida	Sí
Eme	¡Caray! ¡Qué familia tan numerosa!

▶ **los padres**   parents

Note also ▶   **el padre** (father) and **la madre** (mother)

▶ **pequeño**   little, small

▶ **pero**   but

▶ **entonces**   then

▶ **la familia**   family

mis padres   my parents. More about '**mis**' on page 75. You may remember the phrase **gallego y castellano son mis dos lenguas** from Unit 1.

Queda uno pequeño   There's one little one. **Quedar** to remain, to be left.

¡Qué familia tan numerosa!   What a big family! (literally, what a family so big!). A family with four children is unusual now in Spain.

PRACTICE

1 How much do you remember of the first two conversations? Check the correct response.

RAQUEL

a.	Raquel vive en	una casa un piso un apartamento
b.	Tiene	una planta dos plantas tres plantas
c.	Tiene	tres dormitorios cuatro dormitorios un dormitorio

ADELAIDA

d.	Adelaida vive en	un dúplex un salón-comedor una casa
e.	Vive en	la calle de Madrid la calle del Rey la calle de la Reina
f.	Tiene salón	y una planta y sala de estar y comedor

ANSWERS P. 50

2 Here's a plan of Adelaida's family. Choose a word from the list below to complete each sentence.

Carmen = Juan

Sandra   Moncho   Adelaida   Andrés

a. Carmen es la _____ de la familia

b. Juan es el _____ de los cuatro hijos

c. Sandra es la _____ mayor

d. Moncho es el _____ mayor de Adelaida y Andrés

e. Andrés es el _____ pequeño

f. Carmen y Juan son los _____

g. Adelaida tiene dos _____

h. Moncho tiene dos _____

ANSWERS P. 50

hermano	hermana	madre	hermanas	padres
padre	hermano	hermanos		

3 On the recording Marisa will ask you about your house and the rooms it has. You'll be practising **tiene** and **tenemos**.

Reme asks Raquel where she lives

Reme	¿En dónde vives?
Raquel	Vivo en Lugo
Reme	¿En dónde?
Raquel	En una calle que se llama Armando Durán
Reme	Ah, ya la conozco. ¿Está cerca del instituto?
Raquel	Sí, está a unos doscientos metros
Reme	Supongo que vas a pie, ¿no?
Raquel	A veces en bicicleta, andando ...

- ▶ **ya** already
- ▶ **conocer** to know
- ▶ **el metro** metre (or the underground)
- ▶ **suponer** to suppose
- ▶ **el pie** foot

Ah, ya la conozco Oh, I (already) know (it). **La** (it) is feminine because it refers to **la calle**. Notice where you place this pronoun. More about this in Unit 4.

Está cerca del instituto It's near the school. If you say near something, **cerca** must be followed by **de**. **De** in turn becomes **del** because of the following **el**. (Try saying **de** and **el** together and you will see why!)

Está a unos doscientos metros It's about two hundred metres away. **Unos** in front of a number gives it the sense of 'about'/'approximately'. **A** in front of a number conveys the idea of 'away'. **A 100 metros del instituto** 100 metres away from the institute. You will be practising larger numbers in Unit 4.

Supongo que vas a pie I suppose that you go on foot. **Vas** (you go) is the **tú** form of **ir** (to go). This very important verb is written out for you in Unit 10, page 152.

a veces en bicicleta, andando ... sometimes by bicycle, sometimes on foot ... (literally sometimes on a bicycle, walking ...). Do you remember **bajando** going down, from Unit 2? This is the same structure, based on **andar** to walk. You'll also need **voy en autobús** I go by bus, **voy en coche** I go by car and **voy en tren** I go by train.

María now asks Eme how many pupils he has in his class

LISTEN FOR...

depende	it depends
mira	look
tengo cuatro grupos distintos	I have four different groups
alumnos más jóvenes	younger pupils

María ¿Cuántos alumnos tienes en clase?

Eme Pues mira, depende, tengo cuatro grupos distintos. En una clase, tengo treinta y uno y luego en otra clase, tengo treinta y cinco y luego en los dos cursos de alumnos más jóvenes, tengo en una, dieciocho y en otra, veintitrés.

▶ **depende**   it depends
▶ **distinto/a**   different
▶ **treinta**   thirty
▶ **treinta y uno**   thirty-one
▶ **luego**   then
▶ **treinta y cinco**   thirty-five
▶ **el curso**   (school) year

Mira   look. From **mirar** to look.

más jóvenes   younger (literally, more young). **Joven** is the singular form. Notice how words ending in a consonant, such as **n**, form the plural by adding **es**.

PRACTICE

4 Listen to Carlos saying the key numbers from 30 to 100. Repeat them after him until you feel confident.

5 Carlos and Marisa will be telling you how far certain towns and cities are from Santiago. As you listen, check off the six numbers you hear against the ones below.

ANSWERS P. 50

70   60   45   150   52   85   75   80   55   65   100   28   33   92

6 Telephone numbers in Spanish are often given in pairs. Listen to the recording and fill in the phone numbers of the following people.

a.   el teléfono de Ana es el _____

b.   el teléfono de Bárbara es el _____

c.   el teléfono de Carlos es el _____

d.   el teléfono de David es el _____

e.   el teléfono de Ester es el _____

ANSWERS P. 50

f.   el teléfono de Francisco es el _____

7 Listen to the recording and then decide whether the following statements are true (**verdad**) or false (**mentira**).

	verdad	mentira
a. Marisa lives in the United States		
b. She lives on Staten Island		
c. She lives on 92nd Street		
d. She teaches Spanish nearby		
e. She goes to work by bus		
f. It's a journey of 2 kilometres		

ANSWERS P. 50

8 Marisa will be asking where you live and work. Eliud will prompt as usual.

Serafín asks Janet about her holiday accommodation

LISTEN FOR...

estrellas   stars

Serafín	¿Está en un hotel o en un apartamento?
Janet	Estoy en un apartamento
Serafín	¿Qué prefiere, un hotel, un apartamento o un camping?
Janet	Un apartamento
Serafín	¿Cómo es el apartamento?
Janet	Pues muy bueno. Tiene tres habitaciones, un salón, terraza. Y usted ¿está en un hotel?
Serafín	Sí, estoy en un gran hotel
Janet	Y ¿cómo es el hotel?
Serafín	Pues es un hotel lujoso de cuatro estrellas
Janet	Ah, pues, muy bien

▶ **el hotel**   the hotel
▶ **preferir**   to prefer
▶ **el camping**   campsite
▶ **la terraza**   terrace
▶ **lujoso/a**   luxury
▶ **la estrella**   star

Hostal CERVANTES
(Baño, Calefacción, TV)

correo@hostal-cervantes.com
www.hostal-cervantes.com

Cervantes, 34 - 2.º
28014 Madrid
Próximo Museo del Prado
Y Hotel Palace

Teléf. 91 429 83 65
Teléf. y Fax: 91 429 27 45
Next to Prado Museum
and Palace Hotel

HOSTAL CERVANTES

D. N. I. 5.367.345-L
CERVANTES, 34 - 2.º
Telefs. 429 27 45 - 479 83 65
28014 MADRID

Madrid, 13 de ENERO de 2003

FACTURA   Núm. 9

Cliente SANDRA TRUSCOTT   D.N.I./C.I.F. 100983550
Domicilio ELMS RD STOCKPORT   Población U.K.   DEBE:

DIAS	CONCEPTO	Precio por día	TOTAL
04	ALOJAMIENTOS	48	192€

HOSTAL RESIDENCIA
CERVANTES
C/ CERVANTES, 34 - 2.º
Tel. 429 27 45
28014 MADRID

BASE IMPONIBLE	178.56
I.V.A. 7 %	13.44
TOTAL	192€

You already know a lot of the vocabulary and structures in this conversation. Notice how Janet and Serafín address each other using the formal **usted**.

¿Qué prefiere?   What do you prefer? **Preferir** is a tricky verb. More about this on page 46.

¿Cómo es el apartamento?   What is the apartment like? (literally, how is the apartment?).

Estoy en un gran hotel   I am in a large hotel. **Grande** shortens to **gran** when it precedes its noun. **Primero** and **tercero** also shorten their forms before a masculine noun. **El primer hombre** the first man, **el tercer piso** the third flat/floor.

Pepe wants a room for the night

LISTEN FOR...	
dos camas	two beds
¿con ducha?	with a shower?
¿con baño?	with a bath?
¿sencilla o de matrimonio?	single or double?
lo siento	I am sorry
¿para cuántas noches?	for how many nights?

Hotel Universal

PLAZA DE GALICIA, 2
Tels. (981) 58 58 00 - 58 51 90 -
58 53 90
15706 SANTIAGO DE COMPOSTELA
(LA CORUÑA)

Pepe	¿Tiene una habitación libre?
Recepcionista	Sí. ¿Cómo la prefiere, sencilla o de matrimonio?
Pepe	De matrimonio, por favor
Recepcionista	Lo siento, pero de matrimonio no tengo. Hay de dos camas
Pepe	De dos camas ... bueno, bueno, vale, vale
Recepcionista	¿Para cuántas noches?
Pepe	Para una, solamente para una
Recepcionista	¿Cómo la prefiere, con ducha o sin ducha?
Pepe	¿Tiene con baño?
Recepcionista	No
Pepe	Bueno, pues entonces con ducha

▶ **libre**   free
▶ **la cama**   bed
▶ **para**   for
▶ **solamente**   only
▶ **¿cómo?**   how, what?
▶ **sin**   without

¿Cómo la prefiere?   What sort of room? (literally, how it do you prefer?). **La** refers to **la habitación**.

¿sencilla o de matrimonio? single or double? You are also likely to hear **individual** (single) and **doble** (double). **De matrimonio** suggests a double bed. This is why the receptionist says she has a double room with two beds.

Lo siento   I am sorry. This is a vital phrase. It comes from **sentir** (to feel) and follows the same pattern as **preferir**.

SOFITEL
ACCOR HOTELS & RESORTS

SOFITEL **MADRID PLAZA DE ESPAÑA**

Tarifas 2002

	€
Habitación Club Single	245
Habitación Club Doble	263
Habitación Prestige Single	275
Habitación Prestige Doble	294
Suite Prado	528
Desayuno (Buffe)	20
Parking (Día)	16

I.V.A. 7% NO INCLUIDO

Tutor, 1 - 28008 MADRID
Teléf. 91 541 98 80
Fax. 91 542 57 36
E-mail:H1320@accor-hotels.com

María checks in

LISTEN FOR...

tengo una habitación reservada a nombre de ...	I have a room reserved in the name of ...
¿me deja el pasaporte?	can I have your passport?
tenga	here you are

María	Hola, buenos días. Tengo una habitación reservada a nombre de Truscott
Recepcionista	Sí, un momento por favor ... Señora Truscott, una persona, habitación individual
María	Sí
Recepcionista	¿Me deja el pasaporte si es tan amable?
María	Sí, tenga
Recepcionista	Tiene usted la habitación cuatrocientas tres
	Está usted en la cuarta planta y el ascensor está a la izquierda de la escalera
María	Gracias
Recepcionista	Gracias, tenga la llave

▶ **reservado/a** reserved
▶ **a nombre de** in the name of
▶ **el momento** moment
▶ **la persona** person
▶ **cuarto/a** fourth
▶ **el ascensor** lift
▶ **la llave** key

¿Me deja el pasaporte? May I have your passport? (literally, to me do you leave/lend the passport?).

si es tan amable if you would be (literally, are) so kind.

Tenga Here you are, here is ... Use this form of **tener** when you are handing something over.

PRACTICE

9 On the recording you will hear a conversation between two friends about María's holiday apartment. Mark the six facilities it has.

▶ **una terraza**

▶ **un jardín**

▶ **un salón**

▶ **dos dormitorios**

▶ **una ducha**

▶ **un baño**

▶ **una cama de matrimonio**

▶ **dos camas**

ANSWERS P. 50

10 Listen to the conversation on the recording. The two people in the hotel both have different requirements. Link up each person with what he or she needs by drawing a line between the person and the facility on offer.

ANSWERS P. 50

11 In *La Guía del Buen Hotel* (*The Good Hotel Guide*), the Gran Hotel Arantaya is highly recommended. Read the description.

Gran Hotel Arantaya ★ ★ ★ ★

El hotel está situado en el campo, a sesenta kilómetros de Montelamancha y tiene instalaciones amplias con jardines y discoteca. Concebido para celebrar banquetes numerosos y reuniones privadas. Destaca el alto confort de sus cien habitaciones, en varias plantas dentro de un viejo edificio renovado.

La Posada Condesa is a little different.

Posada Condesa ★ ★

Tiene solamente siete habitaciones, todas distintas: un ejemplo para muchos pequeños hoteles con encanto. Muy cerca de la ciudad de Albacete pero apartado del tráfico urbano. Agradable terraza-jardín en verano.

New vocabulary

el campo	the countryside
la reunión	meeting
destacar	to stand out
el verano	summer

ANSWERS P. 50 Now decide whether the following statements are **verdad** or **mentira**.

	verdad	mentira
a. The Arantaya is in the countryside		
b. It is 70 kilometres from Montelamancha		
c. It is a large hotel with over 100 rooms		
d. It is built all on one floor		
e. The Posada Condesa has 6 bedrooms		
f. It is an excellent example of its type		
g. You can hear the traffic noise from Albacete		
h. It has facilities for sitting out in summer		

Vivir to live

The last of the three categories of verbs is those ending in **-ir**. **Vivir** is a typical example. Have a look at the present tense.

vivo	I live
vives	you live (informal)
vive	s/he lives
vive	you live (formal)
vivimos	we live
vivís	you live (informal plural)
viven	they live
viven	you live (formal plural)

Another **-ir** verb which you will come across is **partir** to leave.

Preferir and **Sentir**
Some verbs in Spanish gain an extra **i** before the **e** in some of their parts. These are called radical or stem-changing verbs. **Preferir** is a typical example.

Preferir to prefer

prefiero	I prefer
prefieres	you prefer (informal)
prefiere	s/he prefers
prefiere	you prefer (formal)
preferimos	we prefer
preferís	you prefer (informal plural)
prefieren	they prefer
prefieren	you prefer (formal plural)

Sentir (to feel) works in the same way: **lo siento**, I am sorry (literally, I feel it).

Prepositions of place

Here is a list of the most common phrases which indicate where things are. You'll see that they all combine with '**de**'. Remember to use **estar** and not **ser** with these.

al lado de	beside
	al lado de María
cerca de	near
	cerca de Madrid
lejos de	far from
	lejos del campo
delante de	in front of
	delante de la casa
detrás de	behind
	detrás del apartamento
debajo de	underneath
	debajo de la mesa (table)
encima de	on top of
	encima de la cama
en	in, on
	en París
enfrente de	opposite
	enfrente del banco

De

You've probably noticed that in Spanish you can't use '-'s' or '-s' when you're talking about who owns what. John's flat or Mary's house has to be translated as:

el piso de Juan   the flat of John
la casa de María   the house of Mary

- Neither can you use the combination **de + el**. Use **del** instead:
  el coche del profesor está delante del colegio
  the teacher's car is in front of the school
  (the same thing happens with **a + el: voy al parque**   I'm going to the park).

12
You're writing cheques for the following amounts:
Write each number out in full.

a. 35 libras (pounds)

_____

b. 120 euros

_____

c. 95 euros

_____

d. 52 libras

_____

e. 88 dólares

_____

f. 68 euros

_____

ANSWERS P. 50

13
Look at these pictures and describe where each person, place or thing is, in relation to the other using the phrases you've just learned.

a. María Tomás

b. Juan Alicia

c. Luis Pedro

d. Santiago Granada

e.

f. STATEN ISLAND NEW YORK PHILADELPHIA

ANSWERS P. 50

14
Try out your stem-changing verbs with **querer**, by matching each part of the verb.

i. yo

ii. Carlos

iii. nosotros

iv. mis padres

v. tú

vi. usted

a. queremos

b. quiero

c. quieres

d. quiere

e. quiere

f. quieren

ANSWERS P. 50

---

el piso	flat
la casa	house
el apartamento	flat
la habitación	room, bedroom
el dormitorio	bedroom
la cocina	kitchen
el salón	sitting room
la sala de estar	living room
el cuarto de baño	bathroom
la familia	family
grande	big
pequeño/a	small
los padres	parents
el padre	father
la madre	mother
bastante	quite, enough
¿Cuántas habitaciones tiene?	How many rooms does it have?
¡caray!	really! goodness!
un hotel de 4 estrellas	a 4 star hotel
un gran hotel	a big hotel
¿Qué prefiere?	What do you prefer?
Prefiero	I prefer
una habitación sencilla/ individual	a single room
doble/de matrimonio	double room
con dos camas	with two beds
con ducha	with a shower
sin ducha	without a shower
con baño	with a bathroom
¿Tiene una habitación libre?	Do you have a room (free)?
¿Para cuántas noches?	For how many nights?
Lo siento	I am sorry
Tengo una habitación reservada a nombre de ...	I have a room reserved in the name of ...
¿Me deja el pasaporte?	May I have your passport?
Tenga	Here you are
la llave	is your key

treinta	30	ochenta	80
treinta y uno/a	31	noventa	90
treinta y dos	32	noventa y tres	93
cuarenta	40	cien	100
cincuenta	50	ciento uno	101
sesenta	60	ciento dos	102
setenta	70		

Hotels

There are an enormous number of different types of hotels and guest houses in Spain. A list of the accommodation facilities in the town or district can usually be obtained from the local tourist offices or, if you are still at home, from a good guide book or the internet. Hotels are divided into five classes and awarded stars accordingly. **Pensiones** (small family-run establishments) are divided into three categories. A **pensión** might also be referred to as a **fonda**, a **casa de huéspedes** or an **hostal** and they do have the advantage of being cheap and central, although they don't usually have a **sereno** or night porter and therefore may not be open if you arrive very late.

In addition to this network, a chain of accommodation has been set up by the Secretariat for Tourism in areas of special interest all over Spain. These establishments are of three types – **paradores**, which are buildings of artistic and historical value, refurbished to provide the comforts of a first class hotel; **albergues de carretera**, which are modern hotels located near main roads and which provide the motorist with a comfortable 'stop-over'; and lastly, **refugios**, located in the countryside.

All hotel prices are fixed centrally, so there is no danger of your having to pay over the odds. The cost of the room is displayed in the room: the price is for the room and not per person. Breakfast is usually not included. Hotels and campsites are required by law to keep complaints forms (**hojas de reclamaciones**) and produce them when required to do so by a client. Your complaint will be investigated by the appropriate inspector.

Travelling around Latin America is a little more problematic. Either you stick to the tourist trail and stay in luxurious but international-style hotels or you can travel on your own initiative and stay in more doubtful accommodation. The exception is Mexico, which has a wider range of hotels because it has a more developed tourist industry. Independent travelling has become quite dangerous recently with the emergence of guerrilla groups such as the **FARC** (**Fuerzas Armadas Revolucionarias de Colombia**) and the **ELN** (**Ejército de Liberación Nacional**) in Colombia. The moral is: don't wander too far off the beaten track. You may regret it.

Hostal - Residencia
CORUÑA
Rafael y Manoli

Paseo del Prado, 12
Teléf. 429 25 43

Suite Prado
APARTHOTEL

TARIFA DE LANZAMIENTO

Manuel Fernández y González, 10
MADRID
5 59

RESIDENCIA LOS ALPES
FUENCARRAL 17-4º DCH.

AND FINALLY...

15 In this exercise you will be practising checking into a Spanish hotel. Eliud will prompt you. You'll be using the following structures:

Para .... noches
Con/sin ducha
Con/sin baño
Tenga

ANSWERS

EXERCISE 1

(a) una casa   **(b)** dos plantas   **(c)** tres dormitorios
(d) un dúplex   **(e)** la calle de la Reina   **(f)** y sala de estar

EXERCISE 2

(a) madre   **(b)** padre   **(c)** hermana   **(d)** hermano
(e) hermano   **(f)** padres   **(g)** hermanos   **(h)** hermanas

EXERCISE 5

92, 100, 80, 85, 60, 150

EXERCISE 6

(a) 33 82 50   **(b)** 59 22 89   **(c)** 18 54 94   **(d)** 78 72 66
(e) 10 64 75   **(f)** 30 24 72

EXERCISE 7

(a) verdad   **(b)** mentira   **(c)** verdad   **(d)** verdad   **(e)** mentira
(f) mentira

EXERCISE 9

un salón, una terraza, una ducha, dos dormitorios, uno con dos camas y otro con cama de matrimonio

EXERCISE 10

The man would like: una habitación para una noche, con ducha y dos camas, en el segundo piso. The woman would like: una habitación para tres noches, con ducha, cama de matrimonio, en el primer piso.

EXERCISE 11

(a) verdad   **(b)** mentira   **(c)** mentira   **(d)** mentira
(e) mentira   **(f)** verdad   **(g)** mentira   **(h)** verdad

EXERCISE 12

(a) treinta y cinco libras   **(b)** ciento veinte euros
(c) noventa y cinco euros   **(d)** cincuenta y dos libras
(e) ochenta y ocho dólares   **(f)** sesenta y ocho euros

EXERCISE 13

(a) María está al lado de Tomás   **(b)** Juan está detrás de Alicia   **(c)** Luis está encima de Pedro   **(d)** Granada está lejos de Santiago   **(e)** El juguete está debajo de la cama **(f)** Staten Island está cerca de Nueva York

EXERCISE 14

i b   **ii** d   **iii** a   **iv** f   **v** c   **vi** e

4 COFFEE – AND BAR SNACKS

WHAT YOU WILL LEARN

▶ How to …
order coffee and snacks
pay the bill
count from one hundred

BEFORE YOU BEGIN

Language learning is a little like doing a jigsaw puzzle. It takes a while before all the pieces fall into place. So don't worry about odd pieces of grammar or items of vocabulary that you can't quite remember or understand. With plenty of practice and exposure to the languge you will piece together each bit to create the whole picture. This is why you need your file – so that you can keep adding new information to what you have already learned.

It is a good idea at this stage to divide up your notes according to some plan that suits you. It might be based on grammar if you are that way inclined, or it could be based on situations (such as the ones you are going to meet in this Unit). Whatever it is, review your notes regularly. Language learning is about maintaining what you already know, as well as learning new information. And don't be afraid to write on your books. They are working documents, designed to help you learn as efficiently and interestingly as possible.

Pronunciation notes

Before **a**, **o** and **u**, pronounce the Spanish letter **c** as in 'car' – but try not to breathe at the same time! Before **e** and **i**, **c** is pronounced as an English 'th' as in 'thumb' – but only in northern and central Spain. In Andalusia and Latin America it is pronounced as a strong **s**. You'll hear both pronunciations in the conversations but you won't be practising the **s** sound till the next Unit.

coca cola   café   doscientos

CAFE DEL CENTRO

COCKTAILS

★CAFES ESPECIALES
★DESAYUNOS
★MERIENDAS
★PASTELERIA
★BOLLERIA
★PLATOS COMBINADOS

Plaza de España, 9

CONVERSATIONS 1

Eme asks his friends what they would like to drink

LISTEN FOR...

¿qué vais a tomar?	what are you going to have?
un cortado	a white coffee
un solo	a black coffee
un café con leche	a large white coffee

Eme	¿Qué vais a tomar? ¿Sandra?
Sandra	Un cortado
Eme	Un cortado para ti. Y tú Delia, ¿qué tomas?
Delia	Un café con leche
Eme	Un café con leche. Y Gerald, un solo, ¿no?
Gerald	Sí
Eme	Vale, así que uno solo, un cortado y dos con leche. Estupendo

▶ **tomar** to take
▶ **la leche** milk
▶ **así que** so

¿Qué vais a tomar? What are you going to have? (literally, to take). Eme is talking to a number of friends, each one of whom he calls **tú**, so he uses **vais**, the plural (**vosotros**) form of **ir** to go.

un cortado, un café con leche: un cortado is coffee with a dash of milk. **Café con leche** is more milky. **Un solo** is a black coffee. You will also hear **uno solo**.

para ti for you. **Tú** changes to **ti** after prepositions (short connecting words like **para** and **con**). More about this on page 74.

This time, the waiter takes the order

LISTEN FOR...

¿qué van a tomar?	what are you going to have?

Waiter	¿Qué van a tomar, señores?
Eme	Pues, dos cafés con leche, un cortado y un solo
Waiter	Muy bien

¿Qué van a tomar? What are you going to have? This time the waiter speaks to the group more formally, as **ustedes**, so **van** is used rather than **vais**.

PRACTICE

1 Without looking back at the conversations, fill in the blanks in the conversation at the café.

Eme: ¿Qué _____ a tomar?

Sandra: Un cortado

Eme: Un cortado para _____ . Y tú, Delia, ¿qué_____?

Delia: Un café con _____

Eme: Un café con leche. Y Gerald, un _____ , ¿no?

Gerald: Sí

Waiter: ¿Qué _____ a tomar, señores?

Eme: Un solo, un cortado y _____ _____ con leche.

ANSWERS P. 64

| solo | vais | dos | van | ti | tomas | leche |

2 Listen to Carlos, Marisa and Eliud ordering coffees. Tick what sort of coffee each person wants.

	café solo	cortado	café con leche
Carlos			
Marisa			
Eliud			

ANSWERS P. 64

3 Now it's your turn to order a coffee. Follow Eliud's prompts.

Unit 4   Coffee – and bar snacks

CONVERSATIONS 2

Isabel asks how much she owes

LISTEN FOR...

¿cuánto le debo?	how much do I owe you?
cuarenta y seis euros	forty six euros
setenta céntimos	seventy centimes

Isabel	¿Cuánto le debo?
Dependiente *(shop assistant)*	Cuarenta y seis euros, setenta céntimos
Isabel	Cuarenta y seis, cuarenta y siete. Tenga.
Dependiente	Y treinta céntimos hacen cuarenta y siete euros
Isabel	Gracias
Dependiente	De nada

▶ **deber** to owe

¿Cuánto le debo? How much do I owe you? Here, **le** means 'to you' and is the polite **usted** form. If you were using the **tú** form, you would say **¿Cuánto te debo?** **Y treinta céntimos hacen cuarenta y siete euros** And thirty centimes make forty seven euros.

Isabel asks for her bill

LISTEN FOR...

una cerveza	a beer
¿cuánto es?	how much is it?

Isabel	¡Oiga! ¿Cuánto es?
Camarero *(waiter)*	Mm ... un cortado, un té con limón, una cerveza y ...
Isabel	Un zumo de naranja
Camarero	Y un zumo de naranja ... bueno pues, son sesenta céntimos, cincuenta y siete, sesenta y seis, y ochenta y cuatro. Son dos euros, sesenta y siete céntimos
Isabel	Tenga. Gracias
Camarero	A usted

a usted thanks to you. This is sometimes said in shops, bars and so on, in reply to **gracias**.

And now Isabel pays the bill for a light snack

LISTEN FOR...

¿cuánto es todo?	how much is everything?
¿cómo dice?	what did you say?
la cuenta, por favor	the bill, please

Isabel	¡Oiga, oiga!, ¿cuánto es todo?
Camarero	¿Cómo dice?
Isabel	La cuenta, por favor
Camarero	Ocho euros, treinta y cinco céntimos

▶ **la cuenta** the bill

¡Oiga! excuse me. This really means 'listen' and is the formal command form of **oír** to listen. We have already had the same word in the **tú** form – **oye**. Use it to attract someone's attention. Alternatively, use 'por favor'.

¿Cuánto es todo? How much is it all? An alternative way of saying **¿Cuánto le debo?**

¿Cómo dice? What did you say? Use this if you didn't hear what was said. Other useful phrases of this sort are: **no entiendo** I don't understand, **lo siento** I am sorry and **despacio, por favor** slowly, please.

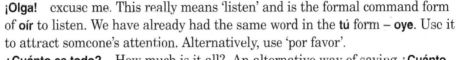

PRACTICE

4

Circle seven numbers Roberto and Diana use in the following recorded conversation.

40		65		48
	79		75	
2		27		84
	20		90	
1		36		56

ANSWERS P. 64

(Note that Spaniards use a comma to separate euros from cents – 1,60€ rather than 1.60€.)

Although used much less frequently now that Spain has the euro currency, you still need to learn the numbers from two hundred to two thousand (they are listed on page 62). Listen to Diana saying those numbers and repeat them after her.

5 You will now hear a conversation on the recording between a waitress and a couple of customers in the Bar Marbella. Reproduced below is the Bar Marbella's menu. Mark what the customers order.

BAR MARBELLA					
zumo de naranja	0,65		bocadillos		sandwiches
cerveza – caña	0,60	draft beer	queso	1,35	cheese
– botellín	0,70	bottled beer	jamón	1,40	ham
vino (vaso)	0,40	by the glass	sardinas	1,10	sardine
whisky	1,20		tapas variadas		bar snacks
café con leche	0,80		calamares	1,20	squid
café solo	0,70		ensaladilla	1,30	Russian salad
pan	0,75	bread	helados	0,90	ice-creams
agua mineral	0,60	mineral water			

ANSWERS P. 64

6 This time you're ordering drinks and snacks. You'll be choosing items from the Bar Marbella's menu. As usual, you will be prompted by Eliud.

Coffee – and bar snacks *Unit 4*

Neni asks her son what sort of ice-cream he would like

LISTEN FOR...

helado	ice-cream
¿de qué son los helados?	what flavour are the ice-creams?
¿de cuál quieres?	which one do you want?

Neni	Alvaro, ¿quieres helado?
Álvaro	¿De qué son los helados?
Neni	De naranja y de caramelo. ¿De cuál quieres?
Álvaro	De naranja y de caramelo
Neni	¿De los dos?

¿Quieres helado? Do you want some ice-cream? You have already practised this verb in Unit 3. Turn back to the Grammar section if you need to revise it.

¿De qué son los helados? What flavour are the ice-creams? (literally, of what are the ice-creams?). Use this expression for asking what things are made of. **¿De qué son los bocadillos?** What sort of sandwiches are they?

caramelo caramel. In the plural (**caramelos**), this means 'sweets'.

Other flavours you may come across are: **chocolate**, **café**, **limón** and **fresa** (strawberry).

¿De cuál quieres? Which do you want? (literally, of which do you want?). Use '**cuál**' when choosing between specific alternatives.

In a bar, the waiter asks a group of friends what they would like to drink...

LISTEN FOR...

vino tinto	red wine
vino blanco	white wine

RESERVA
1 9 8 9

R I O J A
DENOMINACION DE ORIGEN CALIFICADA

Campo Viejo

75cl.e   BODEGAS   12.5%Vol
CAMPO VIEJO SA
LOGROÑO RIOJA ALTA ESPAÑA
PRODUCE OF SPAIN

Camarero	Hola, buenas tardes. ¿Qué vais a tomar?
Marta	Para mí una cerveza
Jordi	Yo, un vino tinto
Maite	Yo, un vino blanco
María	Eh, para mí un zumo de naranja
Camarero	Vale, una cerveza, un vino tinto, un vino blanco y un zumo de naranja. Y de comer, ¿qué queréis? ➤

Marta	Para mí, una de jamón
Jordi	A mí ponme una de queso
Maite	Yo, una de ensaladilla
María	Yo no voy a tomar nada
Camarero	Muy bien, una de jamón, una de queso. Y tú, ¿ensaladilla o calamares?
Maite	Ensaladilla, sí
Camarero	Vale, de acuerdo, muy bien

Use **tinto** only for wine. The usual word for red is **rojo**.

Y de comer, ¿qué queréis? What do you want to eat?

Para mí, una de jamón. Una refers to **tapa** or bar snack. A ham one for me.

Jamón is usually either **jamón serrano** (smoked ham) or **jamón York** (boiled ham).

Ponme una de queso Give me a cheese one. **Ponme** is from **poner** to put. **Pon** is the **tú** command form and **me** is tagged on the end.

ensaladilla (rusa) Russian salad. This is cooked vegetables in mayonnaise.

Yo no voy a tomar nada I'm not going to have anything (literally, I'm not going to take nothing).

calamares are squid. They either come in ink (**en su tinta**) or fried (**fritos**).

PRACTICE

7 Now for the bill at the Bar Marbella. Some of the words are omitted in the transcript below. Listen carefully to the recording and then fill in the blanks. Rewind to check that you were right.

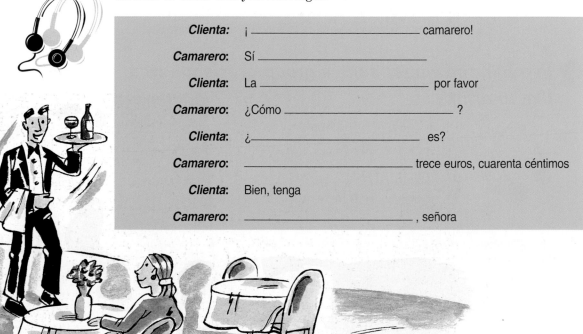

Clienta:	¡ _____ camarero!
Camarero:	Sí _____
Clienta:	La _____ por favor
Camarero:	¿Cómo _____ ?
Clienta:	¿ _____ es?
Camarero:	_____ trece euros, cuarenta céntimos
Clienta:	Bien, tenga
Camarero:	_____ , señora

8 In this conversation between a waiter and a customer, the customer's part hasn't been printed. Can you complete the conversation, choosing the correct response from the box below? Then listen to the recording to see if you were right.

Camarero:	Buenos días, señora, ¿qué va a tomar?
Señora:	_____
Camarero:	Tenemos bocadillos de queso, de jamón ...
Señora:	_____
Camarero:	Bien. ¿Algo más?
Señora:	_____
Camarero:	Sí, por supuesto
Señora:	_____
Camarero:	Son de caramelo, naranja, café y chocolate
Señora:	_____
Camarero:	¿Y algo de beber? ¿Café? ¿Zumos?
Señora:	_____
Camarero:	¿Un botellín o una caña?
Señora:	_____

No, una cerveza   ¿Hay helados?   ¿Qué bocadillos tiene?
Una caña   ¿De qué son?   Bueno, un bocadillo de queso
Bueno, pues, uno de chocolate

9 And now it's your turn to order. Eliud will prompt.

GRAMMAR AND EXERCISES

Something about pronouns

Where in English 'it' or 'them' is used to avoid repeating the name of the object or person under discussion, in Spanish you simply use the appropriate word for 'the' and place it in front of the verb. (The only exception is **el**, which changes to **lo**.) Look at the examples:

> **Conozco la calle**
> I know the street
> **La conozco**
> I know it
> **Conozco el centro de París**
> I know the centre of Paris
> **Lo conozco**
> I know it
>
> **¿Conoces las islas de Escocia?**
> Do you know the Scottish islands?
> **Las conozco**
> I know them
> **Estudio los efectos de la polución**
> I am studying the effects of pollution
> **Los estudio**
> I am studying them

When using an indirect pronoun (*to* him, *to* her, *to* them and so on), use either **le** or **les**.
¿Cuánto le debo? How much do I owe (to him, her, you)?
Les hablo en francés I speak to them in French

Verbs with irregular first person forms

A number of verbs in Spanish are perfectly regular in the present tense – except for the first person or '**yo**' form. Four examples are:

dar to give
doy I give
Le doy diez euros todos los días
> I give him ten euros every day

hacer to do, I to make
hago I do, I make
Hago las camas de toda la familia
> I make all the family's beds

saber to know (a fact)
sé I know
Lo sé I know (it)

conocer to know (a person, country)
conozco I know
Lo conozco bien I know it well

It can be difficult to know when to use **conocer** and **saber**. One rule of thumb is to use **saber** when you know a fact and **conocer** for knowing a person or a place.

Sé que está en París. I know he's in Paris. BUT
Conozco París. I know Paris.

10 Write out these amounts in full.

a. 1,40 euros

_____

b. 3,50 euros

_____

c. 7,90 euros

_____

d. 10,75 euros

_____

e. 21,35 euros

_____

f. 25,70 euros

_____

ANSWERS P. 64

11 Would you use **saber** or **conocer** in these sentences? Fill in the blanks with the correct form of the verb. Remember that **saber** follows the normal pattern for **-er** verbs (see Grammar, Unit 2, except for the '**yo**' part).

a. Yo _____ bien Chicago

b. ¿Tú _____ donde está tu hermana?

c. ¿(Tú) _____ a Conchita?

d. (Yo) no _____ qué hacer

e. (Ellos) _____ muy poco italiano

f. (Nosotros) _____ todos a Juan

g. (Ella) no _____ muy bien Irlanda

ANSWERS P. 64

12 **No lo veo** I can't see it ... There are lots of other items that you can't see either. Complete each sentence with the correct form of 'it' or 'them'.

a. ¿El café?

No _____ veo.

b. ¿La ensaladilla?

No _____ veo.

c. ¿El botellín?

No _____ veo.

d. ¿Los bocadillos de jamón?

No _____ veo.

e. ¿Las cervezas?

No _____ veo.

ANSWERS P. 64

El sabor de Baileys nos llevó a un mundo lleno de emociones. Hoy seguimos disfrutándolo juntos.

EL SABOR DE TUS EMOCIONES

KEY WORDS
AND PHRASES

Oiga	Excuse me
¿Cuánto es todo?	How much is everything?
La cuenta por favor	The bill, please
¿Cómo dice?	What did you say?
Lo siento	I am sorry
No entiendo	I don't understand
despacio por favor	slowly, please
¿Quieres ...	Do you want ...
helado	ice-cream
vino tinto	red wine
vino blanco	white wine
un vaso de vino	a glass of wine
una caña	a draft beer
un bocadillo	a sandwich
tapas	bar snacks
jamón	ham
calamares fritos	fried squid
queso	cheese
ensaladilla	Russian salad
¿De qué es ...?	What is ... made of?
¿De qué son ...?	What are ... made of?
¿De cuál quieres?	Which one do you want?
¿Qué vais a tomar?	What are you going to have? (informal)
¿Qué van a tomar?	What are you going to have? (formal)
¿Qué tomas?	What are you having? (**tú**)
¿para ti?	for you?
para mí	for me
¿Cuánto le debo?	How much do I owe you?
¿Cuánto es?	How much is it?
la cuenta	the bill
un cortado	coffee with a dash of milk
un solo	black coffee
un café con leche	milky coffee
un té	tea
un té con limón	lemon tea
un chocolate	chocolate (drink)
una bebida	drink (in general)
una tónica	a tonic water
un zumo de manzana	an apple juice
un zumo de naranja	an orange juice
una cerveza	beer

doscientos/as	200	setecientos/as	700
trescientos/as	300	ochocientos/as	800
cuatrocientos/as	400	novecientos/as	900
quinientos/as	500	mil	1,000
seiscientos/as	600	dos mil	2,000

DID YOU KNOW?

SPANIARDS use bars and cafeterias much more frequently than other nations. They arrange to meet their friends there rather than at home, they go out for an apéritif (even if they are dining at home) or, as we find out later in the course, they have an after lunch coffee in a bar rather than making it themselves. Even school students will go out to a bar to have a coffee in between lessons. It used to be the fashion for Spaniards to meet at regular times in certain bars or cafés to discuss politics, poetry or important issues of the day. The Café Gijón in Madrid was famous for these literary coteries, or **tertulias**, and they still exist though on a smaller and less formal scale. You will also see one or two of the old-style **casinos** or gentlemen's clubs where prominent townspeople meet to drink, chat and read the press.

On a more practical note, if you want to 'wash your hands', a bar or a cafeteria is a good place. There is always one nearby and toilets are kept scrupulously clean. Most bars also have telephones – just ask the waiter where it is. Strictly speaking, you don't even have to patronize the bar – but don't overdo going to the same place just to use their facilities! Tipping is still expected in Spain, but you don't usually have to pay for your drinks until you leave (though this too is changing). If you want a cheaper drink, sit at the bar rather than at a table and choose a café off the main squares and avenues.

Tapas, which is what the group of friends ordered in this Unit, are offered with pre-lunch or pre-dinner drinks. These used not to be charged for, although you may find that you pay separately for them in the more touristy areas of Spain. They are a good way of sampling regional dishes without committing yourself to a full meal.

Typical offerings include the following: **tortilla** is Spanish omelette made with eggs, onions and potatoes. **Boquerones** are fresh baby anchovies, fried and eaten whole – as are **chanquetes** (whitebait). You may find **merluza rebozada**, hake in egg batter or any variety of shellfish, ranging from **gambas** (prawns) to **almejas** (clams) or **mejillones** (mussels). **Chorizo** is always available. This is a spiced sausage and there are many different recipes used, but all contain pork, paprika (**pimentón**) and salt. **Chorizo de lomo** typically contains larger pieces of pork and if your **chorizo** is **picante**, it is highly spiced.

By law, menus must be displayed outside or in the window of the restaurant. Remember that a restaurant will be empty at 1.00 pm not because it's unpopular but because Spaniards eat much later. (See Unit 10.) Otherwise, a good rule of thumb as to whether a restaurant is good or not is to check how many people are already there. If it's full, it's probably excellent. In both Spain and Latin America, it is quite customary to be invited out to eat rather than in your host's home. Take care about when you are expected. **Hora inglesa** and **hora española** are not the same! In some parts of the Spanish-speaking world you may be invited for 8.00 pm but not eat until 11.00 pm. As the time before you eat will be spent drinking **aperitivos**, some people solve the problem of hunger and hangovers by having a light meal before they set out.

AND FINALLY...

13 You're in a cafeteria ordering various things to eat and drink for yourself and for a friend. Eliud will prompt you with what you have to say. You'll be practising:

items of food and drink

tenga

ANSWERS

EXERCISE 1

Eme: ¿Qué vais a tomar? **Sandra:** Un cortado **Eme:** Un cortado para ti. Y tú, Delia, ¿qué tomas? **Delia:** Un café con leche **Eme:** Un café con leche. Y Gerald, un solo, ¿no? **Gerald:** Sí **Waiter:** ¿Qué van a tomar, señores? **Eme:** Un solo, un cortado y dos con leche.

EXERCISE 2

Carlos milky coffee, Marisa black coffee, Eliud coffee with a dash of milk

EXERCISE 4

1, 40, 79, 65, 2, 84, 20.

EXERCISE 5

botellín, zumo de naranja, un bocadillo de queso, calamares fritos

EXERCISE 10

(a) un euro, cuarenta céntimos
(b) tres euros, cincuenta céntimos
(c) siete euros, noventa céntimos
(d) diez euros, setenta y cinco céntimos
(e) veintiún euros, treinta y cinco céntimos
(f) veinticinco euros, setenta céntimos

EXERCISE 11

(a) conozco **(b)** sabes **(c)** conoces **(d)** sé **(e)** saben **(f)** conocemos **(g)** conoce

EXERCISE 12

(a) lo **(b)** la **(c)** lo **(d)** los **(e)** las

5 NO RIGHT TURN

WHAT YOU WILL LEARN

▶ How to say ...
something about where you live
what you may and may not do
more about directions

BEFORE YOU BEGIN

It is a good idea to listen to each recording several times before going on. Repetition, including reading the answers to written exercises out loud and repeating the oral exercises several times, is the key to successful language learning, because words and structures need to be internalized before you will be able to use them with confidence and at natural speed. This is why courses which promise you a quick fix and rapid results are unlikely to prove effective in the long term.

If you do find yourself reaching a plateau, go back and review the earlier material. This not only gives you a boost in confidence (because you will understand it so much more easily) but you will maintain the language you have already learned. Material learned early in the course is just as useful on an everyday basis as is the more difficult language you will learn later on.

Pronunciation notes

The **s** in Spanish is usually pronounced like that in the English 'serpent' and has a rather hissing sound. Before **b**, **d** and **g**, however, the **s** is more like an English **z**. Say 'dezde' rather than **desde**. In some parts of the Spanish-speaking world (especially in the Canary Islands and Andalusia) the **s** drops altogether in favour of a sound like the English 'h'. Be careful, therefore, that you don't board a plane to La Palma instead of La(s) Palma(s)!

lejos   significa   España   inglés   esquina   desde

Eme asks Ricardo how he gets into Lugo

LISTEN FOR...

un pequeño pueblo	a small town
lejos	far
¿cómo haces para venir al colegio?	how do you get to school?

Eme	Oye, Ricardo, tú, ¿dónde vives?
Ricardo	En un pequeño pueblo cerca de Lugo. Se llama Rábade
Eme	Rábade
Ricardo	Mm
Eme	¿Y está muy lejos de aquí?
Ricardo	No, está a unos once kilómetros
Eme	Ah, y ¿cómo haces para venir al colegio todos los días?
Ricardo	Pues vengo todos los días en bus
Eme	En bus. Muy bien

▶ **el pueblo**   town, village
▶ **¿cómo?**   how?
▶ **hacer**   to do, to make
▶ **venir**   to come
▶ **el colegio**   school
▶ **el día**   day
▶ **el bus**   bus

¿Está muy lejos de aquí? Is it very far from here? **Lejos** far, **cerca** near. If you want to say near or far *from* somewhere, you need to use **de** as well: **cerca de Londres, lejos de Dallas.**

a unos once kilómetros   about eleven kilometres away. Use **unos/unas** for 'approximately, about ...'

¿Cómo haces para venir al colegio?   How do you get to school? (literally, how do you do to come to school?). **Hacer** (to do, to make) is also irregular. You will find it on page 60.

todos los días   every day. Although **día** looks like a feminine word, it is in fact masculine.

Pues vengo en bus.   Well, I come by bus. You will also hear **autobús. Venir** (to come) is irregular. You will find it on page 182. Remember **en tren** (by train), **en coche** (by car) and **en bicicleta** (by bike).

VIAJES AMADO LUGO, s.a.

Viajes Amado Lugo, S.A.
AGENCIA DE VIAJES
GRUPO A - TITULO XG-94

César

Obispo Aguirre, 2
Teléf. 23 17 30
        22 94 42
Telex 86133
27002 LUGO

IATA

RENFE

- BILLETES DE FERROCARRIL
- PASAJES AEREOS Y MARITIMOS
- RESERVA DE HOTELES Y APARTAMENTOS
- EXCURSIONES (AEREAS Y AUTOCAR)
- ALQUILER DE COCHES SIN CONDUCTOR
- ORGANIZACION DE CONGRESOS

Jordi tests Marta on the highway code

LISTEN FOR...

¿qué significa esta señal?	what does this sign mean?
no se puede circular	traffic prohibited
girar	to turn
parar	to stop
adelantar	to overtake

Jordi	Marta, ¿qué significa esta señal?
Marta	Eh, no se puede circular a más de cuarenta (kilómetros por hora)
Jordi	¿Y ésta?
Marta	No se puede parar aquí
Jordi	¿Y ésta?
Marta	No se puede entrar por esta dirección
Jordi	¿Y ésta otra?
Marta	No se puede girar a la derecha
Jordi	¿Y ésta?
Marta	No se puede girar a la izquierda
Jordi	¿Y ésta?
Marta	Eh, no se puede adelantar
Jordi	¿Y ésta?
Marta	No se puede circular en bicicleta

▶ **significar** to mean
▶ **la señal** the sign
▶ **circular** to travel
▶ **por** along
▶ **parar** to stop
▶ **entrar** to enter
▶ **girar** to turn
▶ **adelantar** to overtake

¿Qué significa esta señal? What does this sign mean? You'll be practising '**¿qué significa ...?**' later in the course.

se puede one can: **no se puede** one cannot, it is prohibited. As you see from the conversation, this expression is followed by the infinitive (the full form) of the verb.

No se puede circular Traffic prohibited (literally, one can not circulate). Use **circular** for cars, buses and so on.

a más de cuarenta at more than forty (kilometres per hour).

¿Y ésta? And this one? As in English, you don't need to keep repeating 'sign'. There's more about **éste/a/os/as** in the Grammar section of Unit 7.

por esta dirección in this direction. **Por** is awkward to translate but often means 'by', 'through' or 'from'. More about this on page 74.

¿Y ésta otra? And this other one?

1 Here's a short extract from a letter to a new friend. Only the verbs are missing. Try filling them in.

vivimos

está

va

voy

vivo

está

es

ANSWERS P. 78

Yo _____ *en Sant Just:* _____ *un pequeño pueblo muy cerca de Barcelona.* _____ *a unos quince kilómetros del centro de la ciudad.* _____ *todos los días en autobús a mi oficina. Mi esposo* _____ *en coche a su trabajo que* _____ *bastante lejos de donde* _____ .

2 Regulations around the swimming pool (**la piscina**) can be quite strict.
What can you do and not do around the pool area?
Write down the regulations in English.

a	No se puede montar en bicicleta en el área de la piscina
	_____
b	No se puede entrar en la piscina sin ducharse
	_____
c	No se pueden llevar zapatos en el área de la piscina
	_____
d	No se puede beber cerca de la piscina
	_____
e	No se puede comer cerca de la piscina
	_____
f	No se puede poner música
	_____

el zapato shoe
poner to put
ducharse to shower

ANSWERS P. 78

3 In this spoken exercise, you will be telling Eliud about how you get to work in the morning.

CONVERSATIONS

Directions to the Plaza de la Magdalena and the Plaza Mayor

LISTEN FOR...

la segunda bocacalle	the second turning
toda la calle adelante	right down the street

Pepe	Por favor, ¿la Plaza de la Magdalena?
Ernesto	La segunda bocacalle a la derecha

▶ **la plaza** square
▶ **la bocacalle** turning

Pepe	Por favor, ¿para ir a la Plaza Mayor?
Recepcionista	Toda la calle adelante,
	Calle Mayor a la izquierda

▶ **para ir ...** in order to go to ...
▶ **todo/a** all

And to the Plaza Galicia, the cathedral and the town hall or Ayuntamiento

LISTEN FOR...

saliendo de aquí	leaving here
¿podría decirme por dónde se va ... ?	can you tell me how to get to ... ?
enfrente	opposite
detrás	behind

María	La Plaza de Galicia por favor
Passer-by	Saliendo de aquí, todo recto, la primera plaza

▶ **salir** to leave

saliendo leaving. The -ing equivalent for **-ir** and **-er** verbs is **-iendo**:
cogiendo taking, **viniendo** coming.
todo recto straight on.

Delia	¿Podría decirme por dónde se va a la catedral?
Passer-by	La tiene usted aquí muy cerca, enfrente, detrás de este edificio, la Caja de Ahorros, está la Catedral

▶ **enfrente**   opposite
▶ **el edificio**   building
▶ **la Caja de Ahorros**   the Savings Bank

¿Podría decirme por dónde se va a la catedral?   Could you tell me how to get to the cathedral? A politer (and more longwinded) version of '**la catedral, por favor**'.

Delia	¿Podrías decirme dónde está el Ayuntamiento?
Passer-by	Allí al lado

▶ **allí**   over there
▶ **al lado**   just here
▶ **allí al lado**   just over there

 Note also ▶ **al lado de**   beside

Podrías ...   This time Delia uses the informal '**tú**' form.

PRACTICE

4   Here's a short quiz for you.

a. give three ways to ask how you get to the Plaza Mayor

   i. _____

   ii. _____

   iii. _____

(There are several possibilities here. We give some in the Answers on page 78.)

b. how do you say

   i. straight ahead? _____

   ii. the first turning? _____

   iii. behind this building? _____

   iv. opposite? _____

5 On the recording you will be given directions to three different places. Find out where you are being sent on the map, by following the instructions.

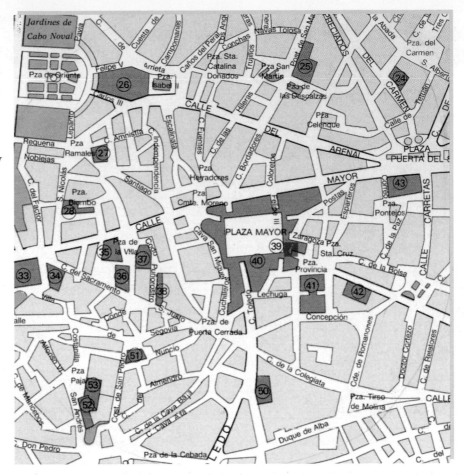

24 Church of El Carmen	38 Basilica of San Miguel
25 Convent of Las Descalzas Reales	39 Plaza Mayor
26 Royal Theatre	40 Cuchilleros Arch
27 Church of Santiago (St James)	41 Santa Cruz Palace. Ministry of Foreign Affairs
28 Church of San Nicolás	42 Church of Santa Cruz
29 Royal Palace	43 Headquarters of the Community of Madrid
30 Cathedral of Nuestra Señora de La Almudena	44 Spanish Theatre
31 Municipal Tourist Board Offices	45 Madrid Athenæum
32 Viaduct	46 Prado Museum
33 Los Consejos Palace. Military Headquarters	47 Convent of Las Trinitarias
34 Church of El Santísimo Sacramento	48 Royal Academy of History
35 City Hall	49 Cervantes Museum. Miguel de la Cuesta Printing House
36 Casa de Cisneros	50 Cathedral of San Isidro
37 Los Lujanes Tower	

ANSWERS P. 78

6 Now you are out and about in the middle of a Spanish city. You'll be asking for directions to the **Plaza Real**, the **Ayuntamiento**, the **Catedral** and the Tourist Office – the **Oficina de Turismo**.

At a service station

Pepe	Oiga, por favor, ¿para ir hacia la carretera de Madrid? ¿Para ir a Madrid?
Gasolinero	Bueno, pues tiene usted que salir por la carretera de la Nacional Uno y está tomando el puente, el puente romano, el puente viejo y después a mano izquierda allí verá los indicadores para Madrid
Pepe	Tengo que cruzar el puente, ¿no?
Gasolinero	Sí, sí, tiene que ir al otro lado del río
Pepe	¿Y luego doblo?
Gasolinero	A la izquierda. (A la izquierda). Y allí verá los indicadores para Ávila y Madrid
Pepe	Aha. ¿Y tengo que pasar por Ávila?
Gasolinero	Pues, sí, puede usted pasar por Ávila, pero no es necesario

- ▶ **hacia**   towards
- ▶ **la carretera**   road
- ▶ **el gasolinero**   petrol pump attendant
- ▶ **el puente**   bridge
- ▶ **romano**   Roman
- ▶ **viejo**   old
- ▶ **después**   then, after
- ▶ **a mano izquierda**   on the left hand (**la mano** the hand)
- ▶ **necesario**   necessary

Tiene usted que salir por la carretera de la Nacional Uno   You have to go out along the N.1 road.

Está tomando el puente   You take the bridge. (Literally, you're taking the bridge.)

Tomar and **coger** both mean 'to take'. **Tome/coja la carretera a la izquierda** take the road on the left. (Don't use **coger** in Latin America: it has another, very vulgar, meaning.)

Allí verá los indicadores   There you'll see the signs.

¿Tengo que cruzar el puente?   Do I have to cross the bridge? **Tener que** to have to
... **Tengo que ir a casa de mis padres** I have to go to my parents' house.

al otro lado del río   to/on the other side of the river. You'll remember the word **río** if you think of **el Río Grande** or Rio de Janeiro.

¿Y luego doblo?   And then do I turn? **Doblar la esquina** to turn the corner.

¿Tengo que pasar por Ávila?   Do I have to go through Ávila?

7 In this exercise you will be practising '**¿tengo que?**' do I have to ...? Look at the instructions and sketches below and fill in the phrase which is most appropriate, using **¿tengo que ... ?** The first one has been done for you.

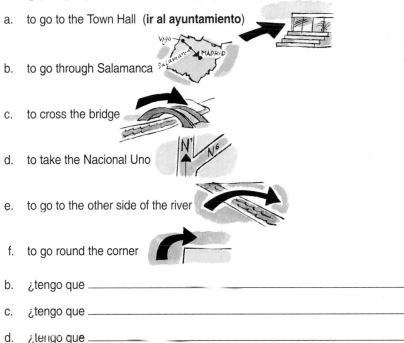

a. to go to the Town Hall (**ir al ayuntamiento**)

b. to go through Salamanca

c. to cross the bridge

d. to take the Nacional Uno

e. to go to the other side of the river

f. to go round the corner

b. ¿tengo que ————————————————————————————?

c. ¿tengo que ————————————————————————————?

d. ¿tengo que ————————————————————————————?

e. ¿tengo que ————————————————————————————?

ANSWERS P. 78

f. ¿tengo que ————————————————————————————?

8 You're going to visit a friend in Spain. Here is part of his letter to you giving directions and he also includes a map for getting to his home in Barcelona.

fácil easy

cuidado (take) care

Following the instructions that your friend sends you in the letter, draw the map that he also included. You'll find our version on page 78.

9 Now you give your friend directions for visiting you.

... es fácil llegar a la casa. Vas todo recto hasta la Plaza de Colón. Cruzas la Plaza. Luego tomas la calle Romero (es la primera bocacalle a la derecha). Vas toda la calle adelante y al final, tomas la calle Bravo. Nosotros vivimos en el número veinte, enfrente del Banco Popular, en la esquina con Cortes Catalanas. Está a un kilómetro, más o menos, de la estación de tren, pero si vienes en coche, ¡cuidado! No se puede aparcar en nuestra calle. Tienes que seguir hasta la próxima bocacalle a la izquierda, calle Cuernavaca. Aquí va el plano junto...

GRAMMAR AND EXERCISES

Poder to be able to

In Unit 3 you learnt about stem-changing verbs (**siento**, **prefiero**, **quiero**). **Poder** is an example of another stem-changing verb where, this time, the **o** changes to **ue**.

puedo	I can
puedes	you can (informal)
puede	s/he can
puede	you can (formal)
podemos	we can
podéis	you can (informal plural)
pueden	they can
pueden	you can (formal plural)

Volver (to return) and **costar** (to cost) work in a similar way.

Always follow **poder** by a verb in the infinitive:
Lo puedo hacer
    I can do it
Se puede
    means 'one/you can' or 'are allowed to':
se puede comer aquí
    one/you can eat here
No se puede
    means 'one/you cannot':
no se puede fumar aquí
    one/you cannot smoke here

Por and *Para*

Por and **para** are often translated by the word 'for' in English, but they are used in different ways and in a variety of situations. Here's a short summary of how and when to use them.

Para
  i. Whenever you can insert the English phrase 'in order to', use **para**:
    ¿Para ir a la catedral?
    How do I get to the cathedral? (In order to get to the cathedral?)

  ii. **Para** also means 'towards':
    Voy para Cuba
    I'm going to(wards) Cuba

  iii. In phrases like: **es para mí** it's for me
    Es un regalo para Juan
    It's a present for Juan

Por
  i. Use **por** to mean 'through', 'along' or 'via':
    por la plaza
    through the square
    por la calle
    along the street
    Voy a Madrid por Salamanca
    I'm going to Madrid via Salamanca

  ii. It's used a lot in set phrases such as:
    por favor
    please
    gracias por (tu carta)
    thank you for (your letter)
    por aquí
    around here

  iii. It's also used in time expressions:
    Voy por dos días
    I'm going for two days
    por la mañana
    in the morning

  iv. Use it when you're talking about how you do things:
    por autobús
    by bus
    llamar por teléfono
    to call by phone, to phone

When in doubt, use **por** – it occurs more frequently than **para**

■ one more note about **para**. One says **para mí** and **para ti**; otherwise use the usual pronoun, **para él** (for him), **para usted** (for you), etc.

Mi(s), Tu(s) and Su(s)

To say 'my' in Spanish, simply use **mi**. If the word you're describing is plural, add an **s**.

mi padre   my father
mis padres   my parents

It's the same for **tu** your
tu hijo   your son
tus hijos   your children/sons

Su means 'his', 'her', 'their' or 'your' (formal). You'll need to look at the whole phrase or sentence to work out the exact meaning. Add an **s** for the plural.

Su familia   his, her, their or your family
Sus familias   his, her, their or your families

You won't be practising this here, but **nuestro** means 'our' and **vuestro** means 'your' when you're talking to people whom you address as **vosotros**.

10 Complete these sentences with the correct form of **poder**, **volver** and **costar**:

a. ¿Cuánto _____ por favor?

b. ¿Cómo _____ a casa, Roberto? ¿Yo?
_____ en autobús

c. María no _____ venir esta tarde

d. _____ ochenta euros

e. Yo no _____ volver por la mañana

f. No se _____ fumar en el comedor

g. Mis padres _____ a Valencia mañana

ANSWERS P. 78

11 Complete these sentences with either **por** or **para**

a. ¿Es _____ mí?

b. ¿_____ al banco?

c. Pasa _____ la Plaza Mayor

d. _____ favor

e. Voy al trabajo _____ autobús

f. Puedes llamar _____ teléfono

g. _____ beber, señor?

ANSWERS P. 78

12 Tick the correct word in brackets:

a. (mi/mis) padres viven en Barcelona, a unos setecientos kilómetros de aquí.

b. ¿Dónde vive (tu/tus) familia?

c. ¿Dónde está (tu/tus) colegio?

d. (mi/mis) pueblo se llama Fontalba

e. (su/sus) hijos van a un colegio privado

f. Señor, (su/sus) taxi ...

ANSWERS P. 78

KEY WORDS
AND PHRASES

¿Qué significa esta señal?	What does this sign mean?
no se puede	one must not, it is forbidden to
circular	go, travel
aparcar	park
girar	turn
doblar la esquina	turn the corner
¿Se puede ir a pie?	Can you go on foot?
en coche?	by car?
en bicicleta?	by bike?
en autobús?	by bus?
vengo	I come
en tren	by train
¿La Plaza de España, por favor?	Plaza de España, please
¿Para ir a la Plaza de España?	How do you get to the Plaza de España?
¿Podría(s) decirme dónde está la Plaza de España?	Can you tell me where the Plaza de España is?

formal	informal	
vaya	ve	go
cruce	cruza	cross
doble	dobla	turn (the corner)
coja	coge	take
tome	toma	take
baje	baja	go down
suba	sube	go up

todo recto	straight on
toda la calle adelante	straight down the street
la primera bocacalle	the first turning
al lado de la catedral	next to the cathedral
en frente del ayuntamiento	opposite the town hall
detrás del Corte Inglés	behind the Corte Inglés
entre Vigo y el Ferrol	between Vigo and Ferrol
en la esquina con Fuentes	on the corner at Fuentes St.
la avenida	avenue
cerca de	near to
lejos de	far from
a unos ... kilómetros	about ... kilometres away
de aquí	from here
depende	it depends
todos los días	every day

Modern Spain

MODERN SPAIN has moved far away from the traditional image of the bullfighter and the flamenco dancer. It is a complex society in which many different life styles co-exist and where attitudes are coloured much more by age than by other factors.

Recent studies have shown that the old rural Spain is fast disappearing. Although agriculture still plays an important part in the Spanish economy, this is 'agribusiness' – exemplified by the acres of plastic tunnelling for producing fruit and vegetables in the Almería region. The profound differences between life styles in the city and in the country have disappeared and it is now difficult to tell who lives where, simply by their way of life. As elsewhere in Europe, small farmers and peasants are rapidly disappearing and their children are being educated into technology and the liberal professions.

Indeed, Spain is fanatical about change, novelty and experimentation. Most of what reaches the country from abroad is welcomed with open arms, especially if it comes from North America. Indeed it is inconceivable that the changes which have taken place since the death of Franco could have taken place elsewhere.

Today, the Spaniard is better fed than ever he or she was when living off the land, lives on average twelve years longer than in the 1950s and is perhaps, the most sexually liberated citizen in Europe. Family size has plummeted so that Spain has one of the lowest birth rates in Europe. Families with one or possibly two children are now the norm and the **familias numerosas** of the past are rapidly disappearing. What is amazing is the adaptability and tolerance of the average Spaniard.

13 Now you'll be asking for directions in a garage just outside Madrid, where you've somehow taken the wrong turning. You'll be practising:

¿está lejos/cerca?
por favor, ¿para ir a ...?
¿tengo que ...?

ANSWERS

EXERCISE 1

Yo vivo en Sant Just: es un pequeño pueblo muy cerca de Barcelona. Está a unos quince kilómetros del centro de la ciudad. Voy todos los días en autobús a mi oficina. Mi esposo va en coche a su trabajo que está bastante lejos de donde vivimos.

EXERCISE 2

it is forbidden   **(a)** to ride bikes   **(b)** to swim without having a shower   **(c)** to wear shoes in the pool area
(d) to drink   **(e)** to eat   **(f)** to play music

EXERCISE 4

(a) i. ¿para ir a la Plaza Mayor?   ii. la Plaza Mayor, por favor
iii. ¿podría decirme por dónde se va a la Plaza Mayor?
iv. ¿me puede decir por dónde se va a la Plaza Mayor?
(b) i. todo recto   ii. la primera bocacalle   iii. detrás de este edificio   iv. enfrente

EXERCISE 5

i. Church of El Carmen   **ii.** Royal Theatre
iii. Basilica of San Miguel

EXERCISE 7

(b) ¿tengo que pasar por Salamanca?   **(c)** ¿tengo que cruzar el puente?   **(d)** ¿tengo que salir por (la carretera de) la Nacional Uno?   **(e)** ¿tengo que ir al otro lado del río?
(f) ¿tengo que doblar la esquina?

EXERCISE 8

EXERCISE 10

(a) cuesta   **(b)** vuelves, vuelvo   **(c)** puede   **(d)** cuesta
(e) puedo   **(f)** puede   **(g)** vuelven

EXERCISE 11

(a) para   **(b)** para   **(c)** por   **(d)** por   **(e)** por   **(f)** por
(g) para

EXERCISE 12

(a) mis   **(b)** tu   **(c)** tu   **(d)** mi   **(e)** sus   **(f)** su

6 TELLING THE TIME

WHAT YOU WILL LEARN

▶ How to …
tell the time
find out about the times of trains and buses
▶ Something about telephones in Spain

BEFORE YOU BEGIN

In order to retain the material that you have learned, you need to review it fairly systematically. A good pattern is the following: look over what you learned on day 1, on day 2, and then again on day 4 and day 7. You should then be able to leave it for another week (day 14) before looking through it once more.

Review this same material two weeks later (day 28) and it should by then have been transferred to your long-term memory! The process of fixing something in your long-term memory takes a long time – hence the need for plenty of revision and review.

Even when material has been transferred to the long-term memory, it may not always be easy to access. This is why you need to keep your newly acquired language constantly on the boil. You can do this by tuning into Spanish stations on the radio or on satellite television – or to the schools' language programmes on British television. At this very early stage you may not understand a great deal, but you *are* listening and having your memory constantly jogged.

Pronunciation notes

The **ñ** (as in **mañana**) is pronounced like 'ny' or the French **gn** in oignon. Make sure it is just one sound. The **ñ** (the accent here is called a tilde) is dear to Spaniards and they have resisted all European attempts to banish it from the computer keyboard. **Peña** (a cliff or rock) and **pena** (grief, sadness) do not mean at all the same thing!

mañana   cumpleaños

niño   niña   año

**Museo Nacional Centro de Arte
Reina Sofía**
C/ Santa Isabel, 52
28012 Madrid
Teléf.: (91) 467 50 62
Fax: 539 68 24

Horario
Lunes a Sábado de 10,00 a 21,00 horas.
Domingos de 10,00 a 14,30 horas.
Martes cerrado.

Transporte
Autobuses: 6, 10, 14, 18, 19, 26, 27, 32, 34, 36, 37, 41, 45, 47, 55, 57, 59, 68, 86, 119.
Metro: Línea 1
RENFE.

Pepe asks how long it takes to get to Vigo by train

LISTEN FOR...

¿cuánto tiempo dura el viaje?   how long does the journey take?

Pepe	¿Cuánto dura el viaje a Vigo, por favor?
Empleada	Diez horas aproximadamente
Pepe	¿Cómo?
Empleada	Diez horas

▶ **durar**   to last
▶ **el viaje**   journey
▶ **la hora**   hour

¿cuánto (tiempo)?   how long? (literally, how much time?). Use **cuánto** with a noun to mean how much? **¿Cuánto dinero?** How much money?
el viaje a Vigo   the journey to Vigo. Vigo is also in Galicia.
¿cómo?   what (did you say)?

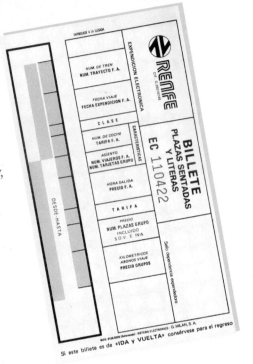

 María asks some people in the street the time

LISTEN FOR...

¿qué hora es?   what time is it?

María	¿Qué hora es, por favor?
Passer-by	Las cuatro y media
María	¿Qué hora es, por favor?
Passer-by	Pues son las cinco menos diez

▶ **¿qué hora es?**   what time is it? (literally, what hour is it?)
▶ **la hora**   hour, time
▶ **medio/a**   half
▶ **son las (once)**   it is (eleven o'clock).
▶ **menos**   minus, less

▶ Telling the time

Telling the time in Spanish is quite easy. Study these examples and read them out loud.

¿qué hora es?	what time is it?
es la una	it's one o'clock
son las dos	it's two o'clock
son las tres	it's three o'clock

Use **es** only for talking about one o'clock. You can guess why.

son las cuatro y cuarto	it's a quarter past four
son las cuatro y media	it's half past four
son las cinco menos diez	it's ten to five (**menos** minus)
son las cinco y diez	it's ten past five

You can specify whether you are talking about the morning, afternoon or evening by using these expressions:

son las seis de la mañana	it's six o'clock in the morning
son las seis de la tarde	it's six o'clock in the afternoon
son las doce de la noche	its twelve o'clock at night
son las doce del mediodía	it's midday

¿a qué hora?	at what time?
a la una	at one o'clock
a las dos	at two o'clock

Use the twenty-four-hour clock for official timetables.

las dieciséis horas	16.00 hours
las veinte horas	20.00 hours
las veintitrés horas diez minutos	23.10

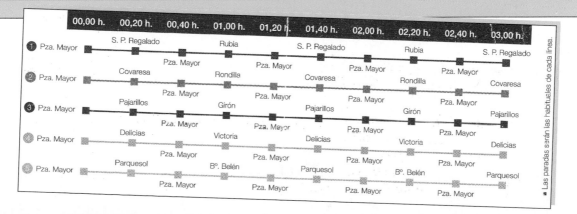

1 On the recording, a number of tourists ask how long the journey takes to various Spanish cities. Jot down the reply in Spanish, writing out the number in full.

   i. Sevilla _____

  ii. Córdoba _____

 iii. Granada _____

 iv. Barcelona _____

  v. Lugo _____

ANSWERS P. 94   vi. Santiago _____

2 Look at these clocks and watches. Write in the correct time underneath each one. The first has been done for you.

  i. _____ *son las cuatro menos cinco*

 ii. _____ _____

iii. _____ _____

iv. _____ _____

 v. _____ _____

ANSWERS P. 94 vi. _____

3 In the spoken exercise, several people stop you in the street to ask the time. Eliud will prompt you.

● **Eme asks Daniel and Adelaida when their birthdays and saints' days are**

LISTEN FOR...

¿cuándo es tu cumpleaños?	when is your birthday?
¿el día de tu santo?	your saint's day?
enero	January
mayo	May
marzo	March
diciembre	December

Eme	Daniel, ¿cuándo es tu cumpleaños?
Daniel	Es el dos de mayo
Eme	El dos de mayo. Y ¿el día de tu santo?
Daniel	El tres de enero
Eme	Ah, muy bien

▶ **¿cuándo?** when
▶ **el cumpleaños** birthday
▶ **(el) mayo** May
▶ **el santo** saint's day
▶ **(el) enero** January

¿Cuándo es tu cumpleaños? When is your birthday? **Cumpleaños** looks plural but is in fact singular.

Es el dos de mayo It's the second of May. To give dates, simply use the following formula 'el + number + de + month'. You don't need to use the word **día**. **El cinco de marzo** the 5th of March.

el día de tu santo your saint's day. Spanish children are often named after a saint and they often celebrate the feast day of that saint as well as their birthday.

Eme	Oye, Adelaida, ¿cuál es el día de tu cumpleaños?
Adelaida	El catorce de marzo
Eme	El catorce de marzo
Adelaida	Sí
Eme	Y ¿el día de tu santo?
Adelaida	El dieciséis de diciembre
Eme	El dieciséis de diciembre. El mío es el doce de diciembre

▶ **(el) marzo** March
▶ **(el) diciembre** December

You'll find a list of the months of the year in the Key Phrases section. They are all masculine.

Septiembre is written with or without a **p**. In either case the **p** is hardly sounded.

▶ *Pepe asks about opening and closing times for El Corte Inglés*

LISTEN FOR...

¿a qué hora se abre?	what time does it open?
¿a qué hora se cierra?	what time does it close?
todos los días de la semana	every day of the week
los sábados	on Saturdays

Pepe	Por favor, ¿a qué hora se abre El Corte Inglés?
Loli	A las diez de la mañana
Pepe	Y ¿a qué hora se cierra?
Loli	A las ocho
Pepe	¿Todos los días de la semana?
Loli	Todos los días de la semana
Pepe	¿Los sábados también?
Loli	Los sábados también
Pepe	Y ¿no cierran ustedes al mediodía?
Loli	No, nunca
Pepe	Nunca. Pero los domingos no abren, ¿no?
Loli	No, no, nunca
Pepe	Nunca

▶ **abrir**   to open
▶ **cerrar**   to close
▶ **la semana**   week
▶ **el sábado**   Saturday
▶ **el mediodía**   midday
▶ **el domingo**   Sunday
▶ **nunca**   never

¿A qué hora se abre El Corte Inglés?   What time does the Corte Inglés open? Don't confuse '**¿qué hora es?**' (what time is it?) with '**a qué hora?**' (at what time?)

Se abre   opens: **se cierra**   closes. More about this in the grammar section on page 196. El Corte Inglés is a big department store with branches all over Spain. The name means 'the English cut/style'.

Y ¿a qué hora se cierra?   And what time does it close? You'll see the word **cerrado** (closed) on shop doors, as well as **abierto** (open).

¿Los sábados también?   On Saturdays too? Use the plural for talking about many Saturdays: if you are referring to one particular day, use '**el**'. **Voy a la discoteca el sábado por la noche** I'm going to the disco on Saturday night.

¿No cierran ustedes al mediodía?   You don't close at midday? Note also **a la medianoche** at midnight.

cerrar is a stem-changing verb, like **preferir** and **sentir**. You'll find a list of the days of the week in the Key Phrases section. Like the months of the year, they don't take capitals.

4 On the recording, Carlos will read out the days of the week. Repeat them after him. Then answer Marisa's questions according to the prompts.

5 Now for the months. When you've repeated them, listen to Carlos giving information which includes various dates. Number them from one to six as you hear them mentioned. You'll be meeting the words **mujer** wife and **mi aniversario de boda** my wedding anniversary.

a. el diecinueve de marzo

b. el dieciocho de enero

c. el seis de febrero

d. el tres de abril

e. el veintiséis de julio

f. el quince de agosto

ANSWERS P. 94

6 In the speaking exercise, Carlos asks you about certain important days and dates in your life. You'll hear **marido** husband.

ENERO		FEBRERO		MARZO
ABRIL		MAYO		JUNIO
JULIO		AGOSTO		SEPTIEMBRE
OCTUBRE		NOVIEMBRE		DICIEMBRE

DIAS BLANCOS · DIA BLANCO DESDE LAS 12 h · DIAS ROJOS
DIAS AZULES · DIA AZUL DESDE LAS 16 h · DIA ROJO DESDE LAS 12 h
DIA ROJO HASTA LAS 16 h
EN TRENES REGIONALES, LOS DIAS ROJOS SE CONSIDERARAN DIAS BLANCOS.

CONVERSATIONS 3

What time does the train leave?

LISTEN FOR...

¿a qué hora sale el tren?	what time does the train leave?
¿a qué hora llega?	what time does it arrive?
sale a su hora	it leaves on time
en punto	punctually

Pepe   ¿A qué hora sale el tren para Salamanca por favor?

Dorita   ¿Por la mañana o por la tarde?

Pepe   Por la mañana y por la tarde por favor

Dorita   Tiene uno a las ocho horas quince minutos, semi-directo con llegada a Salamanca a las doce horas treinta minutos, y por la tarde tiene otro semi-directo, a las dieciséis horas quince minutos, con llegada a Salamanca a las veinte horas treinta minutos

Pepe   Por favor, ¿a qué hora llega a Salamanca el de la tarde?

Dorita   A las veinte horas treinta minutos

Pepe   Y ¿sale el tren siempre a su hora?

Dorita   Sí, sale en punto

Pepe   Gracias

▶ **salir**   to leave
▶ **la llegada**   arrival
▶ **el semi-directo**   stopping (train)
▶ **llegar**   to arrive

salir (to leave) is like a number of Spanish verbs which are irregular only in the first person or **yo** form of the present tense: **salgo** I leave. Combine **salir** with **de** in expressions such as: **salgo de la casa** I leave the house.

por la mañana   in the morning: **por la tarde**   in the evening. Use **de** rather than **por** where you mention specific times of day. **A las seis de la mañana** at six o'clock in the morning.

Notice how **la llegada** (arrival) is related to the verb **llegar** to arrive; **salida** (exit or departure) is similarly related to **salir** to leave.

a su hora   on time. This is a useful expression to know when enquiring about arrival (**la llegada**) and departure (**la salida**).

Sale en punto   It leaves punctually (literally, on the dot).

Madrid Puerta de Atocha - Ciudad Real - Puertollano - Córdoba - Sevilla Santa Justa												
MADRID (Pta. de Atocha)	7,00	7,15	8,00	9,15	11,00	13,15	14,00	16,00	17,00	19,00	19,15	21,00	22,15
CIUDAD REAL	7,53	8,09	·	10,09	·	14,09	·	·	17,53	·	20,09	21,53	23,09
PUERTOLLANO	8,08	8,30	·	10,30	·	14,30	·	·	18,08	·	20,30	22,08	23,30
CORDOBA	8,53	·	9,47	·	12,47	·	·	17,47	18,53	20,47	·	22,53	·
SEVILLA (Sta. Justa)	9,45	·	10,38	·	13,38	·	16,30	18,38	19,45	21,38	·	23,45	·

Sevilla Santa Justa - Córdoba - Puertollano - Ciudad Real - Madrid Puerta de Atocha											
SEVILLA (Sta. Justa)	·	7,00	·	8,00	·	11,00	14,00	·	16,00	17,00	19,00	·	21,00
CORDOBA	·	7,44	·	8,44	·	11,44	·	·	16,44	17,44	19,44	·	21,44
PUERTOLLANO	7,00	8,27	9,00	·	12,00	·	·	17,00	·	18,27	·	21,00	22,27
CIUDAD REAL	7,16	8,42	9,16	·	12,16	·	·	17,16	·	18,42	·	21,16	22,42
MADRID (Pta. de Atocha)	8,15	9,45	10,15	10,38	13,15	13,38	16,30	18,15	18,38	19,45	21,38	22,15	23,45

Todos los servicios se prestan diariamente. AVE - RENFE se reserva el derecho de modificar la denominación de los trenes (Valle, Llano, Punta, Lanzadera) sin previo aviso.

Juan wants to make a call to Wolverhampton

LISTEN FOR...

¿qué tengo que hacer?	what do I have to do?
tiene que marcar...	you have to dial...
esperar el tono	wait for the tone
la llamada	the call
el abonado	the subscriber

Juan	Por favor, quiero hacer una llamada a Wolverhampton. ¿Qué tengo que hacer?
Telefonista	¿A dónde?
Juan	Wolverhampton, en Inglaterra
Telefonista	En Inglaterra. ¿Sabe usted el número de la ciudad?
Juan	El uno nueve cero dos
Telefonista	Pues, entonces, tiene que marcar el cero cero, esperar el tono, el cuatro, cuatro, uno, nueve, cero, dos y el del abonado

▶ **la llamada**   call
▶ **el número**   number
▶ **la ciudad**   city
▶ **marcar**   to dial
▶ **esperar**   to wait
▶ **el tono**   the tone
▶ **el abonado**   subscriber

¿Qué tengo que hacer?
What do I have to do? You will remember that **tengo + que** means 'I have to'. Notice how the telephonist replies saying **'tiene que ... esperar'**: you have to ... wait.
el del abonado   the subscriber's number (literally, the one of the subscriber).
44 is the code to the UK from the Continent. The code to the USA is 1. The international dialling code is 00.

7 On the recording you'll hear a number of train announcements. Listen carefully to where the trains come from and then fill in their times of arrival (in figures only), and their platform numbers in the timetable below. Listen right through at least once, before you try to write anything.

ANSWERS P. 94

el andén   platform

Procedencia	Llegada	Andén
SALAMANCA		
VALENCIA		
MADRID		
LA CORUÑA		
VIGO		
BURGOS		

8 **Telefónica** (the Spanish Telephone Company) has been having a publicity drive recently. Read through the information about making calls to Spain from any country in the world and then answer the questions in English.

ESPAÑA DIRECTO

Desde teléfonos públicos o privados. Sin problemas de dinero o monedas. Porque la llamada es atendida en castellano y una vez aceptada será abonada en España. Por comodidad. Por economía. Para tu tranquilidad y la de tu familia y amigos.

➤ Llama a cualquier hora: el precio es el mismo

➤ No se tienen que pagar recargos de cabinas u hoteles
➤ Es más barato que el Cobro Revertido
➤ Sin problemas de idioma

Para más información, llame gratis al teléfono 900 105 105 (Centro de Atención para Comunicaciones Internacionales).

▶ **la moneda**   change
▶ **una vez**   once, one time
▶ **cualquier**   any
▶ **el recargo**   charge
▶ **u**   or (replaces **o** in front of **o-** or **ho-**)
▶ **el Cobro Revertido**   reverse charge service

a. What sort of telephone can you use for this service?

_____

b. What money problems do you avoid?

_____

c. What language is used?

_____

d. Who pays for the call?

_____

e. Which number do you call for more information?
    (Write out the answer, in Spanish, in full.)

ANSWERS P. 94

_____

9 Now you try making a phone call from the Reception desk at your Spanish hotel.
The presenter will prompt you as usual.

GRAMMAR AND EXERCISES

Expressing dates

Look at how people talk about their birthdays and saints' days:

el (día) dos de mayo
> the second of May

el tres de enero
> the third of January

There are a number of points to make about dates:

- days of the week and months of the year don't have capitals

- use cardinal numbers (**dos**, **tres**, **cuatro**) instead of ordinal ones (**segundo**, **tercero**, **cuarto**). The only exception is the first of the month, when you can say either:
  el uno de (junio) or **el primero de (junio)**

- if you're giving the date on a letter, then follow this formula: **Caracas, 24 de marzo de 2003**

- if you mention the day of the week, you don't need to repeat the article (**el**): **el domingo, veintinueve de julio**.

Tener que

You have already met and practised the verb **tener** to have. In this Unit it occurs again, this time followed by **que**. In this sense, it expresses obligation: **Tengo que** I have to. It is always followed by the infinitive of the verb. **Tengo que salir** I have to leave.

Infinitives

An infinitive is the fullest form of the verb. In English it is always preceded by 'to': to speak (**hablar**), to be (**ser/estar**). In Spanish the word for 'to' disappears, but the endings on the verb tell you that it is in the infinitive form. This is the form you will find in the dictionary.

10

a.
i.

voy al trabajo _____

ii.

estoy en la oficina _____

iii.

como en un restaurante _____

iv.

voy a casa _____

v.

veo la televisión _____

vi.

voy a la cama _____

ANSWERS P. 94

b. At what time do *you* do those same activities?

11 Today is Monday and you are in a dreadful hurry. How do you say you need to do the following things?

Hoy, lunes…

a. I have to leave home at 8.00 in the morning

_____

b. I have to go to the Corte Inglés

_____

c. I have to be at the university at 11.00

_____

d. I have to lunch with my mother at midday

_____

e. I have to work in the office in the afternoon

_____

f. I have to dine with my boyfriend in the evening

_____

g. I have to arrive at home at midnight

_____

ANSWERS P. 94

12 Here are some important days and dates in Spain. Can you express them as words?

a. 15th of August (**la Asunción**)

_____

b. 8th of December (**la Inmaculada**)

_____

c. 25th of December (**Navidad**)

_____

d. 1st of January (**Año nuevo**)

_____

e. 6th of January (**los Reyes**)

_____

f. 7th of July (**San Fermín**) in Pamplona

_____

g. 1st of May (**día del Trabajo**)

_____

h. 12th of October (**día de la Hispanidad**) or Columbus Day

_____

ANSWERS P. 94

KEY WORDS
AND PHRASES

¿Cuánto (tiempo) dura el viaje?	How long does the journey last?
Diez horas aproximadamente	Approximately ten hours
¿Me puede(s) decir los horarios de los autobuses?	Can you tell me the bus times?
adiós	goodbye
hasta luego	see you later
¿A qué hora se abre el Corte Inglés	What time does the Corte Inglés open
se cierra	close
abren ustedes	do you open
cierran ustedes?	do you close?
cerrado	closed
abierto	open
a las diez de la mañana	at ten in the morning
de la tarde	in the evening
de la noche	at night
al mediodía	at midday
a la medianoche	at midnight
nunca	never
mañana por la mañana	tomorrow morning
mañana por la tarde	tomorrow afternoon
los días de la semana	the days of the week
el domingo	Sunday
el lunes	Monday
el martes	Tuesday
el miércoles	Wednesday
el jueves	Thursday
el viernes	Friday
el sábado	Saturday
¿Cuándo es tu cumpleaños?	When is your birthday?
tu santo?	your saint's day?
Mi cumpleaños es el 3 de abril	My birthday is April 3rd
los meses del año	the months of the year
enero	January
febrero	February
marzo	March
abril	April
mayo	May
junio	June
julio	July
agosto	August
se(p)tiembre	September
octubre	October
noviembre	November
diciembre	December
con llegada a ...	with an arrival time of ...
con salida a ...	with a departure time of ...
El tren sale a las diez	The train leaves at 10.00
llega	arrives
en punto	on the dot

Time ...

One of the main things which surprises non-Spaniards when they first visit Spain is the time at which things happen. Generally speaking, events take place two or even three hours later than the usual time in the rest of Europe. People tend to have lunch at 2.00 pm (or even 3.00 pm in the south) and dinner not much earlier than 10.00 pm in the evening. This means that Spaniards tend to go to bed later than other Europeans but they don't seem to lie in any later in the mornings! It helps to think of certain time expressions in relation to meals. Although **mediodía** literally means midday, it really means about lunchtime (that is, 2.00 or 3.00 pm). Similarly, **la tarde**, which is always translated as afternoon, is any time until the evening meal. **Clases de tarde** are what we would call the typical evening class which starts at 7.00 pm.

Spanish shops often open between 9.00 and 10.00 am and close at 1.30 pm

for lunch. They re-open at 4.00 pm and close at 7.30 or 8.00 pm. It is of course a good idea to check these opening hours when you first arrive in a town or city because there are often regional variations. Large department stores don't usually close at midday: more and more are opening from 10.00 am till 4.00 pm on a Sunday as well.

Schools follow much the same pattern of the long lunch break. Many children go home to lunch because of this: there are certain areas where pressure on school places is such that there are two sessions. The morning session finishes at 2.00 or 2.30 pm and the afternoon one begins at around 4.00 pm. Entirely different pupils and teachers attend each session. At Nuestra Señora de los Ojos Grandes in Lugo, whose sixth formers we interviewed for this course, the evening session does not end till 11.00 pm at night!

This of course means that people who dropped out of school earlier can take up their studies again.

Check in the newspapers for cinema and theatre schedules. You may find at busy cinemas that there is a **sesión continua** (continuous showing) but even if not, the last show does not usually start till about 11.00 pm.

During the summer in southern cities, Spaniards work the **jornada intensiva** or intensive day. This means that they start early and finish the day's work at 3.00 pm. After lunch and a siesta, they are then free to enjoy the cool air of the evening and to go dancing or **de paseo** (for a stroll). Don't worry that you won't be able to adapt. The long lunch hour means that, even if you don't take a siesta, you can rest for a couple of hours. You will then feel revived for the evening's activities!

AND FINALLY...

13 In this exercise you'll be practising times and dates once again. This time you're enquiring about buses to Málaga. You'll be using the following words and phrases:

¿a qué hora sale el autobús para ...?
¿a qué hora llega ...?
mañana por la mañana
¿sale a su hora?
¿tengo que ...?

SERVICIO COMBINADO TREN+BUS
30 de Junio al 15 de Septiembre de 2003

| SALIDA BUS PEÑISCOLA | PROCEDENCIA DEL TREN | DESTINO DEL TREN | BENICARLO | | VINAROS | | PEÑISCOLA |
			LLEGADA DEL TREN	SALIDA BUS	LLEGADA DEL TREN	SALIDA BUS	LLEGADA BUS
6.40	VINAROS	MADRID	7.11	–	–	–	9.15
7.45	VALENCIA	BARCELONA	8.32	8.45	–	–	10.15
8.45	BARCELONA	ALICANTE	9.29	9.45	–	–	10.45
9.15	VALENCIA	MONTPELLIER	9.54	10.15	–	–	11.15
9.45	BARCELONA	MALAGA/GRANADA/ALMERIA	10.37	10.45	–	–	11.45
10.15	ALICANTE	BARCELONA	10.56	11.15	–	–	12.45
11.15	BARCELONA	ALICANTE	11.50	12.15	–	–	13.45
11.30	MADRID	BARCELONA	–	–	12.45	12.55	13.45
12.15	PORTBOU	ALICANTE	12.50	13.15	–	–	14.15
12.45	PORTBOU	MADRID	13.26	13.45	–	–	14.15
12.45	ALICANTE	PORTBOU	13.34	13.45	–	–	15.15
13.45	CARTAGENA	CERBERE	14.35	14.45	–	–	15.45
14.15	CERBERE	CARTAGENA	14.53	15.15	–	–	17.15
15.45	MADRID	PORTBOU	16.40	16.45	–	–	17.45
15.30	BARCELONA	MADRID	–	–	16.49	16.55	18.45
17.15	BARCELONA	ALACANT/MURCIA	17.58	18.15	–	–	19.45
17.00	MURCIA/ALACANT	BARCELONA	–	–	18.36	18.55	19.15
17.45	BARCELONA	ALICANTE	18.42	18.45	–	–	20.15
18.45	MALAGA/GRANADA/ALMERIA	BARCELONA	19.19	19.45	–	–	20.15
18.45	ALICANTE	BARCELONA	19.32	19.45	–	–	20.45
19.15	BARCELONA	ALICANTE	19.57	20.15	–	–	21.15
19.45	ALICANTE	BARCELONA	20.40	20.45	–	–	22.45
21.15	MONTPELLIER	VALENCIA	21.53	22.15	–	–	23.15
–	MADRID	VINAROS	22.27	22.45	–	–	

ANSWERS

7 I'D LIKE TO BUY ...

WHAT YOU WILL LEARN

▶ How to ...
>   *describe and ask for objects simply*
>   *pay by credit card*

▶ and how not to buy – gracefully!

BEFORE YOU BEGIN

As the number of new words you meet is increasing, you may wonder how you should be recording them in written form. Most people write lists with the foreign word on one side of their notebook and its equivalent on the other. Although this might work for some people, it's not really so sensible as all these words are out of context – that is, you don't know how they are used. Many words require certain constructions after them – perhaps a preposition such as **a** or **de** or a certain form of the verb – and your word list won't give you any indication of this. Also, since many foreign words don't have exact equivalents in English (and vice versa), the one-word translation may well be inaccurate.

Try different ways of recording vocabulary:

■ including each word in a sentence which gives you a good idea of how and where the word is used

■ grouping words according to their 'fields' or subjects. In this unit, all words which deal with food, for example, could be put together. This has the added advantage of making the words easier to memorize.

Pronunciation notes

In Spanish, there's no difference between the sounds of the letters **b** and **v**. **Botar** (to throw out) and **votar** (to vote) are pronounced exactly the same. So how *is* the sound pronounced? At the beginning of a word, it's very much like an English **b**. Elsewhere, pronounce it very lightly. You hardly need to open your lips at all. Listen to Roberto and imitate his pronunciation.

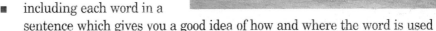

bonito **vale** **huevos** **verde** **cabeza**

▶ *Eme is looking for a gift in a ceramics shop*

LISTEN FOR...

un regalo	a present
azul	blue
marrón	brown
verde	green
¿te puedo pagar con tarjeta?	can I pay by credit card?

Eme	Hola
Dependienta	Hola
Eme	Mira, quería comprar un regalo, una figurita quizá
Dependienta	Muy bien
Eme	O una cabeza, ¿no?
Dependienta	Sí, las hay de hombre y mujer y con color azul
Eme	Ésta es bonita, ésta azul y marrón, ¿no?
Dependienta	Sí, lleva también color verde
Eme	Sí, ésta está bien ... y ¿te puedo pagar con tarjeta?
Dependienta	Sí, ¿Visa o Master?
Eme	Es Visa
Dependienta	Bien, vale
Eme	Muy bien, gracias

- ▶ **comprar**   to buy
- ▶ **el regalo**   present
- ▶ **la figura**   figure
- ▶ **la cabeza**   head (here, a ceramic head)
- ▶ **quizá**   perhaps
- ▶ **el hombre**   man
- ▶ **la mujer**   woman, wife
- ▶ **el color**   colour
- ▶ **marrón**   brown
- ▶ **llevar**   to carry
- ▶ **pagar**   to pay
- ▶ **la tarjeta**   card

Quería comprar un regalo   I want(ed) to buy a present. Eme uses a past tense to express diffidence or tentativeness.

una figurita   a little figure. The ending **-ito(s)** or **-ita(s)** means 'little/nice'.

Un regalito a small present. **Unas figuritas**   some (nice) little figures.

Lleva también color verde   It also has some green (literally, it carries also colour green). A word about adjectives of colour. If used with the word **color** (as here), they agree with **color** (**color blanco**). If used just with a noun, they usually change according to the gender of the noun – **una figura blanca** a white figure.

Use '**llevar**' in another important phrase: **me llevo éste** I'll take this one. **Éste/ésta/éstos/éstas** means 'this' or 'these ones'. There's a full explanation of this point in the Grammar section.

¿Te puedo pagar con tarjeta?   Can I pay you by credit card? You can substitute the formal **le** for **te** in this phrase, if you wish.

Javi's looking for a suitcase

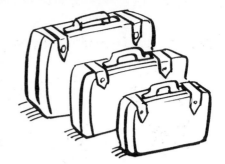

LISTEN FOR...

más o menos	more or less
una maleta	a suitcase
paja	rattan
caro	expensive
lo voy a dejar	I'm going to leave it
si no te importa	if you don't mind

Javi	Hola, ¿qué hay? Buenos días
Dependiente	Buenos días
Javi	Mira, quería una maleta
Dependiente	Y ¿de qué tamaño la quería más o menos? ¿Grande...?
Javi	No muy grande. Éstas de aquí, ¿cuántos tamaños hay?
Dependiente	Hay tres, la grande, la mediana y la pequeña. Son de paja y de cuero
Javi	De paja y de cuero
Dependiente	Sí
Javi	Son bonitas. ¿Cuánto cuesta la mediana?
Dependiente	La mediana cuesta noventa y seis euros, cincuenta céntimos
Javi	Ah, es un poco cara. Y la pequeña me resulta muy pequeña. Lo voy a dejar si no te importa
Dependiente	De acuerdo. Muchas gracias
Javi	Gracias
Dependiente	Adiós

▶ **la maleta** suitcase
▶ **aquí** here
▶ **la paja** straw, rattan
▶ **el cuero** leather
▶ **caro/a** expensive
▶ **resultar** to turn out
▶ **dejar** to leave
▶ **importar** to matter
▶ **de acuerdo** fine

de paja y de cuero (made) of rattan and leather. To say something is made of a particular material use 'es/son de'. **Es de poliester** it's made of polyester. **Son de algodón** they're (made of) cotton.

Es un poco cara It's rather expensive. You should also know the word **barato/a** cheap.

La pequeña me resulta muy pequeña The little one is too small for me (literally, the little one for me turns out very small). If you want to express things more simply, you can say '**Es muy pequeña**'.

Lo voy a dejar I'm going to leave it (literally, it I am going to leave).

si no te importa if you don't mind (literally, if not to you it matters).

PRACTICE

1 Below you will see a sales slip with the number of items bought and their cost – but the name of each item is missing. Fill them in after you've listened to the extract on the recording.

REGALOS Y MODA S.A.	
CANTIDAD	PRECIO
2	50€
2	70€
1	70,50€

What was the total amount to be paid? Write it out in full.

ANSWERS P. 110

_____

2 Fill in your part of the conversation from the choices in the box below.

Dependienta: Hola, buenos días

Tú: Buenos días _____
Dependienta: ¿De qué tamaño más o menos?

Tú: _____
Dependienta: Sí, ésta es muy bonita – es de cuero

Tú: _____
Dependienta: Cuesta – a ver – doscientos veinte euros

Tú: _____
Dependienta: Sí – bueno, tenemos éstas que están muy bien de precio

Tú: _____
ANSWERS P. 110
Dependienta: De acuerdo

> 1. lo voy a dejar si no le importa
> 2. quiero una maleta grande
> 3. es un poco cara
> 4. quería una maleta
> 5. ¿cuánto cuesta?

3 Now you'll be having a similar conversation with a shopkeeper on the recording. This time you're buying a ceramic figure. Maika will prompt you with the details.

Delia is buying groceries

LISTEN FOR...

aceitunas	olives
un bote	a tin
no me queda	I don't have any left
así	like this
negro	black

**ACEITUNAS
LA ESPAÑOLA,** 150 GRS.
P. NETO ESCURRIDO

Delia	Quería unas aceitunas verdes y negras
Dependienta	Verdes y negras. ¿Con hueso?
Delia	Sí, con hueso
Dependienta	¿Este tamaño te va bien?
Delia	¿Éstas qué son? ¿Las verdes?
Dependienta	Sí
Delia	Las negras, un bote más pequeño
Dependienta	Más pequeño, no me queda
Delia	No te queda, bueno pues, grande
Dependienta	¿Así?
Delia	Sí

▶ **la aceituna** olive
▶ **negro** black
▶ **el hueso** bone (here: stone, pit)
▶ **el bote** tin, can (generally used for tall, cylindrical objects)

¿Este tamaño te va bien? Is this size all right for you? (literally, this size to you goes well?).
¿Éstas qué son? Which ones are these?
un bote más pequeño a smaller tin (literally, a tin more small). (Use '**más**' for the equivalent of '-er' endings in English. **Más grande** bigger.)
No me queda I don't have any left (literally, to me it does not remain).

Delia goes on to buy a couple of tins of sardines

LISTEN FOR...

latas	tins
almejas	clams
zanahoria	carrot
rallada	grated

Delia	Quería también unas sardinas. Dos latas de sardinas	
Dependienta	¿Sardina grande o pequeña?	
Delia	Pequeña	
Dependienta	¿Así?	
Delia	Así, muy bien. Y ¿almejas tienes?	
Dependienta	Sí, almejas. ¿Al natural?	
Delia	Al natural sí, al natural mejor. Y zanahoria	
Dependienta	Sí. ¿Entera o rallada?	
Delia	Rallada, rallada... Unos espárragos	
Dependienta	¿Blancos?	
Delia	Blancos, sí, de los pequeñitos	

▶ **también**   also

▶ **la lata**   tin (generally used for flat, square objects)

▶ **la almeja**   clam

▶ **al natural**   nothing added, plain

▶ **mejor**   better

▶ **la zanahoria**   carrot

▶ **entero/a**   entire, whole

▶ **rallado/a**   grated

▶ **el espárrago**   asparagus

▶ **blanco/a**   white

al natural mejor   better, plain. This rather laconic remark merely means that Delia prefers to have her tinned clams with no additional sauces. They probably come in brine.

PRACTICE

4 **Verdad o mentira?** What can you remember about Delia's purchases? Remember that **comprar** means to buy. You'll be practising adjectives as well as new food vocabulary

	verdad	mentira
a. Delia compra aceitunas negras y verdes		
b. Las quiere sin hueso		
c. No quedan botes pequeños de aceitunas negras		
d. Delia compra tres latas de sardinas		
e. Las latas de sardinas son grandes		
f. También compra zanahorias enteras		
g. Y espárragos blancos y pequeños		

ANSWERS P. 110

5 On the recording, you'll hear a customer asking for various items in a grocery shop. Circle the eight items below which are mentioned. *New vocabulary*: **una barra** a loaf of bread, **aceite** oil.

ANSWERS P. 110 What was the total bill? _____

6 In the speaking exercise you'll be asking for a variety of different foods at a grocery shop. You'll need two new words: **arroz** rice and **cebollas** onions.

Buying milk and oil

LISTEN FOR...

vegetal   vegetable
girasol   sunflower
maíz   maize

Isabel	¿Cuánto cuesta la leche por favor?
Tendero	La leche, noventa céntimos litro y medio, y setenta un litro
Isabel	¿Tiene botellas de litro? ¿Y de medio litro no tiene?
Tendero	No, de medio litro no hay
Isabel	De medio litro no. Y las botellas de aceite, ¿de qué tamaño son?
Tendero	De litro o de dos litros
Isabel	Y ¿es aceite de oliva o aceite vegetal?
Tendero	Hay aceite de oliva, aceite de girasol y aceite de maíz
Isabel	¿Cuál es el más caro?
Tendero	El más caro, el de oliva

▶ **la leche**   milk
▶ **el tendero**   shopkeeper
▶ **la oliva**   olive
▶ **vegetal**   vegetable
▶ **el girasol**   sunflower
▶ **el maíz**   maize

¿Tiene botellas de litro?
Do you have litre bottles?
Botella is a largish bottle and **botellín** a
small one, usually for beer.
¿De qué tamaño son?   What size are they? Size in clothing
is **talla: ¿Qué talla tiene usted?** but for shoes (**zapatos**) use
número: ¿Qué número tiene usted?
¿Cuál es el más caro?   Which is the most expensive? **El más
barato** the cheapest.

At the grocery store

LISTEN FOR...

¿a cómo es la mortadela?	how much is the mortadela sausage?
una bolsa de patatas fritas	a packet of crisps
un paquete de sal gorda	a packet of cooking salt
una docena	a dozen

Isabel	¿Cuánto es la coca-cola pequeña? Ah, sí, noventa céntimos. Vale. Tres botellas de leche y un litro de aceite
Tendero	Sí, cinco euros, treinta y nueve céntimos
Isabel	Una lata de aceitunas negras
Tendero	Son setenta y tres céntimos
Isabel	Una docena de huevos y doscientos gramos de mortadela. ¿A cómo es la mortadela?
Tendero	A cuatro euros el kilo. Son ochenta céntimos
Isabel	Vale. Una bolsa de patatas fritas
Tendero	Cincuenta y dos céntimos
Isabel	Y un paquete de sal gorda

▶ **la docena** dozen
▶ **la bolsa** bag
▶ **la patata frita** crisp
▶ **el paquete** packet

¿A cómo es la mortadela? How much is the mortadela (today)? Another way of asking '**¿cuánto cuesta?**'

sal gorda coarse or cooking salt. **Gordo** usually means fat. **El gordo de Navidad** is the big lottery prize drawn at Christmas.

PRACTICE

7 Which words in columns A and B go together?
Match up the correct item in each column with a line.

A		B	
a.	un kilo	i.	de leche
b.	tres botellas	ii.	de mortadela
c.	una docena	iii.	de cerveza
d.	una barra	iv.	de tomates
e.	un paquete	v.	de pan
f.	dos latas	vi.	de patatas fritas
g.	500 gramos	vii.	de sal
h.	seis botellines	viii.	de sardinas
i.	una bolsa	ix.	de huevos

ANSWERS P. 110

8 On the recording you will hear a conversation between a sales assistant and a difficult customer. The transcript still has some omissions. Listen to the conversation and then fill in the missing phrases.

Dependiente:	Buenas tardes
Señora:	Buenas tardes. A ver... una _____ de aceitunas
Dependiente:	Sí, tenemos aceitunas _____ y _____
Señora:	Negras por favor. Una lata _____
Dependiente:	Lo _____ , sólo tenemos latas grandes
Señora:	Pues no. Vivo sola, no puedo _____ una lata entera. A ver, otra cosa. Sí. Quiero _____
Dependiente:	¿Una _____ así?
Señora:	Uy, también es muy grande. ¡Oiga! ¿Más _____ no tiene?
Dependiente:	No, no nos _____ más – son las siete de la tarde y...
Señora:	Bueno, bueno, no importa... Trescientos _____ de mortadela... ¿a cómo es la mortadela?
Dependiente:	A _____ el kilo
Señora:	¡Uy, es muy cara! ¿No tiene nada más _____ ?
Dependiente:	Más baratos son los _____ – a _____ la docena
Señora:	Vale, vale, media _____ de huevos – ¡ de los grandes eh!

ANSWERS P. 110

I'd like to buy ... *Unit 7*

9 Read through this recipe and then answer the questions.

Atún estofado Tuna stew

Ingredientes para 4 personas

600 gramos de atún
aceite de oliva
2 cebollas medianas
6 pimientos verdes pequeños
6 tomates grandes
sal

Lavar y cortar las cebollas, los pimientos y los tomates. Calentar el aceite de oliva y freír la cebolla y el pimiento durante diez minutos. Añadir el tomate y la sal. Lavar y cortar el atún y ponerlo en la cazuela. Cocinar durante un cuarto de hora. Es un plato muy rico.

lavar	to wash
cortar	to cut
calentar	to heat
freír	to fry
la cazuela	cooking pot
cocinar	to cook

a. How many people can you serve with this dish?
b. What size onions do you need?
c. What colour must the peppers be?
d. What is the first step?
e. How long must you fry the onions and peppers?
f. How long do you let the tuna mixture simmer?

ANSWERS P. 110

Este, esta, estos and estas (this, these)

Because these words are adjectives, they must agree with their nouns. Here are some examples of the four options:

este pan	this bread
esta lata	this tin
estos huevos	these eggs
estas bolsas	these bags

As in English, you don't always need to name the object itself.

Quiero esta postal y – a ver – ésta también
I want this postcard and – let's see – this one too.
(When you use **este** without a noun, i.e. as a pronoun, it needs to have an accent.)

- Use **esto** when you're talking generally rather than about specific things. It translates phrases such as 'all this':
  esto no me gusta
  I don't like this (in general)

The word **ese** (that) works in exactly the same way:

ese aceite	that oil
esa maleta	that suitcase
esos botes	those tins
esas manzanas	those apples
eso	that (in general)

Comparatives and superlatives

If you wish to say that something is bigger, better, or brighter than something else, use **más ... que**.

Juan es más alto que Isabel
Juan is taller than Isabel

If you want to say something is the biggest, best or most intelligent, add **el**, **la**, **los** or **las** as appropriate.

Isabel es la niña más alta de la familia
Isabel es la más alta
Isabel is the tallest girl (in the family)

Some everyday adjectives have their own comparatives:

bueno	good	**mejor**	better
malo	bad	**peor**	worse
grande	big	**mayor**	bigger, older
pequeño	small	**menor**	smaller, younger

To say someone is as (big) as, use **tan (grande) como**:
Guillermo es tan grande como Daniel
William is as tall as Daniel

10 Read through these four exchanges. Circle the item to which each customer was referring:

i. **Tendero:** ¿Cuál quiere usted?
   Teresa: Éste por favor
   una lata de sardinas   una maleta   un paquete de sal

ii. **Tendero:** ¿Cuál quería usted?
   María: Quería ésa
   una figura   un plato   un vaso

iii. **Tendero:** ¿Qué quería?
   Luisa: Um... éstas
   manzanas   espárragos   tomates

iv. **Tendero:** ¿Qué número tiene?
   Carmen: Éstos me están bien
   zapatos   botas   naranjas   arroz

ANSWERS P. 110

11 The words in these sentences are out of order. Write the correct version underneath:

a. barra por estos de esta y huevos favor pan

_____

b. sardinas estas negras quiero esta de y lata aceitunas

_____

c. manzanas melón esas ese quería y

_____

d. favor botella girasol aceite de de por esa

_____

e. muy no – ese es pan quiero grande

_____

ANSWERS P. 110

12 By reading the six statements below, try to put these six people in order of height:

Isabel García   (13)

Leonor García   (15)

María García   (48)

Guillermo García   (49)

Ana Suárez   (13)

Daniel López   (16)

i. La persona mayor es la más alta

ii. Leonor es más alta que su hermana

iii. Leonor no es tan alta como su novio

iv. La más pequeña de la familia es María

v. Ana es más alta que la hermana menor

vi. Ana no es tan alta como la hermana mayor

ANSWERS P. 110

Señor Gordinflón

Señor Delgaducho

Quería unas aceitunas	I'd like some olives
un litro de leche/aceite	a litre of milk/oil
un kilo de manzanas	a kilo of apples
naranjas	oranges
arroz	rice
cebollas	onions
una lata de sardinas	a tin of sardines
pequeña	small
grande	big
más pequeña	smaller
más grande	bigger
unas almejas	some clams
zanahorias	some carrots
ciento veinticinco gramos de	125 grams of ...
doscientos cincuenta gramos de	250 grams of ...
quinientos gramos de	500 grams of ...
¿Este tamaño te va bien?	Is this size all right?
No me queda(n)	I don't have any left
Estos dos paquetes me llegan	These two packets will be fine
¿así?	like this?
detrás de ti	behind you
¿algo más?	anything else?
nada más	nothing else
un regalo	a present
una figurita	a little figure
una cabeza	a head
el color	colour
azul	blue
marrón	brown
verde	green
rojo/a	red
negro/a	black
blanco/a	white
amarillo/a	yellow
Éste/a es bonito/a	This one is pretty
Éstos/éstas son bonitos/as	These ones are pretty
¿Le/te puedo pagar con tarjeta?	Can I pay by credit card?
más o menos	more or less
una maleta	a suitcase
¿de qué tamaño?	what size?
¿Qué talla tiene Vd.?	What size are you? (clothes)
¿Qué número tiene Vd.?	What size are you? (shoes)
paja y cuero	rattan and leather
Es un poco caro/a	It's rather expensive
Es barato/a	It's cheap
Lo/la voy a dejar	I'm going to leave it
si no le/te importa	if you don't mind

SPAIN AND LATIN AMERICA are a paradise for souvenir hunters. As there are so many crafts which are particular to certain areas, it is difficult to generalize about which items are best buys. It's better to consult the local tourist office in the area that you are visiting – or simply to browse in the market. You will soon find out what is made in the region. Steer away from souvenir shops which are crowded around the main tourist attractions. As you no doubt already know, their products tend to be expensive, mass-produced and shoddy. Think too about what will look good when you get home. Huge colourful ceramic pots look wonderful in the Mexican sun but somehow out of place under grey skies. Since they are often not very well fired, they may also crack with the arrival of the winter frost.

Metric measurements

Here are a few conversions in case you are not quite attuned yet.

1 kilo	= 2.2 lbs.
½ kilo	= 1.1 lb.
250 grams	= 8 oz.
150 grams	= 5 oz.
600 ml.	= 1 pint
250 ml.	= 9 fl. ounces.

A bottle of beer (**un botellín**) usually contains 33 centilitres (12 fluid ounces) although smaller bottles of beer are also sold which contain 25 centilitres (9 fluid ounces).

If you are self-catering, you may need to know the fahrenheit and centigrade equivalents for your cooker. Centigrade temperatures are about half the fahrenheit equivalent: so if you normally cook a roast at 425° F, you need to adjust your thermostat to 220°.

Most people who are self-catering probably buy food in the supermarket (**el supermercado**), where you only need to know how to read your receipt (**el recibo**)! However, open-air markets (**el mercado**) are much more fun and the variety of fresh fruit and vegetables is much greater than in the supermarket. **Hipermercados** are to be found on the edge of town in the **centro comercial** and they are widely used by Spanish housewives. Oddly enough, many shop there every day, rather than doing a weekly or monthly shop. This may be because not so many Spanish women work outside the home as in the rest of Europe and the trip to the shops still forms part of their daily routine.

AND FINALLY...

13 You'll be using many of those new words and structures for shopping. You'll need the following:

una docena de ...
medio kilo de ...
¿a cómo es ...?
250 gramos de ...

ANSWERS

EXERCISE 1

dos figuras, dos cabezas, una maleta de paja. The full cost is ciento noventa euros, cincuenta céntimos.

EXERCISE 2

the order of each reply is: 4, 2, 5, 3, 1.

EXERCISE 4

(a) verdad   **(a)** mentira   **(c)** verdad   **(d)** mentira   **(e)** mentira
(f) mentira   **(g)** verdad

EXERCISE 5

You should have circled: loaf of bread, ham, tins of olives, milk, cheese, ice cream, sardines and eggs. The total bill was 10,57 euros.

EXERCISE 7

(a) iv   **(b)** i   **(c)** ix   **(d)** v   **(e)** vii   **(f)** viii   **(g)** ii
(h) iii   **(i)** vi

EXERCISE 8

lata, verdes y negras, pequeña, siento, comer, pan, barra, pequeña, queda, gramos, cuatro euros, barato, huevos, un euro, docena.

EXERCISE 9

(a) four   **(b)** medium   **(c)** green   **(d)** to wash and cut the vegetables   **(e)** ten minutes   **(f)** a quarter of an hour

EXERCISE 10

i. un paquete de sal   **ii.** una figura   **iii.** manzanas
iv. zapatos

EXERCISE 11

(a) estos huevos y esta barra de pan por favor
(b) quiero esta lata de sardinas y estas aceitunas negras
(c) quería esas manzanas y ese melón
(d) esa botella de aceite de girasol por favor
(e) no quiero ese pan – es muy grande

EXERCISE 12

Guillermo is the tallest, then Daniel, Leonor, Ana, Isabel and María.

IN EL
CORTE INGLÉS

**WHAT
YOU WILL
LEARN**

▶ How to ...
go shopping for clothes
ask for certain medicines

▶ and the names of a variety of items of clothing

**BEFORE
YOU
BEGIN**

At the beginning of the course, the vocabulary was often similar in sound and meaning to the English equivalent. But now that you are meeting words which are not so obvious, don't rush to the dictionary immediately you come across one you don't know. Try to guess its meaning first, either by looking at the context in which it appears, or at the form of the word itself. Is it a verb or a noun? You can recognize which is which from the ending. What job does it do in the sentence?

Knowing this will help you discover its meaning. Only look up the word if all else fails – or if you need to check a gender. You need to develop your comprehension strategies for both reading and listening because, however well you get to know Spanish, there will always be words and phrases that you come across for the first time. This is because language is constantly evolving; also, in the case of Spanish, there are so many speakers of Spanish all over the world (300 million and increasing) that standardization is almost impossible.

Pronunciation notes

■ Before **e** and **i**, the Spanish **g** is pronounced like the 'ch' in the Scottish 'loch' – that is, a guttural sound in the throat. **J** is also pronounced this way.
Gerona, Giralda

■ After **a**, **o** and **u** and with consonants, **g** sounds just like the English 'g':
Grande, gordo

■ In between vowels the **g** sound almost fades away:
Nicaragua, agua

Buying sports equipment

LISTEN FOR...

deporte	sport
pelotas	balls
medias	socks or stockings
camiseta	tee-shirt
chandal	tracksuit

CALCETIN
DEPORTE
HOMBRE

Reebok

3 UNIDADES, TALLA UNICA

5,95

Pepe	¿Venden ustedes artículos de deporte?
Dependiente	Sí, sí. Los tenemos aquí en la planta baja
Pepe	¿Venden ustedes cosas para tenis?
Dependiente	Sí, sí, vestidos, pantalones, pelotas, raquetas ... de todo, vamos ...
Pepe	Y ¿venden ustedes también artículos para fútbol?
Dependiente	Botas, medias, camisetas, pantalones, chandal, balones, todo, todo
Pepe	Muchas gracias
Dependiente	De nada

▶ **el artículo**   article
▶ **el deporte**   sport
▶ **la cosa**   thing
▶ **el tenis**   tennis
▶ **el vestido**   dress
▶ **la pelota**   ball (small)
▶ **el balón**   ball (large)
▶ **la raqueta**   racquet
▶ **el fútbol**   football
▶ **la bota**   boot
▶ **las medias**   stockings
▶ **el chandal**   tracksuit

DEPORTIVO NIÑO **Reebok**
MOD. TRANSITION COURT

76,70

¿venden ustedes?   do you sell?
la camiseta   tee shirt. You also ought to know the words **camisa** shirt and **blusa** blouse.
Pantalones cortos are shorts (**corto** short).

María is buying sweaters for her husband ...

LISTEN FOR...

¿me podría(s) mostrar?	could you show me ...?
dibujado	patterned
liso	plain
cuello	neckline

María	Señorita, ¿me podrías mostrar algún suéter de caballero, por favor?
Jefa	¿Cómo lo quiere, de angora, de jaquard, dibujado, liso?
María	Liso y ... ¿qué colores tienes?
Jefa	Los tienen en tonos pastel, desde el verde, naranja, geranio, rosa ...
María	Bueno
Jefa	¿Algún cuello en especial?
María	¿Cuello en pico tienen?
Jefa	No, en pico no, sólo cuello Perkins y cuello vuelto
María	Muy bien. Gracias

- **la angora**   angora wool
- **el jaquard**   jacquard weave
- **dibujado**   patterned
- **liso/a**   plain
- **geranio**   geranium
- **rosa**   pink
- **el cuello en pico**   V neck
- **el cuello Perkins**   crew neck
- **el cuello vuelto**   roll neck

¿Me podría(s) mostrar algún suéter de caballero?   Could you show me some men's sweaters? Although María uses the informal address (**tú**), it's safer for you to use **usted**. The **tú/usted** distinction is rather blurred, but when in doubt, always use the formal **usted**.

jefa   manageress or boss. The masculine form is **jefe**.

¿algún cuello en especial?   any neckline in particular? **Cuello** also means neck.

1 Who is buying what? Match up the person with the item they might have bought at Tiendas Mani. You'll need to know the words **azul marino** navy blue.

a. un suéter de niño, liso, color naranja

b. unas botas de fútbol y un balón

c. un suéter de angora, de color rosa, con cuello vuelto

d. un vestido corto y blanco y una raqueta

e. un chandal azul marino

i.   Diego Maradona

ii. Steffi Graf

iii. Javier (de diez años)

iv. Maricarmen, la hermana mayor de Javier

v.   Pablo, profesor de deporte

ANSWERS P. 124

2 Listen to the conversation between Carlos and Marisa as Carlos packs his suitcase. Five items of clothing from the card below are mentioned. Tick off those which you hear.

suéter	camisa		camiseta	chandal
vestido	medias	botas	mantilla	zapatos

ANSWERS P. 124

3 Now you'll be enquiring about sports equipment in a Spanish department store. You'll need: **¿venden Vds.?** and **¿tienen Vds.?**

CONVERSATIONS

◗ *Asking for advice in a menswear department*

LISTEN FOR...

deseo comprar	I would like to buy
¿podría aconsejarme?	could you advise me?
¡cómo no!	certainly

Jefe	Buenas tardes
Pepe	Buenas tardes. Por favor, deseo comprar una chaqueta pero no sé qué tipo de chaqueta. ¿Podría aconsejarme?
Jefe	Sí, ¡cómo no! Podríamos aconsejarle una chaqueta de cheviot, es propia de esta época. No es ni muy gruesa ni es muy fina
Pepe	¿Tiene de otros colores? Porque ...
Jefe	Tenemos varios tonos de color, como son los grises, los verdes, los marrones o las clásicas blazers azul marino

▶ **el cheviot**   lamb's wool (from the Cheviot breed of sheep)
▶ **el tono**   shade
▶ **ni ... ni ...**   neither ... nor ...

Deseo comprar una chaqueta   I wish to buy a jacket. Pepe may also wish to buy a **corbata** (tie) to go with his jacket.

¿Podría aconsejarme?   Could you advise me? The assistant replies **podríamos aconsejarle** we could advise you. This tense is called the conditional but you only need recognize it at this stage.

Es propia de esta época   It's right for this time of year.

No es ni muy gruesa ni es muy fina   It's neither too thick nor too thin. Note this use of **muy**, too.

porque   because. **¿por qué?** (two words and an accent on **qué**) means why?

las clásicas blazers (en) azul marino   classic blazers in navy blue. The word **blazers** is of course borrowed from the English.

And now Pepe is looking for some trousers to go with the jacket

LISTEN FOR...	
estoy buscando	I am looking for
vamos a tomar la medida	let's take your measurements
¿para ahora?	for now?
el verano	summer

Pepe	Estoy buscando unos pantalones
Jefe	Sí, ¿para usted? ¿... o es para ...?
Pepe	Sí, para mí ...
Jefe	Para usted. Vamos a tomar la medida, por favor, para saber su talla ... Sí, cuarenta y dos
Pepe	Um, ¿qué tipo de pantalones tiene?
Jefe	¿Usted lo desea para ahora o lo prefiere para verano?
Pepe	Para verano
Jefe	Para verano

▶ **buscar**   to look for
▶ **el tipo**   type
▶ **la medida**   measurement
▶ **ahora**   now
▶ **el verano**   summer

Estoy buscando unos pantalones
I'm looking for some trousers
The word **pantalón** is often used in the singular too. You may also wish to know the word **el cinturón** belt.

Vamos a tomar la medida, por favor, para saber su talla   Let's measure you, please, to find out your size. Pepe is a size 42 (equivalent to a 32-inch waist). Use **talla** for clothes and **número** for shoes. **¿Qué número tiene usted? El treinta y nueve.**

¿Usted lo desea para ahora o lo prefiere para verano?   Do you want them for now or do you prefer them for the summer?

The other seasons of the year are **el otoño** (autumn), **el invierno** (winter) and **la primavera** (spring). Eliud will pronounce them for you on the recording.

4 Have a look at these fashion sketches. Link up each sketch with its Spanish description. You'll need to know:

largo/a long
la falda skirt
arriba above, top

ANSWERS P. 124

1. pantalón con blusa estilo militar

2. minivestido estilo túnica, la parte de arriba en forma de camiseta

3. falda larga con sandalias estilo romano

4. suéter, dibujado con cuello en pico, con chaqueta estilo masculino

5. pantalón corto con medias largas y zapatos de cuero

6. sombrero grande, de paja

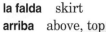

5 Match up the questions in the left-hand column with the answers on the right. Practise reading them out loud once you've done the exercise.

1. ¿qué talla tiene?
2. ¿venden ustedes cosas para el tenis en esta planta?
3. ¿tienen ustedes suéteres de señora?
4. ¿qué número tiene?
5. ¿tiene camisas en azul marino?
6. estoy buscando una chaqueta. ¿Me podría aconsejar?

i. sí, ¿es para el verano o para el invierno?
ii. el treinta y nueve
iii. sí, cómo no. Los tenemos en tonos pastel y también en colores más oscuros
iv. la cuarenta
v. no, los artículos de deporte están todo en la tercera planta
vi. no, sólo en blanco, verde y rojo

ANSWERS P. 124

6 Now you will hear Carlos shopping. Listen to the conversation as many times as you like and then answer the questions below in English. You'll hear a new word, **probar** (to try on) and a useful phrase '**me quedo con (éstos)**' I'll have (these).

a. What does Carlos wish to buy?
b. What does he think his size is?
c. What shade of blue does he ask for?
d. How many types of material does the saleswoman offer him to start with?
e. What is wrong with the first garment he tries on?
f. What is wrong with the next one?

ANSWERS P. 124

At the chemist's

LISTEN FOR...

dolor de estómago	stomach-ache
comprimidos	pills
jarabe	syrup
malas digestiones	indigestion

Pepe	¿Tiene alguna medicina para el dolor de estómago por favor?
Farmacéutica	Sí, sí, ¿cómo lo quería, en comprimidos, jarabe? ¿Qué es, para ardor de estómago, dolor, malas digestiones?
Pepe	Es para malas digestiones
Farmacéutica	Pues sí, hay unos comprimidos Polidasa.
Pepe	Y ¿tiene algún bronceador?
Farmacéutica	Sí, bronceadores, sí

▶ **la farmacéutica**   the chemist (woman)

Note also ▶ **el farmacéutico**   the chemist (man)

▶ **el comprimido**   tablet, pill

¿Tiene alguna medicina para el dolor de estómago?
Have you any medicine for a stomache-ache? Note also: **tengo dolor de estómago** I have a stomache-ache; **tengo dolor de cabeza** I have a headache; **tengo dolor de muelas** I have toothache.
¿Cómo lo quería?   How did you want it?
jarabe   syrup: **jarabe para la tos** cough mixture.
¿para ardor de estómago, dolor, malas digestiones?   for heartburn, pain, indigestion? (You can use the singular form for indigestion if you prefer – **mala digestión.**)
comprimidos Polidasa   Polidasa tablets. Polidasa is a brand name.

7 Listen to another conversation which takes place at the chemist's. Marisa has a number of holiday problems. Can you note down in English the four items which Carlos mentions? (He's playing the chemist.) You'll need three more items of vocabulary:

la fiebre   a temperature, fever
la diarrea   diarrhoea
la insolación   sunstroke

a. _____

b. _____

c. _____

ANSWERS P. 124   d. _____

8

¿DIGESTIONES PESADAS?
¿ARDOR DE ESTÓMAGO?

Lo que necesita usted es el digestivo **STOMOPAZ**
STOMOPAZ es rápido y eficaz: alivio rápido para el estómago.
Neutraliza la acidez del estómago desde el primer momento.
¡Ayuda a hacer la digestión!

(Lea las instrucciones y consulte a su médico o farmacéutico)

pesado   heavy
el digestivo   product to help you digest
eficaz   effective
el alivio   relief
ayudar a   to help

a. What two symptoms does STOMOPAZ help to alleviate?
b. It has two specific functions. What are they?
c. How quickly does it work?

ANSWERS P. 124   d. What two things should you do before taking STOMOPAZ?

9 You're at the chemist's enquiring about one or two problems. You'll need:
tengo ...
   fiebre
   dolor de estómago
   dolor de cabeza

Adverbs

Adverbs are like adjectives in that they describe words; the difference is that adverbs describe verbs rather than nouns. We are often able to recognize them in English by the ending -ly: slowly, quickly, clearly.

Spanish adverbs are usually formed by adding **-mente** to the feminine form of the adjective. Look at these examples:

rápido	quick
rápidamente	quickly
sólo	alone
solamente	only
probable	probable
probablemente	probably
posible	possible
posiblemente	possibly

Some common adverbs don't work in this way. Here are a few of the more usual ones:

mal:
Habla mal   S/he speaks badly

bien:
Estudia bien   S/he studies well

despacio:
¡Despacio por favor!   Slowly please!

demasiado:
Bebe demasiado   S/he drinks too much

bastante:
Trabaja bastante bien   S/he works quite well

More about pronouns

You looked at some pronoun forms (**lo**, **la**, **los**, **las** etc.) in Unit 4. Here are a few more pronouns which you also need to learn.

me	me, to me
te	you, to you (informal)
nos	us, to us
os	you, to you (informal plural)

¿Me quieres?	Do you like/love me?
¡Claro que te quiero!	Of course I love you!
¿Nos llevas?	Are you taking us?
¡Claro que os llevo!	Of course I'm taking you!

Usually, these pronouns precede the verb. However, if you have an infinitive, they are often tagged on to the end. There is an example of this in this Unit when Pepe asked for advice: **¿podría aconsejarme?** (could you advise me?).

Decir to say

This is another verb which has **g** in the **yo** form – **digo** (I say) – like **hago** (I do), **salgo** (I leave) and **pongo** (I put). In the present tense the **e** changes to an **i** in most of the forms. Look at the full verb and underline the two parts where **e** does *not* change.

digo	I say
dices	you say (informal)
dice	s/he says
dice	you say (formal)
decimos	we say
decís	you say (informal plural)
dicen	they say
dicen	you say (formal plural)

Pedir (to ask for) and **servir** (to serve) also change in the stem like this in the present tense.

> **¿Qué pides?**   What are you ordering?
> **¿Le sirvo algo?**   Shall I serve you something?

10

Make as many sentences as you can with the adverbs and verbs that follow: e.g.
Hablo mal el alemán I speak German badly.

You'll find six possibilities on page 124, but you will be able to think of more yourself.

VERBOS	ADVERBIOS
hablar	rápidamente
trabajar	solamente
comer	despacio
beber	demasiado
vivir	bastante
comprar	mal
ir	bien
pasar	corrientemente
escribir	fácilmente

a. _____

b. _____

c. _____

d. _____

e. _____

f. _____

ANSWERS P. 124

11

Here are six sentences, all of which use **decir**, **pedir** or **servir**. Write in the translation:

a. ¿Pedimos cerveza o vino blanco?

_____

b. ¿Les sirvo ahora?

_____

c. ¿Le digo la verdad?

_____

d. Dice que no quiere ir

_____

e. Yo pido una coca-cola y después un helado de vainilla

_____

f. ¡Esto no sirve!

_____

ANSWERS P. 124

12

Add the correct Spanish pronouns in the spaces. Look at this example:

¿_____ vemos el domingo? te vemos el domingo?
shall we see *you* on Sunday?

a. ¡No _____ quiero ver más por aquí!
   I don't want to see *you* here again!

b. _____ veo el lunes, si queréis
   I'll see *you* on Monday if you like

c. Ella _____ escribe todos los días
   She writes to *me* every day

d. Mamá _____ quiere mucho a todos
   Mummy loves *us* all very much

e. Quiero decir _____ que no voy hoy por la tarde
   I want to tell *you* (formal) that I am not going this afternoon

f. ¿_____ puedes pagar ahora por favor?
   Can you pay *me* now please?

g. ¿_____ da el menú por favor?
   Can you give *us* the menu please?

ANSWERS P. 124

KEY·WORDS
AND PHRASES

el vestido	dress
la bota	boot
el zapato	shoe
sección zapatería	shoe department
las medias	socks, stockings
el chandal	tracksuit
la camisa	shirt
la camiseta	tee-shirt
el suéter	sweater
Deseo comprar una chaqueta	I'd like to buy a jacket
Estoy buscando un(os) pantalon(es)	I'm looking for some trousers
¿Qué tipo de [pantalon(es)] tiene?	What sort of [trousers] do you have?
¿Tiene de otros colores?	Do you have any other colours?
¿Me podría(s) mostrar algún suéter de caballero?	Could you show me some men's sweaters?
¿Podría aconsejarme?	Could you advise me?
¿Me lo/la puedo probar?	Can I try it on?
Vamos a tomar la medida	Let's take your measurements
su talla	your size (clothes)
su número	your size (shoes)
Es propio/a de esta época	It's suitable for this time of year
para primavera	for spring
para verano	for summer
para otoño	for autumn
para invierno	for winter
(no) muy grueso	(not) very heavy
(no) muy fino	(not) very lightweight
¿Cómo lo quiere?	How would you like it?
de angora	in angora
de jaquard	in jacquard (weave)
dibujado	patterned
liso	plain
cuello en pico	V neck
cuello vuelto	roll neck
azul marino	navy blue
gris	grey
marrón	brown
rosa	pink
la aspirina	aspirin
el jarabe	syrup
el comprimido	pill
la medicina	medicine
el dolor de cabeza	headache
el dolor de estómago	stomach-ache
la fiebre	fever, temperature
la diarrea	diarrhoea
la insolación	sunstroke
la mala digestión	indigestion

Clothing

SIZES DIFFER between Spain and the United Kingdom and the charts below should serve as a useful guide.

Men's clothes					
UK	36	38	40	42	44
Spain	46	48	50	52	54

Men's shirts				
UK	14	15	16	17
Spain	36	38	40	42

Women's clothes					
UK	10	12	14	16	18
Spain	40	42	44	46	48

Shoes										
UK	3	4	5	6	7	8	9	10	11	
Spain	35½	36½	38	39	41	42	43	44	45	

Spanish people take great pride in looking as well turned out as they can. Although trainers and sports clothes are as popular in Spain as elsewhere, don't make the mistake of dressing over-casually, especially if you are in the city.

Small children especially are often dressed immaculately – often in white – and their parents still have the opportunity of having their shoes shined in the street or in a café by the **limpiabotas**.

If you are feeling under the weather but don't think you need to consult a doctor, do go to a **farmacia** to ask the chemist's advice. Spanish chemists have a long training and are highly regarded health professionals. They will be able to recommend a variety of medicines for simple problems such as those which you met in this unit. You won't see the full range of products in a **farmacia** that you normally find in a British chemist's shop. If you're looking for cosmetics or dress jewellery, then you'll need to go to a **perfumería**. And by the way, **droguerías** are not drug stores nor do they sell any sort of drugs. They sell items for cleaning your house or holiday apartment, such as bleach, soap powder and so on.

AND FINALLY...

13 You're in a department store buying a sweater for your daughter. You'll be using:

estoy buscando ...
liso/dibujado: rosa/azul

ANSWERS

EXERCISE 1
(a). iii **(b)** i **(c)** iv **(d)** ii **(e)** v

EXERCISE 2
suéter, camisa, camiseta, medias, chandal

EXERCISE 4
(a) 2 **(b)** 4 **(c)** 5 **(d)** 3 **(e)** 6 **(f)** 1

EXERCISE 5
1 iv   2 v   3 iii   4 ii   5 vi   6 i

EXERCISE 6
(a) a pair of trousers **(b)** 46 **(c)** navy blue **(d)** three
(e) they're too small **(f)** they're the wrong colour

EXERCISE 7
(a) aspirins **(b)** syrup **(c)** tablets **(d)** suncream

EXERCISE 8
(a) indigestion and heartburn **(b)** to neutralize acid and to ease digestion **(c)** as soon as you take it **(d)** read the instructions and consult your doctor or chemist.

EXERCISE 10
(a) hablo francés corrientemente **(b)** bebe demasiado
(c) Juan come muy despacio **(d)** vamos bien
(e) trabajan mal **(f)** vivimos bastante bien

EXERCISE 11
(a) Shall we order beer or white wine? **(b)** Shall I serve you now? **(c)** Shall I tell him/her/you the truth?
(d) S/he says s/he does not want to go **(e)** I want to order a Coca-Cola and then a vanilla ice-cream. **(f)** This is no good/no use!

EXERCISE 12
(a) ¡No te quiero ver más por aquí! **(b)** Os veo el lunes, si queréis **(c)** Ella me escribe todos los días **(d)** Mamá nos quiere mucho a todos **(e)** Quiero decirle que no voy hoy por la tarde **(f)** ¿Me puedes pagar ahora por favor?
(g) ¿Nos da el menú por favor?

AROUND
AND ABOUT

WHAT YOU WILL LEARN

▶ How to ...
hail a taxi
ask for petrol in a service station
get your oil and tyres checked
get a puncture repaired

BEFORE YOU BEGIN

In this unit, you will be meeting more new vocabulary to enable you to travel in a Spanish-speaking country, so here are some strategies for learning and retaining vocabulary.

Try a multi-sensory approach – that is, read, write and say out loud any word that you find difficult. Do this until you can recall it at will. You can try

writing out words in different colours (blue for masculine and red for feminine!) or even doing small sketches to help illustrate them. These techniques are useful for those of you who have a visual memory.

Try to find a connection with English. As you know by now, many words in Spanish and English are related. If there is no obvious connection – invent one! If you can't remember the word **piso** for example, imagine entering a flat and seeing hundreds of cans of peas – and oh! how surprised you are! Often the sillier and more extravagant the image, the more you are likely to remember.

Write out difficult words on small cards and flick through them when you have a spare moment – in the bus queue or while waiting for the train. Some people put stickers with vocabulary items on the fridge door or on a mirror that they look in every day. Try some of these ideas and find out which ones work for you.

Pronunciation notes

D has two sounds in Spanish. At the beginning of words it is similar to the English but pronounced with the tongue firmly against the teeth. Elsewhere (and especially between vowels) it becomes very soft and almost disappears.

donde   Madrid   nada   ida   día

CONVERSATION

Hailing a taxi

LISTEN FOR...

¿queda libre?   are you free?

Pepe	¡Taxi!, ¿queda libre?
Taxista	Sí, señor, ¿para dónde va Vd.?
Pepe	Al ayuntamiento por favor
Taxista	Muy bien

▶ **libre**   free

al ayuntamiento   to the town hall.
A + el (to the) telescope to give **al**.
The same happens with **de + el**
(of the): **del**.

Pepe	¡Taxi, taxi!, ¿está libre?
Taxista	Sí, señor, ¿adónde va Vd.?
Pepe	A la catedral por favor
Taxista	Muy bien

▶ **¿adónde?**   where to?

a la catedral   to the cathedral. This combination remains as it
is, as do **a los** to the (masculine plural) and **a las** to the (feminine plural).

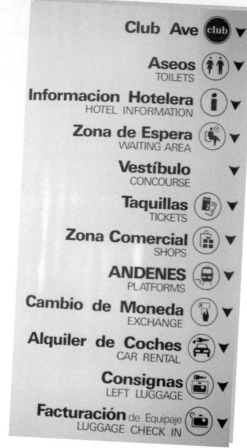

Club Ave (club) ▼

Aseos 🚹🚺 ▼
TOILETS

Informacion Hotelera (i) ▼
HOTEL INFORMATION

Zona de Espera ▼
WAITING AREA

Vestíbulo ▼
CONCOURSE

Taquillas ▼
TICKETS

Zona Comercial ▼
SHOPS

ANDENES ▼
PLATFORMS

Cambio de Moneda ▼
EXCHANGE

Alquiler de Coches ▼
CAR RENTAL

Consignas ▼
LEFT LUGGAGE

Facturación de Equipaje ▼
LUGGAGE CHECK IN

PRACTICE

1 On your recording, listen to six different people telling the taxi driver where they want to go. Jot each destination down below:

a. _____

b. _____

c. _____

d. _____

e. _____

ANSWERS P. 140   f. _____

2 You're buying a new car. Work out what each feature offers and then list them in order of importance for you. 1 will be your most important, 11 the least. There are no answers to this question.

precio final desde 12.000€. ☐

16 válvulas ☐

alarma antirrobo ☐

retrovisores eléctricos ☐

maletero muy amplio ☐

3 años de garantía ☐

radiocassette BARONI (2x25W) ☐

aire acondicionado ☐

faros con regulación eléctrica ☐

volante regulable ☐

cierre centralizado ☐

el retrovisor	mirror
el maletero	boot
el faro	light
el volante	steering wheel

3 Almost all the words in this crossword cropped up either in the previous two conversations or in exercises 1 and 2.

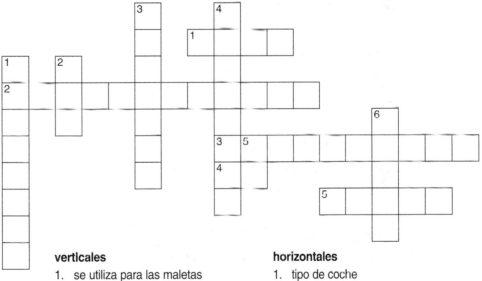

se utiliza(n) is/are used

verticales
1. se utiliza para las maletas
2. significa 'very' en español
3. se utiliza para guiar el coche
4. iglesia grande en una ciudad
5. 'the' (masculino) en español
6. un taxi si no hay personas dentro

horizontales
1. tipo de coche
2. el Town Hall
3. se utiliza para mirar la carretera y los coches
4. 'to the' en español
5. se utilizan de noche

ANSWERS P. 140

4 You're finding your way around Madrid by taxi. Listen to Eliud's prompts and tell the driver where you want to go. You will be using **a + la** (**calle, catedral**) and **al** (**Prado, banco**).

Luis enquires about air fares to Madrid

LISTEN FOR...

en avión	by air
la semana que viene	next week
¿en qué vuelo?	on which flight?

Luis	Quería ir a Madrid en avión el martes de la semana que viene
Agente de viajes *(travel agent)*	¿En qué vuelo? ¿Le digo los que hay?
Luis	Sí. ¿A qué hora salen?
Agente de viajes	Vamos a ver ... (las) siete cincuenta, (las) nueve quince, (las) trece cero cinco, (las) diecinueve cuarenta, (las) veinte quince y (las) veintiuna
Luis	Y ¿qué precio tienen?
Agente de viaje	Noventa euros ida y ciento veinte ida y vuelta
Luis	Muy bien, muchas gracias
Agente de viaje	De nada, buenos días

▶ **el avión**   aeroplane
▶ **el vuelo**   flight
▶ **la ida**   single
▶ **la ida y vuelta**   return

el martes de la semana que viene   Tuesday of next week (literally, Tuesday of the week that's coming).
las siete cincuenta...   The travel agent should really say 'a las ...' at ....
De nada, buenos días   It's a pleasure, good day. Notice how you can use **buenos días** to say 'goodbye' as well as 'hello'.

Buying a train ticket to Madrid

LISTEN FOR...

un billete para Madrid	a ticket for Madrid
ése sirve	that one will do

Javi	Por favor, un billete para Madrid
Empleada	¿Para qué día lo desea?
Javi	Para mañana
Empleada	Mañana, ¿a qué hora quiere salir usted?
Javi	¿Por la noche es posible?
Empleada	Sí. Por la noche tiene usted uno a las once de la noche
Javi	Bueno, ése sirve
Empleada	¿En qué clase le doy? ... ¿Qué clase desea, preferente o turista?
Javi	¿Cuánto cuesta? ¿Cuál es la diferencia?
Empleada	Aproximadamente unos doce euros. Cincuenta en preferente y treinta y ocho en turista
Javi	Bueno, en turista, por favor
Empleada	En turista. ¿Ida y vuelta quiere usted?
Javi	No, sólo ida, sólo ida
Empleada	Sólo ida, ¿no? Son treinta y ocho euros

- ▶ **el billete**   a ticket
- ▶ **la clase**   class
- ▶ **la diferencia**   difference
- ▶ **preferente**   first class
- ▶ **turista**   second or tourist class

¿Para qué día lo desea?   For what day do you want it?
por la noche   at night. **Por la mañana** in the morning; **por la tarde** in the afternoon. If you mention a specific time, however, you need to replace **por** by **de**. **A las ocho de la mañana** eight o'clock in the morning.
Ése sirve   That one will do (**servir** to serve). Remember that **servir** is a stem-changing verb (see the Grammar section in Unit 8).
¿En qué clase le doy?   Which class shall I give you?

5 Play the last conversations through again and answer the questions below. Try not to look at the transcript. Write each number out in full and say it out loud as you do so.

a. What time did the first plane leave for Madrid?

_____

b. And the last?

_____

c. How much was the first class fare to Madrid?

_____

d. And the second class fare?

_____

ANSWERS P. 140

6 Carmen wants to go to Madrid, one afternoon mid-week. She does not want to arrive later than ten o'clock in the evening or start earlier than three o'clock in the afternoon. Which flight should she take?

a. Hay un vuelo a las cuatro de la tarde el sábado que llega a las dieciocho horas cinco minutos.

b. Hay otro el lunes que sale a las dos de la tarde y llega a las cuatro al aeropuerto de Barajas.

c. Luego hay uno que sale los martes a las quince horas cincuenta que llega a Madrid a las diecisiete horas quince minutos.

d. Y por último, hay uno que sale los jueves a las catorce horas treinta minutos y que llega a las dieciséis cuarenta.

ANSWER P. 140

7 Listen to the recording, where you will hear four short conversations. Tick the grid below according to each traveller's requirements. You'll need to know **andén** platform. You'll also hear the words **Talgo** (express) and **AVE** (high speed train), which are different categories of Spanish trains.

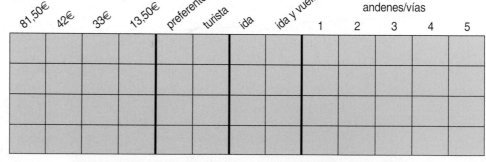

	81,50€	42€	33€	13,50€	preferente	turista	ida	ida y vuelta	andenes/vías 1	2	3	4	5
Manuel													
Y's name													
Beatriz													
X's name													

ANSWERS P. 140

8 Now *you* try buying a ticket for the night train to Valladolid. You'll need: **ése sirve** that one will be fine, **turista** and **ida solamente**.

CONVERSATIONS 3

At the petrol station

> ### LISTEN FOR...
>
> | | |
> |---|---|
> | **¿quiere que lo rellene?** | do you want it filled up? |
> | **veinte litros de súper** | twenty litres of four star |
> | **el nivel de aceite** | the oil level |
> | **la presión de las ruedas** | the tyre pressure |
> | **el parabrisas** | the windscreen |

Gasolinero	¿Quiere que lo rellene?
Pepe	No, sólo quince li... no, veinte litros de súper, por favor
Gasolinero	Sí, claro, aquí tiene, veinte litros de súper. ¿Quiere que le mire el nivel del aceite?
Pepe	No, gracias, no es necesario
Gasolinero	Y ¿quiere que compruebe la presión de las ruedas?
Pepe	Sí, las ruedas, sí por favor, especialmente las dos de delante
Gasolinero	Vale. ¿Quiere que le limpie el parabrisas?
Pepe	Sí, sí, porque está muy, muy, muy sucio, sí
Gasolinero	De acuerdo. Ahora se lo haré

▶ **el gasolinero** pump attendant
▶ **rellenar** to fill
▶ **mirar** to look at
▶ **el nivel** level
▶ **necesario** necessary
▶ **comprobar** to check
▶ **la rueda** tyre
▶ **sucio** dirty
▶ **de acuerdo** all right

¿Quiere que lo rellene? Do you want me to fill it up? This is rather a complicated structure (the subjunctive) which you need only recognize for the moment. To get your tank filled up, just say **'(35/40) litros de súper, por favor'**.

veinte litros de súper 20 litres of four star. Ask for fuel either by the litre or by price. **Treinta euros de súper** thirty euros' worth of four star. **Cincuenta euros de sin plomo** fifty euros' worth of lead-free.

You will only find this sort of 'Rolls-Royce' service in smaller, provincial garages. In the city, most garages are self-service.

¿Quiere que le mire el nivel del aceite? Do you want me to look at/check the oil level? This is a similar construction – as is: **¿Quiere que compruebe la presión de las ruedas?** Do you want me to check the tyre pressure? and **¿Quiere que le limpie el parabrisas?** Do you want me to clean the windscreen? **Quiere que** makes the following verb change its ending. Don't worry about it at this stage.

las dos de delante the front two; **las dos de atrás** the back two.

Ahora se lo haré I'll do it for you now. **Haré** I will do.

Having a tyre repaired

LISTEN FOR...

¿pueden repararme (Vds.) una rueda?	can you repair a wheel for me?
sería conveniente	it would be a good idea
esperar	to wait
¿dejo...?	shall I leave...?
más adelante	further on

Pepe	Oiga, ¿pueden repararme Vds. una rueda? que no llevo rueda de repuesto...
Gasolinero	De acuerdo, entonces, ¿la necesita para ahora mismo?
Pepe	Sí, sería conveniente, porque no me gusta viajar sin rueda de repuesto
Gasolinero	Bien, ¿puede esperar como un cuarto de hora o así?
Pepe	Sí, si es sólo cuestión de un cuarto de hora, sí, pero si es más, pues me voy y vuelvo dentro de un rato
Gasolinero	No, no, será como un cuarto de hora o media hora
Pepe	Estupendo, muy bien. Entonces espero. Ahora mismo... ¿Dejo el coche aquí o lo llevo un poco más adelante?
Gasolinero	No, puede dejarlo allí mismo

- ▶ **la rueda de repuesto** spare wheel
- ▶ **de acuerdo** all right
- ▶ **entonces** then
- ▶ **ahora mismo** straight away
- ▶ **conveniente** desirable, advisable
- ▶ **esperar** to wait
- ▶ **dentro (de)** within
- ▶ **dejar** to leave

¿Pueden repararme Vds. una rueda?   Can you repair a wheel for me? Should anything else need repairing, simply substitute the name of the object for '**rueda**'. **¿Pueden repararme Vds. este neumático?** Can you mend this tyre for me? (Pepe uses '**rueda**' where, strictly speaking, '**neumático**' would be more accurate.) You can also substitute the word **reparar** for other verbs: **¿Pueden mirarme este reloj?** Can you look at this watch for me? It's also useful to know '**tengo un problema con (los frenos)**' I have a problem with (the brakes) and '**no funciona(n)**' it/they don't work.

Sí, sería conveniente   Yes, that would be a good idea.
Vuelvo dentro de un rato   I'll come back in a short while.
Será como un cuarto de hora   It'll be about a quarter of an hour.
Lo llevo un poco más adelante   I'll take it a bit further on.
Puede dejarlo allí mismo   You can leave it right there.

9 Here's one side of a conversation between you and a petrol pump attendant. The pictures will guide you as to what to write.

¿Sí, señora?   Oiga ¿ _____ ?

Lo siento, sólo tenemos súper o normal.

Bueno _____

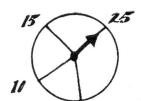

¿Miro el aceite? _____

¿Limpio el parabrisas? Sí, _____

¿Compruebo la presión de las ruedas? Sí, _____

Bien, buen viaje. _____

ANSWERS P. 140

10 In the summer, magazines and newspapers are full of advice about what to do before going on holiday (**antes de salir de vacaciones**). Read this article about checking over your car...

Mecánica:
Ahora, días antes de salir de vacaciones, es importante revisar los elementos importantes de su coche.

Neumáticos:
son el único punto de contacto entre el coche y el asfalto. De ellos depende en gran parte la seguridad. El dibujo debe tener una profundidad mínima de 1,6 milimetros y siempre hay que llevar las presiones correctas.

Frenos:
compruebe las pastillas de los frenos de su coche y también el líquido de frenos. Si su coche tiene más de tres años, es conveniente cambiarlo.

Faros:
todos los faros e intermitentes del coche tienen que funcionar y estar reglados convenientemente.

Limpiaparabrisas:
compruebe que funciona

correctamente. Si no limpia uniformemente el cristal, cámbielo.

Batería:
compruebe que los bornes no tienen restos de ácido.

Rueda de repuesto:
compruebe la presión de la rueda de repuesto.

El día antes de salir, *compruebe:*
el nivel de aceite, agua y líquido limpiaparabrisas y la presión de las ruedas

la seguridad	safety
el dibujo	tread (here, otherwise *drawing*, *sketch*)
la profundidad	depth
la pastilla de frenos	the brake lining
e	and (replaces **y** in front of **i-** and **hi-** but not **hie-**)
los intermitentes	indicators
reglado/a	adjusted
cambiar	to change
los bornes	terminals

Now, answer the following questions:

a. How many days before setting off should you check over your car?

b. What two things must you check on the brakes?

c. How thick should the tread be on the tyres?

d. Under what circumstances should you change the windscreen wipers?

e. What must not remain on the terminals?

ANSWERS P. 140 f. What four things should you do the day before setting out?

11 Now you're on the road in Spain and need certain services at the petrol station. Carlos will prompt you. You'll need: **sin plomo, ¿dónde pago? sucio** and **no es necesario**.

Madrid-Atocha

E.M.T. DE MADRID, S.A.
C.I.F.:A-28/046316

Fecha: 10-01-03   Hora: 17:03

BILLETE SENCILLO

1.10 Euros

Autobús: 00446
M.Expendedora: 10188
Línea: 027   Viaje 017
Nº Billete: 043431
IVA y SOV incluídos.
Consérvese a disposición de los
empleados que lo soliciten.
#03.002#

GRAMMAR AND EXERCISES

Asking questions

As you know, there are several different ways of asking questions in Spanish. Here's a summary of what you've already learned:

- use a questioning tone of voice (rising intonation): **¿vives aquí?**
- change the word order: **¿eres tú?** rather than **tú eres**.
- use a tag word such as '**¿no?**' or '**¿verdad?**'
- use question words such as **¿cómo?** and **¿dónde?**

Here are some other question words. Notice that they always have an accent.

¿Qué quieres?
What do you want?

¿Por qué lo quieres?
Why do you want it?

¿Cómo lo quieres?
How do you want it?

¿Cómo es (tu piso)?
What's (your flat) like?

¿Cuándo lo quieres?
When do you want it?

¿Dónde lo quieres?
Where do you want it?

¿Cuál quieres?
Which do you want?

¿Cuánto quieres?
How much do you want?

¿Cuántos quieres?
How many do you want?

¿Quién lo quiere?
Who wants it?

¿De quién es?
Whose is it?

Coping and repair strategies

Here's a list of useful words and phrases which will get you out of a linguistic jam.

¿cómo?
what? pardon?

¿Cómo dice?
What did you say?

¿Qué significa ... ?
What does ... mean?

¿Cómo se dice ... en español?
How do you say ... in Spanish?

despacio
slowly

Lo siento
I'm sorry

No comprendo
I don't understand (situations in general)

No entiendo
I don't understand (language)

Perdone/oiga/por favor
Excuse me (asking for attention)

Perdóneme
I'm sorry (for doing something wrong)

Personal pronouns – *el mío* (mine) ... *el tuyo* (yours)

Singular		Plural	
el mío	mine	**los míos**	mine
la mía		**las mías**	
el tuyo	yours (**tú**)	**los tuyos**	yours (**tú**)
la tuya		**las tuyas**	
el suyo	his, hers, yours (**Vd.**), theirs	**los suyos**	his, hers, yours (**Vd.**), theirs
la suya	his, hers, yours, theirs	**las suyas**	his, hers, yours, theirs
el nuestro	ours	**los nuestros**	ours
la nuestra		**las nuestras**	
el vuestro (**vosotros**)	yours	**los vuestros**	yours
la vuestra		**las vuestras**	

Remember that these words act in the same way as adjectives and so 'agree' with the word they describe.

Tu coche y el mío
> your car and mine

MI bicicleta y la suya
> my bike and his/hers/yours(**Vd.**)/theirs

12 Here's a quiz to test your general knowledge – and how to ask questions in Spanish. Model answers are on p. 140.

a. ¿Cuándo es tu cumpleaños?
b. ¿Cómo es tu casa?
c. ¿Cuántas habitaciones tiene?
d. ¿Qué significa 'trabajar' en inglés?
e. ¿Cómo se llama la capital de España?
f. ¿Quién es Elizabeth segunda?
g. ¿Dónde está el Museo del Prado?

13 Match up the questions and the replies:

i. ¿Funciona el parabrisas?
ii. ¿Puedo dejar el coche aquí?
iii. ¿A qué hora sale el avión a Málaga?
iv. ¿Para ir a la plaza de España?
v. ¿Cuánto cuesta el billete a Alicante?
vi. ¿Para cuándo quieres el reloj?

a. A las nueve horas quince minutos
b. Veinte euros
c. Para el viernes
d. No, no funciona muy bien
e. Sí, ¡cómo no!
f. Se puede ir en autobús o en metro

ANSWERS P. 140

14 What would you say if you had the following problems?
(Some situations have several possibilities.)

a. someone is speaking too quickly

_____

b. someone asks you a question to which you don't know the answer _____

c. you bump into someone in the street

_____

d. you want to know what a particular word means in Spanish _____

e. you want to get someone's attention

_____

f. someone gives you a long complicated explanation – and you've understood nothing!

_____

ANSWERS P. 140

KEY WORDS
AND PHRASES

¿Queda libre?	Are you free?
¿Está libre?	Are you free?
¿Para dónde?	Where are you going?
¿Adónde va Vd.?	Where are you going?
el (lunes) de la semana que viene	(Monday) of next week
los lunes	on Mondays
el vuelo	flight
¿en qué vuelo?	on what flight?
por la mañana	in the morning
tarde	afternoon
noche	at night, during the night
un billete para Madrid	a ticket for Madrid
¿para qué día?	for what day?
¿A qué hora quiere usted salir?	What time do you want to leave?
¿preferente o turista?	first or second class?
la ida	single (ticket)
la ida y vuelta	return (ticket)
súper	four star
normal	three star
sin plomo	lead-free
veinte litros de súper	twenty litres of four star
¿Quiere que lo rellene?	Do you want it filled up?
el nivel de aceite/agua	the oil/water level
el líquido de frenos	brake fluid
la presión de las ruedas	tyre pressure
el parabrisas	windscreen
el limpiaparabrisas	windscreen wiper
el faro	headlight
el cierre	lock
el maletero	boot
el retrovisor	mirror
el intermitente	indicator
el neumático	tyre
el freno	brake
el volante	steering wheel
¿Pueden repararme Vds. una rueda?	Can you repair a wheel?
¿Pueden mirarme este reloj?	Can you look at this watch for me?
Tengo un problema con ...	I have a problem with ...
No funciona/n	It/they doesn't/don't work
Sería conveniente	It would be a good idea
un poco más adelante	a bit further on

Driving in Spain

GETTING AROUND BY CAR is one of the best ways of seeing the country, although communications in some of the further flung areas can be poor and the distance between towns can be great. However, there are certain things to remember before you set off. You will need your driving licence, insurance certificate and vehicle documentation. You also need a green card and bail bond in case of accident. This is available from your insurance company or broker and is supplied free up to a certain number of days per year. In any case, check with your insurance broker as to what is required before driving in Spain, as the situation at the moment is quite fluid. You should also carry a portable red triangle as a warning signal in case you have to park the car in an emergency. There are two important things to watch out for when driving. First, it is compulsory to wear seat belts; second, the alcohol limit is set lower than in some other countries (0.5g per 1000 cubic cms).

There is now an impressive network of motorways in Spain (labelled with the prefix A for **autopista**), for which you have to pay a toll. Unfortunately, there are no concessions on these tolls for visitors to Spain. Current details on motorway prices can be requested from ASETA, Estebañez Calderón 3, Madrid 20. The network is being continually extended, so do make sure you have an up-to-date map.

Fuel

Petrol in Spain comes in two grades – **súper**, which is equivalent to four star, and **normal**, equivalent to three star. Lead-free (**sin plomo**) is of course readily available. Diesel is **gasoleo**. Although fuel is officially sold by the litre, you can also ask for it in euros. If you are off the beaten track, it is worth topping up when you can. Until recently, fuel was a state monopoly in Spain under the acronym CAMPSA. Fuel sales have now been deregulated and the price is no longer the same wherever you go.

The name of the Spanish railway network is RENFE (**Red Nacional de Ferrocarriles Españoles – www.renfe.es**) and it organizes a bewildering number of train services. RENFE's showpiece used to be the Talgo, a luxury train for which a supplement is payable. It is still an excellent train which provides a fast, comfortable, intercity ride. It has however been superseded by the AVE (**alta velocidad española**) or high speed train, which is similar in style to the French TGV or Japanese bullet train. It was built especially for the International Fair in Seville in 1992 and links Madrid with Seville. You might also like to take the EUROMED, a fast train which travels down the coast from Barcelona to Alicante in three and a half hours. (By the way, it is often easier to buy train tickets at travel agencies rather than at the railway station, where there may be a long queue.) On certain days throughout the year, known as **días azules**, there are several reductions for all categories of passengers. It is worth enquiring at railway stations, RENFE offices or travel agencies for these special offers. Buses are a cheap, popular and efficient way of getting around, especially on short trips, although there are long distance routes also.

AND FINALLY...

15 You have one or two problems whilst on the road in Spain. See if you can solve them. You'll be using:

¿pueden repararme ustedes ...?
tengo un problema con ...
no funciona(n)

ANSWERS

EXERCISE 1

(a) calle San Antonio, 15   **(b)** al Museo del Prado
(c) a la Plaza Mayor   **(d)** al bar Marbella
(e) a la oficina de turismo   **(f)** al hotel Santa Ana

EXERCISE 3

verticales: **1.** maletero   **2.** muy   **3.** volante   **4.** catedral
5. el   **6.** libre.
horizontales **1.** taxi   **2.** ayuntamiento   **3.** retrovisor   **4.** al
5. faros.

EXERCISE 5

(a) a las siete cincuenta   **(b)** a las vientiuna (horas)
(c) cincuenta euros   **(d)** treinta y ocho euros

EXERCISE 6

Carmen should take flight c.

EXERCISE 7

Manuel – preferente, ida y vuelta, andén dos, treinta y tres
euros. Diana – turista, ida, vía uno, cuarenta y dos euros.
Beatriz – turista, ida, andén tres, trece euros, cincuenta
céntimos. Roberto – preferente, ida y vuelta, andén cuatro,
ochenta y un euros, cincuenta céntimos.

EXERCISE 9

¿Sí, señora? Oiga, ¿tiene extra? Lo siento, sólo tenemos súper
o normal. Bueno, veinticinco litros de súper por favor. ¿Miro el
aceite? Sí, por favor. ¿Limpio el parabrisas? Sí, está muy
sucio. ¿Compruebo la presión de las ruedas? Sí, las dos de
delante. Bien, buen viaje. Gracias, adiós.

EXERCISE 10

(a) a few   **(b)** the brake linings and the fluid
(c) 1.6 millimetres   **(d)** if they do not clean uniformly
(e) traces of acid   **(f)** check the oil and water level and the
windscreen wiper fluid, check the tyre pressure.

EXERCISE 12

(a) mi cumpleaños es el tres de abril   **(b)** es grande y
moderna   **(c)** tiene diez habitaciones   **(d)** significa 'to work'
(e) se llama Madrid   **(f)** es la reina de Inglaterra
(g) está en Madrid

EXERCISE 13

i d   **ii** e   **iii** a   **iv** f   **v** b   **vi** c

EXERCISE 14

(a) despacio, por favor   **(b)** no sé – lo siento
(c) perdóneme/lo siento   **(d)** ¿qué significa ...?
(e) ¡oiga por favor!   **(f).** ¡no entiendo!

10 TABLE TALK ...

WHAT YOU WILL LEARN

▶ Something about restaurants in Spain
▶ What the **tenedor** system is all about
▶ More about directions

BEFORE YOU BEGIN

One of the most difficult things at this stage of learning a new language is keeping up the momentum. Try some of these tips for keeping your motivation up. Keep your books to hand, near your favourite armchair, so that picking up where you left off is easy and you don't waste time organizing yourself. Try to listen to the odd radio programme in Spanish (or even television if you have access to satellite or cable). Even if you don't understand too much of what is going on, you will be attuning your ear and getting used to Spanish sounds and intonation. Rather than having the occasional blitz, try to spend just ten or fifteen minutes a day in study. 'Little and often' is much more likely to maintain your interest. Go out to a tapas bar or a Latin American restaurant and try ordering your meal in Spanish. This will show you that your hours of study *are* paying off and encourage you to continue learning.

Pronunciation notes

The **p** in Spanish is never aspirated: that is, it sounds like the **p** in Spain but not in pain. (Try saying both these words aloud to see what we mean.) Listen to Carlos and Marisa giving you the Spanish versions of the international game of ping-pong!

ping   pong   por   para   sopa

María asks Reme if she knows of a good restaurant

LISTEN FOR...

¿qué tipo de comida sirven?   what sort of food do they serve?
un precio bastante razonable   quite a reasonable price

María	¿Me puede recomendar algún restaurante en Lugo?
Reme	Sí, por ejemplo, el Mesón de Alberto
María	Y ¿qué tipo de comida sirven?
Reme	Toda clase de comidas, regionales, españolas, extranjeras ...
María	Y ¿es muy caro?
Reme	No, es un precio bastante razonable

▶ **recomendar**   to recommend
▶ **por ejemplo**   for example
▶ **el tipo**   type
▶ **la comida**   food, (main) meal
▶ **la clase**   kind
▶ **regional**   regional
▶ **extranjero/a**   foreign
▶ **razonable**   reasonable

¿Me puede recomendar algún restaurante en Lugo?   Can you recommend me a restaurant in Lugo? **Algún/alguna** any. **Algunos/as** any, some.

 And now María asks Eme the same question

LISTEN FOR...

ya la ves en seguida   you'll see it immediately
lacón con grelos   shoulder of pork with turnip tops

María	¿Me puedes recomendar algún restaurante en Lugo, por favor?
Eme	Pues sí, el Verruga es bueno
María	Y ¿dónde está?
Eme	Está en la calle de Los Vinos. Mira, por esa calle coges la primera a la izquierda y ya lo ves en seguida
María	Y ¿qué tipo de comida sirven?
Eme	Pues de todas clases, pero ya que estás en Lugo, yo te recomiendo el lacón con grelos que es un plato magnífico

▶ **coger**   to take
▶ **ya**   already
▶ **ver**   to see
▶ **en seguida**   immediately
▶ **ya que ...**   seeing that ..., given that ...
▶ **el lacón**   shoulder of pork

▶ **los grelos**   turnip tops

▶ **el plato**   dish, plate

por esa calle   along that road

coges la primera a la izquierda   you take the first on the left. You can also use 'tomar' here. (**Coger** is a taboo word in Latin America.)

ya lo ves en seguida   you see it immediately

ya que estás en Lugo   now that you're in Lugo. **Ya** means 'already' but is often used as a filler to give the idea of immediacy.

yo te recomiendo   I recommend to you. **Recomendar** is a stem-changing verb. See the Grammar section in Unit 3, for verbs in which **e** becomes **ie**.

el lacón con grelos   shoulder of pork with turnip tops. This is one of the great regional dishes of Galicia.

María asks about the tenedor system

> ## LISTEN FOR...
>
> | | |
> |---|---|
> | **distintos tenedores** | different forks |
> | **limpias** | clean |
> | **aceptables** | acceptable |

> **María**   Por favor, ¿me podrías decir qué quiere decir esto de los distintos tenedores?
>
> **Manolo**   Sí, pues mira, los restaurantes están clasificados con tenedores. Este restaurante tiene tres tenedores, entonces significa que la comida es buena, que las cocinas están limpias y que el precio pues no es excesivamente barato
>
> **María**   Y ¿qué me dices de un tenedor entonces?
>
> **Manolo**   ¡Hombre!, pues, los restaurantes de un tenedor son aceptables

▶ **decir**   to say

▶ **querer decir**   to mean

▶ **el tenedor**   fork

▶ **clasificado**   classified

▶ **entonces**   so, then

▶ **significar**   to mean

▶ **limpio/a**   clean

¿Qué *quiere decir* (tenedor)? ¿Qué *significa* (limpio)? Both italicized terms are translated by the word 'mean': What does (**tenedor**) mean? What does (**limpio**) mean? You'll be practising this construction in exercise 3.

los distintos tenedores   different forks. In Spain, restaurants are classified according to the number of forks they have been awarded.

pues mira   well look ...

La comida es buena   The food is good. **Comida** means food in general or the main meal of the day – which in Spain is at lunchtime.

¿Qué me dices de ...?   What can you tell me about ...?

1   Here is a conversation which is similar to the first two conversations in this unit. Only the verbs are missing. Can you supply them?

María   ¿Me _____ recomendar un restaurante en Lugo?

Reme   Sí, el Mesón de Alberto por ejemplo

María   ¿Qué clase de comida _____ ?

Reme   Toda clase – comida regional, extranjera, típica ...

María   ¿_____ muy caro?

Reme   No, _____ un precio razonable

María   Y ¿dónde _____ ?

Reme   _____ en la calle de Los Vinos. _____ la primera a la izquierda y ya lo _____ en seguida

María   ¿Y la comida _____ buena?

ANSWERS P. 156   *Reme*   Muy buena. Yo te _____ el bacalao al pil-pil

2   Using the conversations you've just studied, work out how you would tell a Spanish person about a restaurant that you are familiar with. Fill in the gaps below and then practise your role out loud until you can say it fluently and from memory. There are sample answers on page 156.

A: ¿Me puede recomendar usted un restaurante aquí?

B: _____

A: ¿Y qué tipo de comida sirven allí?

B: _____

A: ¿Y la comida es cara o barata?

B: _____

A: ¿Y dónde está?

B: _____

A: ¿Y la comida es buena en general?

B: _____

A: ¿Me recomienda algún plato en especial?

B: _____

3   On the recording you'll be asking Marisa about the meaning of certain words and phrases by using **¿qué significa ...?**

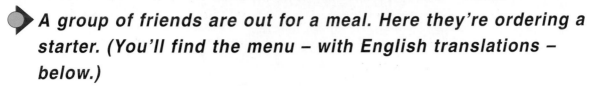

A group of friends are out for a meal. Here they're ordering a starter. (You'll find the menu – with English translations – below.)

LISTEN FOR...

entremeses	hors d'oeuvres
sopa del día	soup of the day
marisco	seafood

Camarera	Hola, buenas tardes, aquí tienen el menú
María	Vamos a ver, de primer plato tenemos consomé con huevo, entremeses y sopa del día. ¿Cuál es la sopa del día?
Camarera	La sopa es de marisco
Marta	Para mí una sopa del día
Jordi	Para mí, a ver, espérate, yo, los entremeses
Manolo	Pues yo voy a tomar una sopa del día
María	Yo también, sopa del día
Camarera	Muy bien

MESON GALLEGO
Menú del día

Primer grupo	First course
sopa del día (sopa de pescado)	soup of the day (- fish soup)
consomé con huevo	consommé with egg
entremeses	hors d'œuvres

Segundo grupo	Second course
ternera a la riojana	Riojan veal
merluza a la romana	hake fried in batter
bacalao a la vizcaína	Vizcayan salt cod
cochinillo asado	roast suckling pig

Postres	Desserts
flan	cream caramel
tarta helada	ice-cream gateau
helados (fresa, vainilla, chocolate, caramelo, naranja)	ice cream (strawberry, vanilla, chocolate, caramel, orange)
melocotón	peach
vino tinto/blanco de la casa	red/white house wine
agua mineral/ sin gas	still mineral water

▶ **el consomé** consommé
▶ **los entremeses** hors d'oeuvres
▶ **el marisco** shellfish, seafood

Aquí tienen el menú Here's the menu. You can use either **menú** or **carta** for menu: **menú** is a little more modern.

de primer plato as a first course. Notice that **primero** loses its final **o** before a masculine, singular noun. The same is true for **tercero**. Note also **cuarto** (4th), **quinto** (5th) and **sexto** (6th). These adjectives are regular. The waiter or waitress will ask you **¿Qué van a tomar de primer plato?** What are you going to have as a first course?

la sopa del día soup of the day

para mí 'for me', which is a key phrase to remember when you're asking for items in a restaurant.

espérate wait a minute

The main course

LISTEN FOR...

ternera a la riojana	Rioja-style veal
merluza a la romana	fried hake with sauce
bacalao a la vizcaína	Biscay-style cod
cochinillo asado	roast suckling pig

Camarera	Y de segundo ¿qué van a tomar?
Marta	Yo, ternera a la riojana
Jordi	Pues yo me pido la merluza a la romana
Manolo	¿El cochinillo asado es muy picante?
Camarera	No, no es muy picante ...
Manolo	Pues un cochinillo asado
María	Yo, casi, bacalao a la vizcaína
Camarera	Entonces es una ternera a la riojana, una merluza a la romana, un bacalao a la vizcaína y un cochinillo asado
Los amigos	Sí, sí, muy bien, eso es

```
        La esquina del Café
GARCIA ESCOBAR, S.L.
C/Jesús,10.-28014- MADRID
Tfno.:91-369-30-84
N.I.F.:B-80788045

 Tiket.:T1-2-81935   Fecha.:12/01/2003
 Mesa/Barra.. :B11
 Hora .: 09:46
 Camarero.. :ROSANA
 Forma de pago:CONTADO

  Concepto            P.Unit Parcial

 2  CHOCOLATE          1,40   2,80
 4  1 CHURRO           0,20   0,80

 Subtotal      3,36
 Iva 7    %    0,24

TOTAL Euros: 3,60

Muchas Gracias.
```

▶ **la ternera** veal
▶ **la merluza** hake
▶ **el cochinillo** suckling pig
▶ **asado** roast
▶ **picante** hot, spicy
▶ **el bacalao** salt cod

¿de segundo? as a second course?
Yo me pido I order for myself, I'll have
Yo, casi, bacalao a la vizcaína I think I'll have the Biscay salt cod. **Casi** means 'almost' and expresses a certain tentativeness.
Eso es That's it. Use this phrase to express agreement.

4 Listen to the conversation between Carlos and Marisa about a couple of restaurants in Madrid, and then fill in the grid.

	tenedores		comida		platos extranjeros
	razonable	caro	andaluza	gallega	
Casa Pepe					
Mesón de Carmen					

ANSWERS P. 156

5 Read this short article about a new soft drink (**refresco**) to be launched by a major American company. Then answer the questions, in Spanish. You don't need to write full sentences.

TOP-HI es una bebida con un sabor a fruta para adolescentes y jóvenes que LAURIE PRODUCTS lanza como su próxima bebida revolucionaria y que la empresa está probando en seis ciudades de Estados Unidos, desde Nueva York hasta San Francisco. LAURIE PRODUCTS espera captar a una generación que está preocupada por los problemas de la vida contemporánea y que gasta 3.000 millones de dólares al año sólo en bebidas.

Pero los 27,8 millones de adolescentes de Estados Unidos son sólo la vanguardia de un mercado mundial de jóvenes de 12 a 20 años, que comprende a casi 1.000 millones de personas. Además, esa masa de adolescentes, sobre todo en países de Asia y Latinoamérica, está mucho más influida por los productos y la cultura popular de Estados Unidos que por los que ven en su propio país. ■

el sabor	taste
lanzar	to launch
la empresa	firm
probar	to try
esperar	to hope
gastar	to spend
el mercado	market
mundial	world
además	what is more
el país	country
propio	own

a. what does the new drink taste of? _____

b. whom is it aimed at? _____

c. in how many cities is it being launched? _____

d. how much do young Americans spend on soft drinks each year?

_____

e. what other markets are also being targeted? _____

f. what influences young people from Asia and Latin America?

ANSWERS P. 156

_____

6 Now try ordering a starter and main course. Eliud will prompt you.

CONVERSATIONS 3̄

Ordering the drinks

LISTEN FOR...	
de beber	to drink
media botella de vino tinto	half a bottle of red wine
agua mineral sin gas	still mineral water

Camarera	Y de beber, ¿qué van a tomar?
Manolo	Pues una botella de vino tinto ¿no?
María	Mm...tal vez blanco, que yo voy a tomar pescado
Manolo	Vale pues, media botella de vino tinto y media botella de vino blanco
Camarera	Bien
Marta	Para mí, agua mineral sin gas. ¿Tiene agua mineral sin gas?
Camarera	Sí, sí. Entonces, bueno, media botella de vino tinto, medio litro de vino blanco y una botella de agua sin gas. Bien
Jordi	¿Y de agua con gas tenéis?
Camarera	También, sí
Jordi	Pues dame una
Camarera	Muy bien, vale, gracias

- ▶ **beber**   to drink
- ▶ **tal vez**   perhaps
- ▶ **el pescado**   fish
- ▶ **medio/a**   half

Y de beber, ¿qué van a tomar?   What do you want to drink? Substitute **de comer**, when you ask what people want to eat.

tal vez blanco, que yo voy a tomar pescado   perhaps white because I'm going to have fish.

media botella   half a bottle. Notice how **medio** agrees with **botella**. Later on, you'll hear **medio litro** a half litre. (The waitress makes a mistake here, as Manolo asked for a half bottle not a half litre of white wine.)

¿Tiene agua mineral sin gas?   Do you have still mineral water? **Agua mineral** comes **con gas** (fizzy) or **sin gas** (still – literally, without gas).

Pues dame una   Well give me one. Jordi should actually say **deme** (the **usted** form of **dame**) as the waitress addressed the group as **ustedes**. More about commands with **usted** in the Grammar section.

And finally the dessert

Jordi	¿Qué hay de postre?
Camarera	Sí, de postre tenemos flan, tarta helada, melocotón y helados
María	Mm... yo no voy a tomar postre
Jordi	Los helados, ¿de qué tienen?
Camarera	Tenemos helado de vainilla, de fresa y de chocolate
Jordi	Pues a ver, bueno, yo uno de chocolate
Camarera	Muy bien
Marta	Para mí, un helado de vainilla
Manolo	Para mí un flan
Camarera	Muy bien, entonces es un flan, un helado de chocolate y un helado de vainilla
Jordi	Muy bien

▶ **el postre**   pudding, dessert
▶ **el flan**   caramel cream
▶ **la tarta helada**   ice-cream cake
▶ **el melocotón**   peach
▶ **la vainilla**   vanilla
▶ **la fresa**   strawberry
▶ **el chocolate**   chocolate

Notice that **flan** is caramel cream and not flan. Caramel cream is a very popular dessert in Spain.

Yo no voy a tomar postre   I'm not going to have any dessert.

Ir to go

This is a very important verb, as it is used frequently not only to mean 'to go' but also to convey the idea of the simple future.
Make sure you know all the parts.

voy	I go
vas	you go (informal)
va	s/he goes
va	you go (formal)
vamos	we go (and let's go)
vais	you go (informal plural)
van	they go
van	you go (formal plural)

Voy a tomar un café   I'm going to have a coffee
vaya(n) is the command form: **vaya(n) por esta calle** go along this street. (Add the '**n**' for the plural.)

Giving opinions with *Me parece que ...*

Spanish likes to use what are called impersonal structures: you've already met one or two like **no me quedan** (I haven't got any left; literally, they don't remain to me) and **me gustaría** (I would like; literally, it would please me). The sentence gets turned around so that what you think is the subject becomes the object and vice versa.
Me parece simply means 'it seems to me' and you can use it to give an opinion or hazard a guess. Look at these examples:

Me parece que sí
I think so
Me parece que no
I don't think so
Me parece que son las dos
I think it's two o'clock
Me parece que está en España
I think he's in Spain
Me parece bien
It seems like a good idea to me

You can also express opinions by using **creo que ...**

Creo que sí
I believe/think so
Creo que no
I believe/think not
Creo que está bien
I believe/think that's fine

Commands with *usted*

If you want to tell someone to do something, you need to use the form of the verb called the imperative. As usual, imperatives (or commands) come in different guises. They vary according to:
i. whether you are talking to one or more people
ii. whether you call these people **tú** or **usted**

In this unit you'll just learn about commands with **usted**. They are easy to form if you follow these steps:

i. start with the first person singular of the present tense.
   Using **decir** (to say) and **bajar** (to go down) as examples you get   **digo**   **bajo**
ii. drop the final **-o**   **dig-**   **baj-**
iii. if the verb ends in **-er** or **-ir**
   add **-a** for **usted**   **diga**   say
   or **-an** for **ustedes**   **digan**   say
iv. if the verb ends in **-ar**
   add **-e** for **usted**   **baje**   go down
   or **-en** for **ustedes**   **bajen**   go down

10 Match up the phrases in each column to make correct sentences:

a. yo voy a

b. Elena y Miguel

c. Carlos va a

d. ¿vas a salir

e. van todos juntos

i. su casa en Málaga

ii. a comer en casa de una amiga

iii. ver a mi madre esta tarde

iv. con tus amigos?

v. ¿adónde vais ahora?

juntos/as   together

ANSWERS P. 156

11 Try answering these questions with sentences which include '**me parece**'. Possible answers are given on page 156.

a. ¿Dónde está Juan?

_____

b. ¿Qué hora es?

_____

c. ¿Van al cine esta tarde?

_____

d. María está en la oficina, ¿no?

_____

e. ¿Y cómo está Pepe ahora?

_____

f. ¿No tiene dinero Pablo?

_____

12 Reread the section on commands and then give directions to a passer-by, using '**usted**'. We've given you the phrases to use below. Tell him or her to:

a. cross the square

b. go down the street

c. go up the stairs

d. catch the bus

e. turn right

f. go straight on

tomar/coger el autobús
subir la escalera
girar a la derecha
ir todo recto
cruzar la plaza
bajar la calle

ANSWERS P. 156

KEY WORDS
AND PHRASES

el menú, por favor	the menu, please
¿Qué tiene de beber?	What do you have to drink?
de comer?	to eat?
¿Qué va(n) a tomar ...	What are you going to have ...
de primer plato?	as a first course?
de segundo plato?	as a second course?
de postre?	as dessert?
Me parece que sí	I think so
no	I think not
Me parece bien	That seems a good idea
Me parece que es ...	I think it's ...
Yo creo que ...	I believe (think) that ...
consomé con huevo	consommé with egg
sopa del día	soup of the day
sopa de marisco	seafood soup
entremeses	hors d'oeuvres
ternera a la riojana	Rioja-style veal
bacalao a la vizcaína	Biscay-style cod
merluza a la romana	battered hake in sauce
picante	hot, spicy
un helado	an ice-cream
de fresa	strawberry
de vainilla	vanilla
de chocolate	chocolate
tarta helada	ice-cream cake
agua mineral	mineral water
con gas	fizzy
sin gas	still
¿Me puede recomendar algún restaurante?	Can you recommend a restaurant?
Yo te/le recomiendo ...	I recommend to you ...
¿Qué tipo de comida sirven?	What sort of food do they serve?
toda clase de comidas	all kinds of food
un plato magnífico	a magnificent dish
un precio bastante razonable	Quite a reasonable price
¿Qué significa ...?	What does ... mean?
¿Qué quiere decir ...?	What does ... mean?
el tenedor	fork
coges	you take
la primera	the first
la segunda	the second
la tercera	the third

Shopping for food and reading menus

SPAIN may be part of the European Union and the Latin American influence is important in North America but there are still many items in foodshops or in restaurants which are unfamiliar to the non-Spaniard. Let's look at fish first.

Fish

Fish is an everyday food in Spain. It is cheap and plentiful, although you will find that prices rise around festival times, especially for shellfish. The most common types are perhaps **besugo** (sea bream), which is often served whole, either grilled or in egg and breadcrumbs, **lenguado** (sole), **merluza** (hake) and **salmonete** (red mullet). Red mullet is usually served baked. Sardines are of course cheap and delicious and often served on the quayside with rough wine and hunks of bread. There are many sorts of fish which are unavailable in this country, so when in doubt, ask.

Meat

Meat cuts are quite different in Spain from elsewhere. Sorting out what is what is quite confusing. Here is a simple list of the most common cuts and what they mean. **Solomillo** is fillet or tenderloin. **Lomo** literally means back and can be both sirloin and fore ribs. **Falda** is skirt or flank and **costillas** are short or spare ribs. Cooked meats of one sort or another are very popular in Spain. You may come across **butifarra**, a sausage made from pork, fat, garlic, cinnamon and cloves – or **morcilla**, similar to black pudding. **Longaniza** is the nearest thing to a pork sausage and contains pork, garlic and herbs. If you are shopping for bacon, there is one golden rule – the darker it is, the saltier it will taste.

Bread and butter

You can buy **pan de molde** or sliced bread everywhere, but you may prefer **una barra** (a French-style loaf). **Mantequilla** (butter) comes salted (**con sal**) and unsalted (**sin sal**). Spaniards don't usually eat bread with butter, but they never eat a meal without bread! Catalans, on the other hand, like **pan con tomate** (bread and tomato) – hunks of bread spread with a mixture of tomato, garlic and olive oil.

Cheese

Spain has a great variety of cheese, of which many are unknown outside the country because they are not exported, but there are some delicious varieties, most of which come from the north. You will see **manchego** in most shops and menus. **Manchego** used to come from La Mancha and traditionally was made from ewes' milk. Now it is industrially made from cows' milk. It is sold either young and fresh or aged with a dry curd. Both are worth trying, especially the aged variety. **Idiazábal** is a variety of cheese made in the Basque country, again from ewes' milk. It has a hard, dark rind and yellow curd. **Requesón** was originally made in Catalonia but is now sold all over Spain. It is a light curd cheese. Finally, when in Galicia, try **teta** or **tetilla**, which comes in the shape of a breast – hence its name. It is made from cows' milk and is mild in flavour.

AND FINALLY...

13 In this exercise you'll be in a restaurant ordering a full meal. You'll practise:

el menú por favor
para mí
para mi mujer

OFERTAS DEL DÍA

1.- Tosta jamón serrano + caña 4'20
2.- Sartenada mejillones + caña 4'75
3.- Sartenada de istorra c/pimientos padrón 4'95
4.- Tosta manchega + caña 4'20
5.- Tortilla de camarón + caña 5'90

DISFRUTE DE NUESTRAS OFERTAS

ANSWERS

EXERCISE 1

puedes, sirven, es, es, está, está, coges, ves, es, recomiendo

EXERCISE 2

A: ¿Me puede recomendar usted un restaurante aquí?
B: Sí, le puedo recomendar The Farmer's Arms.   **A:** ¿Y qué tipo de comida sirven allí?   **B:** Sirven platos tradicionales, típicos de esta región.   **A:** ¿Y la comida es cara o barata?
B: La comida es bastante barata.   **A:** ¿Y dónde está?
B: Está en King Street, en el centro de la ciudad, cerca de la catedral.   **A:** ¿Y la comida es buena en general?   **B:** Sí, muy buena.   **A:** ¿Me recomienda algún plato en especial?
B: Sí, yo le recomiendo el 'ploughman's lunch' que es pan, queso y 'pickle'. Con una cerveza, es muy bueno.

EXERCISE 4

Casa Pepe has one fork, it's reasonably priced, it serves Andalusian food and also foreign dishes. El Mesón de Carmen has four forks, is expensive and serves food from Galicia but not foreign dishes.

EXERCISE 5

(a) fruta   **(b)** los jóvenes y adolescentes   **(c)** seis
(d) 3.000 millones de dólares   **(e)** Asia y Latinoamérica.
(f) la cultura americana.

EXERCISE 7

(a) iii   **(b)** v   **(c)** vi   **(d)** i   **(e)** iv   **(f)** vii   **(g)** ii

EXERCISE 8

Una San Miguel para mí. Un buen vino tinto de Rioja para Juan. Un vino blanco para Pablo. Un jugo de naranja para Ana. Un café solo para Pepe y agua mineral con gas para Carmen.

EXERCISE 9

Camarero: Buenas tardes señores, ¿qué van a tomar?
Señor: ¿Nos da el menú?
Camarero: Aquí tiene.
Señora: ¿De qué es la sopa?
Camarero: Tenemos sopa de pescado y gazpacho.
Señor: Bueno, el gazpacho para mí. ¿Y para ti, Luisa?
Señora: A ver ... melón con jamón.
Camarero: Gazpacho y melón. Bien. ¿Y de segundo?
Señor: Mm ... bacalao a la vizcaína. ¿Luisa?
Señora: Para mí, lacón con grelos.
Camarero: ¿Y de postre qué van a tomar?
Señor: Helados para los dos.
Camarero: Helados, muy bien.

EXERCISE 10

(a) iii   **(b)** v   **(c)** i   **(d)** iv   **(e)** ii

EXERCISE 11

(a) me parece que está en la cama   **(b)** me parece que son las tres y media   **(c)** me parece que sí   **(d)** me parece que sí
(e) me parece que está bien   **(f)** me parece que no

EXERCISE 12

(a) cruce la plaza   **(b)** baje la calle   **(c)** suba la escalera
(d) tome/coja el autobús   **(e)** gire a la derecha
(f) vaya todo recto

11
LIKES –
AND DISLIKES

WHAT YOU WILL LEARN

▶ How to …
say you like or dislike something
talk about the sort of person you are

BEFORE YOU BEGIN

Many people wonder what they can do about improving their accent. The key to speaking well is listening. Try listening for sound rather than for content and think about intonation – that is, the music of the language. Lowering or raising your voice in the right places helps you achieve a more authentic accent and can help hide the fact that individual sounds are not always accurate. Pitch is also important in Spanish – speakers in the peninsula (especially women) tend to have lower voices than people in Britain or in the United States.

Intonation patterns of course change all over the Spanish-speaking world but in peninsular Spanish the voice tends to drop at the end of the sentence. This can be difficult for non-Spaniards to understand because it means that the end of the sentence is sometimes unclear. Within the sentence, however, the voice tends to rise, especially if listing a number of items. Try practising these patterns yourself. You can record yourself and then listen back to the result.

Pronunciation notes

The Spanish **t** resembles the sound **p** in that it is not aspirated or 'breathy'. You'll hear the contrast between the English 'cup of tea' and the Spanish '**un té**' on your recording.

té   trabajo   típico   tengo   televisión

Unit 11   Likes – and dislikes   157

Does Janet like Spain?

LISTEN FOR...

¿le gusta España?	do you like Spain?
sí, me gusta muchísimo	yes, I like it a lot
¿le gusta viajar?	do you like travelling?

Serafín	¿Le gusta España?
Janet	Sí, me gusta muchísimo
Serafín	¿Le gusta viajar?
Janet	Sí, también

▶ **gustar** to like
▶ **viajar** to travel
▶ **también** also

¿Le gusta España? Do you like Spain? Use **¿le gusta?** to say 'do you like?' (literally, to you pleases Spain?). If you're speaking informally, say **¿te gusta España?**

Me gusta muchísimo I like it a lot (literally, to me it pleases a lot). Add **-ísimo/a** to the end of an adjective to strengthen the meaning. **Buenísimo** very good; **malísimo** very bad.

¿Le gusta viajar? Do you like travelling? Verbs immediately following an expression with **gustar** are always in the infinitive.

For a fuller explanation of this structure, read the Grammar section in this unit.

Does Janet like housework?

LISTEN FOR...

cocinar	to cook
coser	to sew
planchar	to iron
lavar	to wash
limpiar	to clean

Pepe	¿Le gusta cocinar?
Janet	Sí, no mucho pero sí me gusta
Pepe	Y ¿le gusta coser?
Janet	Sí, muchísimo
Pepe	¿Le gusta planchar?
Janet	No, no, no, no, lo odio
Pepe	¿Le gusta lavar?
Janet	Lavar ¿en qué sentido? ¿Lavar ropa? ▶

Pepe	Lavar la ropa
Janet	No, es un trabajo duro
Pepe	¿Le gusta limpiar la casa?
Janet	Sí, sí me gusta

- **cocinar** to cook
- **coser** to sew
- **planchar** to iron
- **odiar** to hate
- **lavar** to wash
- **el trabajo** work, job
- **duro/a** hard
- **limpiar** to clean

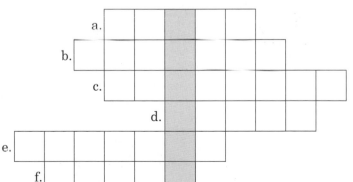

¿Le gusta cocinar? Do you like cooking? Notice how the infinitive is translated into English in phrases with '(**me**) **gusta**'.

No, no, no, lo odio No, I hate it. It's equally important to be able to express dislikes. If you want to be really emphatic, repeat the word '**no**'.

¿en qué sentido? in what sense? **Lavar** can be used in two ways – **lavar la ropa** to wash clothes and **lavarse** to wash oneself.

You'll learn about the latter meaning in Unit 13. If you want to say 'to wash up', use **fregar los platos**.

Note also **las faenas de la casa** housework.

PRACTICE

1 Fill in the blanks with the appropriate verbs or word from the conversations and an activity which many of us like doing will appear in the grey column.

a. to wash
b. to cook
c. to iron
d. the young woman in the conversation
e. to clean
f. to sew

ANSWERS P. 172

2 Read through the conversations again and make a list of the phrases which express liking or disliking. Put them in order from 1 (where you like something very much) to 4 (where you really hate it). Then look at page 172 for the order in which we placed them.

1. _____

2. _____

3. _____

4. _____

3 On the recording Antonio is listing his likes and dislikes. Listen to what he has to say and then fill in the grid below.

Does Antonio like?	Sí	No
vino blanco		
vino tinto		
café solo		
café con leche		
Madrid		
Valencia		
las vacaciones		
el trabajo		
el norte de España		
el sur de España		
helado de fresa		
helado de chocolate		
la carne (meat)		
el pescado		

ANSWERS P. 172

4 Now Marisa asks you what sorts of jobs you like and don't like doing at home.

Serafín asks Janet about her food preferences

LISTEN FOR...

me encanta	I love it
la lechuga	lettuce
muy bien frita	very well cooked

B&B

Campo Viejo

Envejecido más de dos años
en barrica de roble
Aged more than two years in oak
Vieilli plus de deux ans en fût
Mehr als zwei jahre im holzfaß gereift

RESERVA

L-04205   8 410302 502881

Serafín	¿Le gusta el vino?
Janet	Sí, me encanta
Serafín	¿Prefiere el vino o la cerveza?
Janet	Prefiero el vino tinto
Serafín	¿Qué tipo de comida prefiere?
Janet	Bueno, carne o huevos o lechuga
Serafín	¿Cómo prefiere la carne?
Janet	Muy bien frita
Serafín	¿Le gustan los huevos?
Janet	Ah sí, muchísimo

▶ **la lechuga**   lettuce

Me encanta   I love it. This is an alternative to '**me gusta muchísimo**' and works in the same way. **Me encanta el vino** I love wine.

muy bien frita   very well cooked. If you're referring to **pescado**, it will be **muy bien frito**.

¿Le gustan los huevos?   Do you like eggs? Note that because **huevos** is plural, **gusta** becomes **gustan**. **¿Le gustan los vinos franceses?** Do you like French wines? (Literally, do French wines please you?)

Serafín asks Janet whether she's ever been to Valencia

LISTEN FOR...

la detesto	I hate it
hay demasiada gente	there are too many people

Serafín	¿Conoce Valencia?
Janet	Ah, sí, me encanta, es una ciudad preciosa
Serafín	¿Conoce la Costa del Sol?
Janet	No, la detesto, no me gusta nada, nada, nada
Serafín	¿Por qué?
Janet	Hay demasiada gente
Serafín	¿Y la costa más al sur?
Janet	No especialmente. No me gusta ni mucho ni poco. Prefiero la costa gallega
Serafín	¿No le gusta el Mediterráneo?
Janet	No me hace mucha gracia
Serafín	Pero las playas del Mediterráneo son estupendas
Janet	Sí, pero hay demasiada gente

▶ **precioso/a**   beautiful
▶ **detestar**   to hate
▶ **la playa**   beach

¿Conoce Valencia?   Have you been to/do you know Valencia? **Conocer** usually means 'to know' but with respect to places can also mean 'to visit'.

No me gusta nada, nada, nada I really hate it. Here's another example of a key word being repeated to emphasize an idea.

Hay demasiada gente   There are too many people. Note that **gente** is feminine and singular.

No me gusta ni mucho ni poco   I neither like nor dislike it. If you're feeling indifferent, this is the expression for you.

No me hace mucha gracia I don't like it very much/I'm not all that keen on it.

5 Here's a jumbled conversation between Beatriz and Tomás about different places in Latin America . Can you unravel it?

¿Pero por qué? La costa es preciosa

¿El país o la ciudad de México?

¿Conoce México?

Está en los Andes ¿verdad?

Y ¿le gusta la costa, Acapulco por ejemplo?

Sí, no está muy lejos de la jungla y del Amazonas

Sí, pero hay muchos turistas

Y el Perú, ¿conoce el Perú?

El país

Sí, lo conozco también. Cuzco es una ciudad maravillosa

¿Acapulco? Lo detesto, es horrible

Sí, lo conozco bien. Me encanta. La ciudad de México también es preciosa

¡Qué exótico!

ANSWER P. 172

6 Listen to Isabel asking Beatriz and Tomás about their food preferences. If either of them likes the foods below, fill in their names.

a. _____ b. _____ c. _____ d. _____

_____ _____ _____ _____

e. _____ f. _____ g. _____

ANSWERS P. 172

_____ _____ _____

7 You try having a conversation with Carlos about the sorts of food you like. Eliud will tell you what to say.

And what do Spaniards think of England?

Pepe	¿Qué es lo que te gusta más de Inglaterra?
María Luisa	Pues realmente lo que más me gusta es el paisaje. Tiene un paisaje muy verde, unos valles y unos parques muy bonitos
Pepe	Y ¿qué es lo que te gusta menos de Inglaterra?
María Luisa	La lengua. La encuentro un poquito difícil
Pepe	¿Es difícil el inglés?
María Luisa	Sí, sí, es difícil

▶ **el paisaje** the countryside
▶ **el valle** valley
▶ **el parque** park
▶ **bonito/a** pretty
▶ **la lengua** language
▶ **difícil** difficult

¿Qué es lo que te gusta más de Inglaterra? What do you like most about England? Literally, what is that which you like most ...? This time Pepe uses the informal '**te**'.

¿Qué es lo que te gusta menos de ...? What do you like least about ...?

La encuentro un poquito difícil I find it a bit difficult. **Encontrar**, here means, 'to find'. It usually means 'to meet/to encounter'. Note how it changes in the stem. You will also need to know **fácil** easy.

Spanish men and the household chores

LISTEN FOR...

¿qué piensa el hombre español del trabajo doméstico?
what does the Spanish man think about household chores?

María Luisa	Vamos a ver qué piensa el hombre español del trabajo doméstico. ¿Te gusta cocinar?
Juan	No, no, es un trabajo para mujeres
María Luisa	Pero entonces ¿te gusta lavar o planchar?
Juan	No, eso menos. Todavía cocinar, si es para freír un par de huevos, pues sí, pero no lavar y planchar – de eso, nada. La cocina, planchar, y lavar, eso son cosas de la casa. Eso es para la mujer
María Luisa	¡Qué español más típico y qué animales!

▶ **pensar**   to think
▶ **el hombre**   man
▶ **el trabajo doméstico**   domestic chores
▶ **todavía**   still, yet
▶ **si**   if
▶ **freír**   to fry
▶ **el par**   couple/pair
▶ **la cosa**   thing
▶ **el animal**   animal

Take this conversation with a pinch of salt! María Luisa is teasing Juan, who belongs to a generation in which men were not expected to help with household chores. Nowadays young men are expected to pull their weight at home.
eso menos   that even less
pero no lavar y planchar – de eso, nada but washing and ironing – certainly not.
¡Qué español más típico!   What a typical Spaniard! Note how to say 'what a ...'
¡Qué día! What a day! **¡Qué bonito!** How pretty!

8 Read what a sample of young Spaniards have to say about their parents – and more especially about their fathers. Important new words are given below: try to guess the others before looking them up in a dictionary.

'El cree que manda pero mandamos mi madre y yo ...'

DIEZ estudiantes de 15 a 17 años de edad del Instituto Doña Sofía de Valladolid han hablado con nosotros durante más de tres horas de la figura del padre con la pasión y ambivalencia típicas de la adolescencia. Está muy claro que les gustaría un padre más presente y dialogante pero que todavía conserva su autoridad. Las chicas defienden más a la madre y están más a favor de la figura paterna los chicos. Aquí hay algunas de las frases más interesantes:

'Con mi padre, no hablo porque pasa de mí'

'El cree que manda pero en realidad mandamos mi madre y yo'

'Cuando le quiero hablar, siempre dice "háblame mañana, que ahora estoy cansado"'

'Quiero más a mi madre pero estimo más a mi padre'

'El padre es como un niño, que cuando llega a casa, lo único que quiere es comer y dormir'

'Mi madre trabaja todo el día y después tiene que soportar a mi padre que no hace nada en absoluto'

la chica   girl
el chico   boy
pasar de   to be uninterested in
mandar   to order (here, to be the boss)
cansado/a   tired
dormir   to sleep
soportar   to put up with

Now look at this list of adjectives which describe people. Some of them are new to you but you will be able to guess them as they look very much like their English equivalent. Tick those characteristics which you think best describe the fathers of the young people in the discussion. We've given four in the Answers on p. 172.

arrogante	español típico
modesto	egoísta
atractivo	antipático
simpático	fuerte
práctico	cansado
tolerante	compasivo
generoso	impaciente
machista	¡un animal!
tranquilo	

9 Now do the same for yourself. Use the following formula: **¿cómo soy yo?** what am I like? **soy ....** Look up any characteristics that apply to you and which don't appear in the list above. And before you begin – look back at Unit 1 to refresh yourself on agreement of adjectives.

10 Now you'll be talking about personality traits with Marisa on the recording.

GRAMMAR AND EXERCISES

Me gusta

In Unit 10, you were introduced to the idea of impersonal structures – that is, to sentences which to an English speaker's ear seem the wrong way around. **Me gusta** is the prime example of this sort of structure. Although it is not difficult to understand how it works, it can take a while to learn how to manipulate the forms with confidence. It helps if you remember that **me gusta** really means 'it pleases (to) me' and **no me gusta** 'it doesn't please (to) me'.

me gusta	I like it
(it pleases me)	
te gusta	you like it
(it pleases you) (informal)	
le gusta	s/he likes it
(it pleases him or her)	
le gusta	you like it
(it pleases you) (formal)	
nos gusta	we like it
(it pleases us)	
os gusta	you like it
(it pleases you) (informal pl.)	
les gusta	they like it
(it pleases them)	
les gusta	you like it
(it pleases you) (formal pl.)	

If you (and all the others!) don't like the object in question – simply put **no** before the phrase. **No me gusta el fútbol** I don't like football. **No me gusta mucho** I don't like it much

What you like can be a noun:
No me gusta el fútbol I don't like football
– or a verb:
No me gusta jugar al fútbol I don't like playing football

If you're talking about more than one thing which you like, then 'it pleases me' turns into 'they please me' – and **gusta** acquires an **-n**.

Me gustan las flores	I like flowers
No me gustan los huevos	I don't like eggs

Sometimes you'll see phrases like '**me gusta a mí**' or '**le gusta a él**'. The **a mí** or **a él** has two functions:

i. to stress who's doing the liking:
    A mí me gusta el vino blanco, pero a ti te gusta el tinto, ¿verdad?
    I like white wine, but *you* like red, don't you?

ii. to make it absolutely clear whom you're talking about. Remember that **le gusta** can refer to either him, her or you. You may have to add the phrase:

a ella	she, to her
a ellas	them, to them (fem.)
a él	he, to him
a ellos	them, to them (masc.)
a usted	you, to you
a ustedes	you, to you (plural)

to clarify whom you mean. **A ella le gusta el mar** *she* likes the sea. **A él le gusta el campo** *he* likes the countryside.

When you're mentioning people's names, you'll also need to add the **a: a mí me gusta el café solo pero a Luisa le gusta con leche**
I like black coffee but Luisa likes it white

Ver to see

veo	I see
ves	you see (informal)
ve	s/he sees
ve	you see (formal)
vemos	we see
veis	you see (informal plural)
ven	they see
ven	you see (formal plural)

¡vamos a ver!   let's see!
¡a ver!   let's see!

11 **¿Gusta o gustan?** Decide which is correct in the following sentences:

a. No me (_____) limpiar la casa

b. ¿Qué te (_____) más, té o café?

c. Me (_____) la carne bien frita

d. Me (_____) ensalada dc tomato con lechuga

e. Me (_____) el vino blanco y el vino tinto

ANSWERS P. 172

12 Here's a conversation between a market researcher and a man or woman in the street about a certain brand of coffee. Can you put the questions and statements in the correct order?

New vocabulary:
añadir to add, **el sabor** flavour

a. ¿No le gusta? ¿Y por qué?
b. No, no me gusta mucho
c. No – es que no me gusta el café – ¡prefiero el té!
d. ¿Le gusta el café Molinox?
e. Usted tiene que añadir un poco más de agua
f. Porque es un sabor muy fuerte

ANSWER P. 172

13 A feel-good exercise. Think of six things you really like (or like doing) and note them down, using phrases like:

A mí me gusta _____ or **Me encanta** _____

a. _____

b. _____

c. _____

d. _____

e. _____

f. _____

You'll find six possible answers on page 172.

KEY WORDS
AND PHRASES

me gusta	I like (it)
me encanta	I love (it)
no me gusta ni mucho ni poco	I neither like nor dislike (it)
no me gusta especialmente	I don't especially like (it)
no me hace mucha gracia	I don't especially like (it)
Lo/la detesto	I hate it
Lo/la odio	I hate it
No me gusta nada, nada, nada	I really hate it
¿Qué es lo que te gusta más de ...?	What do you like most about ...?
¿Qué es lo que te gusta menos de ...?	What do you like least about ...?
Lo que más me gusta es	What I like most is the
el paisaje	countryside
Lo que menos me gusta es	What I least like is
el clima	the climate
el tráfico	the traffic
la contaminación	the pollution
¡Qué español más típico!	What a typical Spanish male!
pienso que ...	I think that ...
viajar	to travel
cocinar	to cook
lavar (la ropa)	to wash (the clothes)
limpiar (la casa)	to clean (the house)
planchar	to iron
coser	to sew
la carne	meat
la lechuga	lettuce
(muy bien) frito/a	(very well) cooked
el parque	park
el valle	valley
el paisaje	countryside
precioso/a	beautiful
bonito/a	pretty
arrogante	arrogant
machista	macho
egoísta	selfish
simpático/a	nice
antipático/a	unpleasant
práctico/a	practical
duro/a	hard
fuerte	strong
tolerante	tolerant
compasivo/a	understanding
generoso/a	generous
impaciente	impatient
cansado/a	tired

The new Spanish woman

BEFORE 1976, women in Spain had few rights. Under the Franco régime divorce was prohibited: divorces which had taken place in the Republic (1931–6) were declared null and void. Married women had to obtain their husband's permission to travel alone, get a job, even open a bank account or buy a house. They had no control over property acquired jointly during their marriage and no legal authority over their children. The Divorce Act of June 1981 changed much of this, but in the teeth of much opposition. In 1982, 22,578 divorces were granted, many of which were between partners who had obtained legal separations under the previous régime. The divorce rate today is not particularly high: the breakdown of the family, as predicted by the Church and the Right, has not come about.

Under Franco, it was a crime to either sell or use contraceptives. Birth control is now openly available to those who want it and can be obtained through the National Health, although there is a sector of the medical profession who will not prescribe contraceptives. These doctors also object to abortion, which, though legally available, is not easy to obtain. The situation is similar to that in the United States in that there is a powerful pro-life lobby and gynaecologists have been

imprisoned for practising abortions. Pro-abortion campaigners are constantly striving to widen the terms of the Abortion Act but this seems unlikely to succeed, given the strength of the opposition.

In some ways, though, Spain has remarkably liberal legislation on women's rights. One organization that exists is the Instituto de la Mujer (Institute for Women), created in order to encourage the participation of women, along with men, in public life at every level. Its publications (on sexism in the language, for instance) make interesting reading. The problem, of course, is that although Spanish legislation is progressive, changing the attitudes of both men and women takes time. This is obvious from what Juan has to say in this unit. However, it must be stressed that his views are not typical and that young Spanish men (among the best educated in Europe) would certainly reject his opinions.

AND FINALLY...

14 In this exercise, you are asked which areas of Spain you like and why. You'll be practising the phrases you have learnt to express likes and dislikes.

ANSWERS

EXERCISE 1

the words across were: **(a)** lavar **(b)** cocinar **(c)** planchar **(d)** Janet **(e)** limpiar and **(f)** coser. The word down was viajar, to travel.

EXERCISE 2

1. me gusta muchísimo   2. me gusta   3. no me gusta mucho
4. lo odio

EXERCISE 3

sí: vino blanco, el café solo, Valencia, el trabajo, el norte de España, helado de chocolate, la carne. No to the rest.

EXERCISE 5

This is the correct order of the conversation: ¿Conoce México?/¿El país o la ciudad de México?/El país/Sí, lo conozco bien. Me encanta. La ciudad de México también es preciosa/Y ¿le gusta la costa, Acapulco por ejemplo?/¿Acapulco? Lo detesto, es horrible/¿Pero por qué? La costa es preciosa/Sí, pero hay muchos turistas/Y el Perú, ¿conoce el Perú?/Sí, lo conozco también. Cuzco es una ciudad maravillosa/Está en los Andes ¿verdad?/Sí, no está muy lejos de la jungla y del Amazonas/¡Qué exótico!

EXERCISE 6

(a) Beatriz, Tomás   **(b)** Beatriz   **(c)** neither of them likes ice-cream   **(d)** Beatriz   **(e)** Beatriz   **(f)** Tomás
(g) Tomás and Beatriz

EXERCISE 8

machista, egoísta, cansado, impaciente

EXERCISE 11

(a) gusta   **(b)** gusta   **(c)** gusta   **(d)** gusta   **(e)** gustan

EXERCISE 12

This is the order of the conversation: **(d)** ¿Le gusta el café Molinox?   **(b)** No, no me gusta mucho   **(a)** ¿No le gusta? ¿Y por qué?   **(f)** Porque es un sabor muy fuerte   **(e)** Usted tiene que añadir un poco más de agua   **(c)** No – es que no me gusta el café – ¡prefiero el té!

EXERCISE 13

Here are some possibilities: A mí me gusta el café con leche con croissants por la mañana. Me encanta viajar en Europa durante el verano. Me gusta la música clásica, la de Berlioz sobre todo. Me gusta ver televisión cuando estoy cansada después de trabajar. Me encantan las novelas de Terry Pratchett. Me gusta estar en el jardín de mi casa en el campo.

12 TALKING ABOUT THE WEATHER

WHAT YOU WILL LEARN

▶ How to ...
  talk about the climate and the weather
  understand weather forecasts

BEFORE YOU BEGIN

Exercises to test your accuracy are very important if you want to speak correctly – but if you simply want to understand and make yourself understood, then you can afford to make mistakes in gender and number. In fact, native speakers make many errors themselves and have no trouble in getting by! Do try, though, to get your verb endings reasonably accurate. As you know, Spanish

does not need the personal pronouns (**yo**, **tú**, **usted**), so if you do use the wrong ending, everyone (including you!) will be very confused. In fact, it may be a good idea to use the pronouns yourself until you feel more confident with verb endings. In this course, the early exercises have been designed to promote accuracy: the last exercise, *And finally ...*, allows you a little more freedom of expression.

Pronunciation notes

Z in Spanish is pronounced in two different ways. In the north and central regions of Spain, say '**th**' as in 'think'. In Southern Spain, the Canary Islands and Latin America, pronounce it like the Spanish **s**. The same is true for '**c**' before the letters '**e**' and '**i**':

Zaragoza **centro** **Galicia** **Andalucía** **cerveza**

◗ *Talking about the climate*

LISTEN FOR...

¿cómo es el clima?	what is the weather like?
bastante lluvioso	quite rainy
seco	dry
suave	mild
caluroso	hot
caliente	hot
frío	cold

Judy	Y ¿cómo es el clima aquí?
Serafín	Pues bueno normalmente
Judy	¿En el norte?
Serafín	En el norte bastante lluvioso
Judy	Y ¿en el sur?
Serafín	Más bien seco y caluroso
Judy	¿En la costa mediterránea?
Serafín	Pues suave y caluroso también
Judy	¿Y en el centro?
Serafín	Más bien extremo. En verano bastante caliente y en invierno, bastante frío

- ▶ **el clima**   the climate
- ▶ **bastante**   quite
- ▶ **lluvioso**   rainy
- ▶ **más bien**   rather
- ▶ **seco/a**   dry
- ▶ **caluroso/a**   hot
- ▶ **suave**   mild
- ▶ **el centro**   the centre
- ▶ **extremo/a**   extreme
- ▶ **caliente**   hot
- ▶ **frío/a**   cold

¿Cómo es el clima?   What is the weather like? (literally, how is the weather?).

1   Listen again to Conversation 1. As you do so, fill in the appropriate Spanish word to describe the weather in each region, on your map below.

ANSWERS P. 186

2   Can you fill in the missing words in these sentences? Two clues: all the words have something to do with the weather and all start with c!

a.   Hace mucho _____ en verano en Andalucía

b.   El _____ es siempre muy bueno en las Canarias

c.   El clima es _____ y seco en el sur

ANSWERS P. 186

d.   En verano es bastante _____

3   What's the climate like in Peru? Complete this paragraph, using the weather symbols to help you.

¿Cómo es el clima en el Perú? Bueno, depende. En el este, en la jungla, es _____

y muy también. En el oeste, en la costa es muy

ANSWERS P. 186

En el centro, en los Andes, es extremo – por la noche es y por el día

4   Now you will be asking Marisa about the climate in the United States. Eliud will prompt as usual. You'll need: **¿cómo es el clima?, la costa, el sur.**

Unit 12   Talking about the weather   175

Talking about the weather in Galicia

LISTEN FOR...

¿hace frío?	is it cold?
¿hace calor?	is it hot?
¿llueve mucho?	does it rain a lot?
bastante sol	quite sunny

María	¿Hace frío aquí en invierno?
Silvia	Sí, normalmente hace mucho frío
María	Y ¿hace calor en el verano?
Silvia	En el verano las temperaturas suelen ser altas aquí en Santiago de Compostela. En la costa, no
María	¿Llueve mucho aquí en Santiago?
Silvia	Sí, normalmente llueve bastante
María	Y ¿qué tal el tiempo estos días?
Silvia	Bueno, un tiempo muy primaveral, bastante sol

► **alto/a** high
► **primaveral** springlike

¿Hace frío? Is it cold? **¿Hace calor?** Is it hot? This is a different question from the one in the previous conversation, which asked about climate – that is, about permanent characteristics. Use **hacer** when talking about the weather on a day-to-day basis. A rule of thumb is: if the person who puts the question uses **es**, reply using **es**. If s/he says **hace**, you do the same.

Las temperaturas suelen ser altas The temperatures are normally high. **Suelen** is from **soler** to be accustomed to: as you see, it is a stem-changing verb (see Unit 3).

Santiago de Compostela. This is the full name for the capital city of Galicia. Most people usually call it Santiago, unless they wish to distinguish it from Santiago de Chile.

¿Llueve mucho? Does it rain a lot? The verb here is **llover** to rain.

¿Qué tal el tiempo estos días? What's the weather like these days? As you see, **¿qué tal?** isn't just used to enquire about people. **¿Qué tal tu libro?** What's your book like? **¿Qué tal las vacaciones?** What were your holidays like?

bastante sol quite sunny. 'It is sunny' would be **hace sol**.

María asks Chus the same question

LISTEN FOR...

otros años, a medias   other years it's average

María	¿Hace frío en invierno aquí?
Chus	Este año sí, antes no hacía
María	Y ¿hace calor en el verano?
Chus	Unos años sí, otros a medias
María	¿Llueve mucho?
Chus	No, no llueve como antes, llueve menos
María	Y ¿qué tal el tiempo estos días?
Chus	Bueno, frío, pero bueno

▶ **el año**   the year
▶ **antes**   before
▶ **antes no hacía**   before it wasn't (cold)
▶ **como**   like

Antes no hacía (frío)   Before it used not to be (cold). **Hacía** is the imperfect tense of **hacer** (to do, to make). This tense is used to describe things in the past or to talk about how things used to be. It's a good idea for you to be able to recognize this form, but you don't need to learn it at this stage.

unos años sí, otros a medias   some years yes, others it's average. **Unas veces sí, otras no** Sometimes yes, sometimes no.

PRACTICE

5   You will have noticed that María asked two different people the same questions – and got different replies. Fill in the grid below, in English, according to how each woman answered.

	Chus	Silvia
a. ¿hace frío en invierno?		
b. ¿hace calor en verano?		
c. ¿llueve mucho?		
d. ¿qué tal el tiempo estos días?		

 ANSWERS P. 186

6 Below you have two charts. The first gives you the average temperature on the Costa del Sol and the second gives the water temperature throughout the year. Some of the figures are missing, however. Listen to the tape and complete the information below. You'll hear the word **grados** degrees.

Temperatura ambiente de la Costa del Sol	
	°C
Temperatura media del invierno	_____
Temperatura media de la primavera	_____
Temperatura media del verano	_____
Temperatura media del otoño	_____
Temperatura media anual	18.7

Temperatura del agua	
	°C
enero	15.1
febrero	14.2
marzo	15.2
abril	16.6
mayo	17.4
junio	_____
julio	_____
agosto	_____
septiembre	21.2
octubre	18.3
noviembre	17.8
diciembre	14.4

ANSWERS P. 186

7 In this speaking exercise you'll be asking about the weather in Keele.

You'll need: **hace frío, hace calor, llueve, ¿qué tal el clima?**

This is Rosa's opinion of her country's climate

LISTEN FOR...

¿qué tal el tiempo en su país? what's the weather like in your country?

Pepe	¿Qué tal el clima en su país?
Rosa	Prefiero no hablar del tiempo en mi país
Pepe	¿Es malo?
Rosa	¡Malísimo!
Pepe	¡Pues en esta parte del país es una primavera eterna!

▸ **el tiempo** weather
▸ **el país** country
▸ **hablar (de)** to speak (about)
▸ **malo/a** bad
▸ **la parte** part
▸ **eterno/a** eternal

Prefiero no hablar del tiempo en mi país I prefer not to speak about the weather in my country. Use the infinitive after **preferir**. **Prefiero ir al cine** I prefer to go to the cinema.
¡Malísimo! Awful! (Very bad!)

 Roy's opinion of the British is not very high

LISTEN FOR...

a veces	sometimes
¡qué va!	what nonsense!
todo el tiempo	all the time

Pepe	¿Vienen siempre en verano?
Roy	Normalmente, pero a veces también venimos en primavera, en otoño y más de una vez durante el invierno
Pepe	¿En invierno hace frío aquí?
Roy	No, ¡qué va! – no tanto como en mi país y llueve mucho menos
Pepe	¿Y llueve mucho en su país?
Roy	Todo el tiempo, en invierno, en otoño, en primavera y en verano
Pepe	¿En verano llueve?
Roy	¡Hombre, claro!
Pepe	¡Vaya! pues lo siento, hombre, lo siento ...

▸ **siempre** always
▸ **a veces** sometimes
▸ **más de una vez** more than once
▸ **durante** during
▸ **¡qué va!** rubbish!
▸ **¡vaya!** well! really!

¿Vienen en verano?   Do you come in summer? You'll find the full forms of **venir** in the Grammar section of this unit.

A veces también venimos en primavera   Sometimes, also, we come in spring.

no tanto como en mi país   not as much as in my country. **Tanto ... como** so/as much ... as.

¡hombre, claro!   of course! use **hombre** (which means 'man') to a woman or a man to express surprise.

PRACTICE

8

Now for a weather forecast on your recording. Before listening, though, look at these symbols with an explanation of what they are in Spanish. ■

 DESPEJADO   NUBOSO   LLUVIA   NIEBLA   TORMENTA   VIENTO

Now, answer these questions:

a.   What sort of weather will Gibraltar have?
b.   ... and Lanzarote?
c.   When will there be mist in Galicia?
d.   What will the maximum temperature be there?
e.   And the minimum?
f.   What sort of weather will Madrid have in the afternoon?
g.   What will it be like at night in Valencia?

ANSWERS P. 186

9   Spain has been suffering from a serious drought (**una sequía**) for several years. Read this short article about the problem.

LA SEQUÍA EN EL SUR DE ESPAÑA ES MÁS GRAVE QUE EL AÑO PASADO

El sur de la Península española tiene una sequía más seria que la del año pasado, excepto en unas zonas de Cáceres donde las lluvias están causando inundaciones.

En el norte los embalses están del 70% al 80% de su capacidad.

El director de Obras Hidráulicas, Martín García Suárez, dice que el abastecimiento de agua a todos los pueblos está asegurado, excepto en Sevilla donde hay restricciones de ocho horas al día (de las diez de la noche a las seis de la mañana).

Según García Suárez 'no se puede hablar de superación de sequía, pues en algunas zonas es incluso peor que hace un año'. ■

New vocabulary

la inundación	flood
el embalse	reservoir
el abastecimiento	supply
asegurado	assured
peor	worse

Are these observations true or false, **verdad o mentira?**   **verdad**   **mentira**

a. Last year's drought was worse than this year's
b. There are floods in some parts of the south
c. The reservoirs in the north are three-quarters full
d. Everybody will have enough water for their needs
e. Seville does not have running water at night
f. The Spaniards are managing to control the water problem

ANSWERS P. 186

10 Your turn to talk about the weather – and why you always go to Spain for your
holidays. You'll need: **venimos**, **el invierno**, **la primavera**, **el otoño**.

Unit 12   Talking about the weather

GRAMMAR AND EXERCISES

Weather expressions

There are different ways of talking about the weather. It's important for you to know the verb **hacer**, so that you can use expressions such as:

hace (mucho) calor
_____
hace mal/buen tiempo
_____
hace sol
_____
hace fresco
_____
hace frío
_____
hace viento
_____

Check back in the unit to ensure that you remember what each one means and then fill in the translation.

You don't always use **hace** + weather terms to talk about the weather. Here are some other possibilities:

Use **es** when talking about the weather or climate in general:

es seco	it's dry
es lluvioso	it's rainy

Hay (there is) is used with nouns:

hay niebla
it's foggy/misty (there's fog/mist)
hay helada
it's frosty
hay nieve
it's snowing (there is snow)
hay tormenta
it's stormy
hay hielo
it's icy

Use **está** with some adjectives:

está cubierto	it's overcast
está despejado	it's clear

Use a continuous verb form when describing what is happening at the moment:

está nevando	it's snowing
está lloviendo	it's raining

And the normal form of the verb to describe what usually happens:

Llueve mucho en invierno	it rains a lot in winter
y también nieva	it also snows

Finally, another useful verb to learn by heart:

Venir to come

vengo	I come
vienes	you come (informal)
viene	s/he comes
viene	you come (formal)
venimos	we come
venís	you come (informal plural)
vienen	they come
vienen	you come (formal plural)

11 Look at these weather symbols and write in the appropriate phrase to describe each one. You may find that you can use a variety of different expressions, so there's no one correct answer.

a.

b.

c.

d.

e.

f.

ANSWERS P. 186

12 Try translating the following sentences:

a. It's snowing in Aspen............................
b. There's fog in London...........................
c. The climate is dry in Mexico.......................
d. It's very cold in the winter here.................
e. It rains a lot in Manchester.......................
f. In the Canaries it's perpetual spring!..............

ANSWERS P. 186

13 Besides talking about the weather, you can use **hacer** with a variety of different expressions:

hacer la cama
hacer una lista
hacer planes
hacer una casa
hacer las maletas
hacer la comida

Make six sentences using these expressions and try to vary which person you use them with. There are some suggestions in the Answers section on page 186.

KEY WORDS
AND PHRASES

¿Cómo es el clima?	What is the weather like?
¿Qué tal el clima?	What is the weather like?
¿Qué tal el tiempo?	What is the weather like?
el clima es ...	the weather is ...
lluvioso	rainy
seco	dry
suave	mild
caluroso	hot
extremo	extreme
bastante caliente	quite hot
bastante frío	quite cold
Hace (mucho) frío	It is (very) cold
Hace calor	It is hot
Hace sol	It is sunny
Hace viento	It is windy
Hace (muy) buen tiempo	It is (very) good weather
Hace mal tiempo	It is bad weather
Llueve mucho	It rains a lot
Nieva mucho	It snows a lot
Está lloviendo	It's raining
Está nevando	It's snowing
Está cubierto	It's overcast
despejado	clear
nuboso	cloudy
hay	there is
(la) tormenta	storm
(la) helada	frost
(la) niebla	fog
(la) nube(s)	cloud
(la) nieve	snow
a veces	sometimes
todo el año	all year
siempre	always

Talking about the weather   *Unit* 12

The Spanish climate

YOU SHOULD NOW KNOW a little more about the Spanish weather after studying this unit. Because Spain is such a large country and so varied in its landscape, the climate is also subject to a great deal of variation from one region to another. So, whatever the season, there is always pleasant weather to be had if you plan your visit carefully.

Spring and autumn are good seasons to go to Spain and, as was mentioned earlier, summer in the north and north-west is not usually as hot as you might expect. Winter on the Mediterranean coast is to be recommended, as many retired people have found out. Madrid and other inland towns such as Toledo and Soria have a typically continental climate, with stiflingly hot summers and very cold winters. One proverb about Madrid goes **'tres meses de invierno y nueve de infierno'** (three months of winter and nine of hell). These cities can be pleasant to visit in the autumn, however, when temperatures are more moderate, the skies are clear and the sunshine is bright.

Old and new methods for keeping cool

One of the major problems which visitors to the Exposición Universal had to face was the soaring temperatures of Seville. The festival organizers used some of the ancient Arab methods for keeping temperatures down: fountains and channels of cool water, and pergolas to keep off the sun's rays. More modern methods were also devised such as giant atomizers which sprayed tiny droplets of water into the air.

Northern Spain

In an earlier unit, Janet mentioned that she particularly liked the northern coast. We have already discussed Galicia, but further to the east there are other interesting places to visit. The coast is especially dramatic because of the backdrop of mountains called the Picos de Europa. Santander is a town well worth visiting in this area: its International University attracts many foreign students in the summer. If you are in England, you can take a direct service by ferry from Portsmouth to Santander. There are some beautiful beaches (especially at San Sebastián) and they provide the perfect setting for the famous regattas. Santander has an international cultural festival in August and nearby you can visit the prehistoric caves of Altamira. San Sebastián itself is an elegant and cosmopolitan seaside town, a Spanish version of Biarritz. It is famous for its film festival held each year in September.

Seville

AND FINALLY...

14 In this conversation, you will be describing the weather in the UK to a Spanish-speaking friend. You'll be using:

hace frío/calor   **llueve**   **el clima es malo/suave**

EXERCISE 1
north: lluvioso; south: seco, caluroso; Mediterranean coast: suave; centre: caliente

EXERCISE 2
(a) calor **(b)** clima
(c) caluroso **(d)** caliente
(There is little difference between **caluroso** and **caliente**. **Caluroso** is more formal.)

EXERCISE 3
(a) lluvioso **(b)** caluroso/caliente **(c)** seco **(d)** frío
(e) caluroso/caliente

EXERCISE 5
Chus: **(a)** this year yes but not in the past
(b) sometimes **(c)** it rains less now than it used to
(d) good weather but cold.   Sylvia: **(a)** very
(b) in Santiago yes, but not on the coast **(c)** yes, quite a lot **(d)** fine, quite sunny

EXERCISE 6
temperaturas **(a)** invierno 13–14 grados, primavera 20 grados, verano 24 grados, otoño 16 grados **(b)** junio, julio, agosto 20–22 grados

EXERCISE 8
(a) moderately windy **(b)** cloudy **(c)** in the morning
(d) 22 degrees **(e)** 10 degrees **(f)** stormy **(g)** quite cold

EXERCISE 9
(a) M **(b)** V **(c)** V **(d)** M **(e)** V **(f)** M

EXERCISE 11
(a) está despejado, hace buen tiempo **(b)** hace viento
(c) está cubierto, hay nubes **(d)** llueve, está lloviendo
(e) hay niebla **(f)** hay tormenta, hace mal tiempo

EXERCISE 12
(a) Está nevando en Aspen **(b)** Hay niebla en Londres
(c) El clima es seco en México **(d)** Hace mucho frío aquí en el invierno **(e)** Llueve mucho en Manchester **(f)** ¡En las Canarias es una primavera eterna!

EXERCISE 13
(a) hago la cama antes de ir a trabajar **(b)** hago una lista de regalos para mis hermanos. **(c)** hacen planes para el verano
(d) hacemos una casa en Málaga **(e)** hace las maletas antes de salir de vacaciones **(f)** mi madre siempre hace la comida para la familia

13 YOUR EVERYDAY ROUTINE

**WHAT
YOU WILL
LEARN**

▶ How to ...
   talk about what you do each day
▶ Something about leisure activities
▶ Some more important verbs

**BEFORE
YOU
BEGIN**

Now that you are on the homeward straight you may be a little worried about keeping on top of the new vocabulary and structures. Earlier on in the course it was easier to control what language was taught and therefore learned; as we move forwards and more language is introduced you may feel that you are forgetting more and making more errors.

This is probably true – but it is something that you can take advantage of. Forgetting items means that you need to retrieve them actively – by looking them up in the dictionary or in your grammar book or by reworking an earlier unit. This means that you are consolidating your knowledge and transferring it to your long-term memory. Don't be worried about any mistakes you make: you will only progress by making errors and gradually learning how to correct them. Some areas of language will automatically correct themselves, through experience and constant repetition. Others will need a little extra attention on your part. The grammar exercises will help you here.

Pronunciation notes

All Spanish words are stressed on one particular syllable. Words ending in a vowel or **-n** or **-s** are stressed on the penultimate (that is, the next to last) syllable. All other words (i.e. those ending in a consonant except **n** or **s**) are stressed on the last syllable. Any word which doesn't follow these rules has a written accent to show where it *is* stressed. Be careful about these rules when you speak because the presence of an accent can radically alter the

meaning of the word: **hablo** I speak, **habló** you (polite form) or s/he spoke. You'll be hearing the following words on your recording:

nacionalidad	**profesión**
levanto I lift	**¡levántate!** (get up!)
termino I finish	**término** the end

Pepe asks Marcos about his daily routine

LISTEN FOR...

me levanto	I get up
me visto	I get dressed
me peino	I do my hair

Pepe	¿Qué hace usted un día normal?
Marcos	Yo me levanto a las seis de la mañana, me visto, me peino, voy al wáter y, arregladito, marcho a la calle al trabajo
Pepe	¿No desayuna?
Marcos	Pasadas dos horas, desayuno
Pepe	¿En su casa?
Marcos	En la calle
Pepe	¿En un bar?
Marcos	En un bar, efectivamente
Pepe	Bien y ¿a qué hora comienza a trabajar?
Marcos	A las ocho de la mañana
Pepe	Y ¿a qué hora termina de trabajar?
Marcos	Al mediodía

¿Qué hace usted un día normal? What do you do on a normal day? Some people prefer to say **¿Qué hace usted *en* un día normal?**

Me levanto a las seis de la mañana I get up at six in the morning. **Levantarse** is a reflexive verb and must have two parts – **me** and **levanto**. Think of it as 'I get myself up'. **Llamarse** (to be called) also works like this: **me llamo** I call myself. More about these verbs on page 196. You might wish to have a look at them now to see how they work.

Me visto (from **vestirse**) I get dressed, **me peino** (from **peinarse**) I do my hair. These are two more examples of reflexive verbs. You will also need **me lavo** (from **lavarse**) I get washed, and **me acuesto** (from **acostarse**) I go to bed.

Voy al wáter I go to the lavatory. This is a little old fashioned now. Most people use the euphemism '**voy al baño**'. **Servicios** (or **aseos**) is the word to use in a public place.

arregladito all ready – from the verb **arreglarse** to get oneself ready. **Me arreglo** (I get ready) is another good phrase to know.

¿No desayuna? Don't you have breakfast? **Desayunar** to have breakfast, and **el desayuno** breakfast. **Desayuno tostadas** I have toast for breakfast.

¿A qué hora comienza a trabajar? What time do you start working? **Comenzar** to begin, **comenzar a** to begin to (do something). You will also hear **empezar,** which means the same. **Empiezo a trabajar** I begin to work.

¿A qué hora termina de trabajar? What time do you finish work(ing)? **Terminar de** to finish. Some verbs (**comenzar a** and **terminar de** are good examples) need a preposition such as **a** or **de** if a verb follows. The second verb must be in the infinitive.

PRACTICE

1 Imagine you are the woman whose morning routine is illustrated below. Out loud, describe what you do and at what time. Then write in your sentence in the space provided. The first one has been done for you. You'll need **salgo de** I leave, and **llego a** I arrive, for this exercise.

ANSWERS P. 200

a. Me levanto a las siete de la mañana.

a. _____ b. _____ c. _____ d. _____

_____

e. _____ f. _____ g. _____

_____

2 Listen to a conversation between Carlos and Marisa about their morning routine. Then fill in the grid below with their replies. You don't have information for every square. **¿a qué hora**

ANSWERS P. 200

	se levanta?	se viste?	desayuna?	comienza a trabajar?	termina de trabajar?
Carlos					
Marisa					

3 In this speaking exercise, Marisa asks you about your own morning routine. You'll be using **salgo a** and **desayuno**.

Now María asks Reme about her day

LISTEN FOR...

vuelvo a casa	I return home
suelo ir a la aldea	I usually go to the village
pronto	early
temprano	early

María	¿Qué haces un día normal?
Reme	Me levanto temprano a las ocho, voy a clase por la mañana, termino bastante temprano, a las doce y media. Vuelvo a casa, paso por el mercado, preparo la comida. Después de comer, suelo ir a la aldea, a darles de comer a los gatos. Aprovecho la ocasión para pasear un rato. Cuando vuelvo, si tengo algo que comprar, aprovecho el viaje para comprar, preparo la cena y al final me voy al gimnasio

▶ **temprano**   early

▶ **preparar**   to prepare

▶ **la comida**   lunch, meal

▶ **el gato**   cat

▶ **pasear**   to take a walk

▶ **un rato**   a short while

▶ **algo**   something

▶ **aprovechar**   to take advantage of

▶ **el viaje**   journey

▶ **la cena**   dinner

▶ **el gimnasio**   gym

Vuelvo a casa   I return home. **Volver** is an important verb which you need to learn by heart. You will find it on page 196.

Paso por el mercado   I drop in at the market. **Pasar por** usually means to go through: **pasar por el parque** to go through the park.

después de comer   after eating. After prepositions like '**después**' or '**de**' and later in the conversation '**para**' you use the infinitive: **aprendo español para viajar** I learn Spanish so I can travel (in order to travel).

Suelo ir a la aldea   I usually go to the village. **Soler** to be accustomed to doing.

Suele visitar a sus padres los domingos He usually visits his parents on Sunday.

darles de comer   to feed them (literally, to give them to eat)

María asks Reme's husband the same question

María	¿Qué haces un día normal, Eme?
Eme	Pues mira, no hago nada divertido. Voy a clase por la mañana, normalmente paso toda la mañana en el colegio, y después vengo a comer a casa y por las tardes, si no tengo trabajo que hacer, acostumbro salir al campo con mi mujer, o incluso jugar al tenis. Y dos días a la semana, voy a jugar al baloncesto con mis amigos por las noches en el pabellón de deportes de la escuela, precisamente

▶ **nada**   nothing
▶ **divertido/a**   exciting
▶ **el campo**   the country(side)
▶ **la mujer**   woman, wife
▶ **incluso**   even
▶ **jugar al tenis**   to play tennis
▶ **jugar al baloncesto**   to play basketball
▶ **el pabellón de deportes**   sports hall

nada divertido   nothing exciting. **nada interesante** nothing interesting.
Voy a clase por la mañana   I go to school (class) in the morning. Reme and Eme do the morning 'shift' at their large comprehensive school in Lugo. Other staff teach evening sessions to a separate cohort of students.
Vengo a comer a casa   I come home to lunch. Although **comer** means to eat, it is used loosely to mean the main meal of the day, that is, lunch.
por las tardes   in the afternoons. It's more usual to say '**por la tarde**'.
Acostumbro salir al campo con mi mujer   I often go out into the country with my wife. **Acostumbrar** to be accustomed to ...
jugar al tenis   to play tennis. **Jugar** is a stem-changing-verb: **juego** I play.
dos días a la semana   two days a week. **Dos horas al día** two hours a day.

PRACTICE

4 In Spain, many people have a break (**un descanso**) from two in the afternoon till five when they return to work. Here's an extract about how Spain's Government ministers (**ministros del gobierno**) and **ejecutivos** (top executives) use their lunch break. Some of the words are new but you should be able to guess them.

hacer footing   to go jogging
madrileño/a   from or in Madrid
la exposición   the exhibition
ver televisión   to watch television

Son las 15.20 del miércoles 25 de noviembre. Llamo por teléfono a la oficina de varios ministros del gobierno. No contestan. ¿Dónde están? Depende de la persona y del día, claro, pero Felipe González almuerza en familia, toma un café, se fuma un cigarro y ve la televisión. José María Aznar aprovecha unos días libres para ir a jugar al squash con su esposa en un club madrileño. Otros ejecutivos hacen footing por el parque del Retiro o juegan al golf. Los que no suelen practicar deportes dedican estas horas a aprender inglés o a visitar exposiciones o a ver televisión. Y el 15% de los españoles hacen la siesta en el sofá de casa o de la oficina. ■

i. On what day of the week does the writer try to contact the ministers?
ii. What three things does Felipe González do after lunch?
iii. With whom does José María Aznar play squash?
iv. What sort of people learn English in their lunch break?
v. Where do people have their siesta?

ANSWERS P. 200

5 On the recording the mother and father of **una familia numerosa** (a large family) are discussing what they and their children are doing today. Fill in the information you hear for each member of the family in English. Listen for what they are doing and when. By the way, **un(a) cliente** is a customer.

	ACTIVIDAD
Carlos	
Marisa	
Carmen	
Pilar	
Marga	
Antonio	
Los padres de Marisa	

ANSWERS P. 200

6 What do you do in your spare time? On your recording you'll be hearing two more expressions: **el fin de semana** the weekend and **el supermercado** the supermarket.

Some friends say what they would like to do....

LISTEN FOR...

la playa	the beach
ir de marcha	to go out
nadar	to swim

Manolo	Quiero tocar la guitarra
María	Quiero ir a la playa
Marta	Yo quiero ir a nadar
Jordi	Quiero jugar al fútbol
Maite	Yo quiero ir de marcha con mis amigos

Quiero tocar la guitarra   I want to play the guitar. Use **tocar** for musical instruments: **tocar el piano, tocar el violín**. Use **jugar** for games: **jugar al tenis** to play tennis, **jugar al baloncesto** to play basketball.

You will notice that some people say **yo quiero** and others simply **quiero**. Use **yo** if you wish to emphasize what *you* would rather do.

PRACTICE

7   Here are some statements made by a number of different people. Match them up with the person most likely to have said them.

a. veo la televisión todos los días después del colegio

b. me gusta coser en el salón donde hace más fresco

c. visitamos los pueblos blancos de Andalucía cuando vamos a España de vacaciones

d. los sábados me encanta ir al cine con mi novia

e. esta tarde vamos con nuestros hijos al partido de fútbol

f. no sé nadar pero me gusta el agua ...

i. John y Carole Metcalfe, de Brighton

ii. Pablo (estudiante), de diecinueve años

iii. Pilar (abuela), de ochenta años

iv. Arantxa, una niña de diez años

v. Pepito, un niño de tres años

vi. Carmen, de cuarenta años

ANSWERS P. 200

KEY WORDS
AND PHRASES

Me despierto	I wake up
Me levanto	I get up (**levantarse**)
temprano	early
Me visto	I get dressed (**vestirse**)
Me peino	I do my hair (**peinarse**)
Me lavo	I get washed (**lavarse**)
Me arreglo	I get ready (**arreglarse**)
Me acuesto	I go to bed (**acostarse**)
¿A qué hora comienza a trabajar?	What time do you start work?
¿A qué hora empieza a trabajar?	What time do you start work?
¿A qué hora termina de trabajar?	What time do you finish work?
Voy a clase	I go to class
a casa	home
al campo	to the country
vuelvo	I return
del mercado	from the market
del supermercado	from the supermarket
suelo ir	I usually go
a la aldea	to the village
al pueblo	to the town
Preparo la cena	I prepare the evening meal
la comida	the lunch
el desayuno	the breakfast
desayuno (tostadas)	I breakfast on (toast)
No hago nada divertido	I don't do anything exciting
interesante	interesting
jugar al tenis	to play tennis
al baloncesto	basketball
al fútbol	football
al golf	golf
al squash	squash
juego	I play
hacer footing	to go jogging
ver televisión	to watch television
ir al cine	to go to the cinema
visitar el pueblo	to visit the town
una exposición	an exhibition
pasear	to go for a walk
ir de marcha	to go out
nadar	to swim
tocar la guitarra	to play the guitar

Personalities

THERE are certain Spanish personalities that you really need to know about if you are going to understand what is happening in Spanish social, political and cultural life. At the top, there is of course the monarchy: don Juan Carlos the king, his wife doña Sofía (who is Greek and related to the Duke of Edinburgh) and their three children. The heir to the throne is príncipe Felipe and he has two older sisters, the **infantas** (or princesses) Cristina and Elena. They are an extremely popular family because of their easy-going democratic style and because of the crucial role which Juan Carlos played on the night of the attempted coup d'état in February 1981. Don Juan de Borbón was Juan Carlos's father. He died in 1993 and was also a much respected figure in Spanish society. He lived in exile for many years and eventually withdrew his claim to the throne in favour of his son. The family shares a common ancestor with the British Royal Family in Queen Victoria.

The press

Newspaper readership is not all that high in Spain and many people prefer to read a local rather than a national newspaper. The popular press does not really exist and most newspapers are serious in style and content. The most widely read paper is *El País*. This is easily obtainable abroad and is a good source of information about contemporary life in Spain. *El País Dominical* (the Sunday edition) is especially useful as it has a colour magazine, supplements for children, a financial section and so on. It also often comes with a **fascículo** (or part work) on the history or geography of Spain. *El País* is a progressive newspaper and retains a high degree of popularity because of its democratic stance during the period of transition after the Franco dictatorship.

ABC is a right-wing newspaper which is the second most widely read newspaper in Spain. On Sundays, it appears with *Blanco y Negro*, its colour magazine and *TeleABC*. *TeleABC* is a useful publication as it has a full listing of radio and television programmes for the following week, on both satellite and terrestrial channels. Other important newspapers are *La Vanguardia* (published in Barcelona) and *El Mundo*, a forward-looking publication founded in 1990. *As* and *Marca* are two sports newspapers which sell almost as many copies as *El País*.

> **Another María talks about whom her new baby daughter will look like**

LISTEN FOR...

morena	dark
menuda	small, slight
alta	tall
los ojos	eyes
inquieta	restless

▶	**la idea**	idea
▶	**moreno/a**	dark
▶	**menudo/a**	small, slight
▶	**alto/a**	tall
▶	**bastante**	quite
▶	**el ojo**	eye
▶	**inquieto/a**	restless, anxious
▶	**vivo/a**	lively
▶	**despierto/a**	alert
▶	**travieso/a**	naughty
▶	**bonito/a**	pretty, nice
▶	**la gente**	people
▶	**la cosa**	thing
▶	**mover**	to move
▶	**el mundo**	world

Guillermo ¿Tienes alguna idea de cómo va a ser físicamente?

María Bueno yo creo que va a ser un poco entre lo que soy yo y lo que es su padre. Es decir que va a ser una niña morena y menudita. Yo también soy morena y menuda. Pero yo creo que va a ser más alta que yo porque el padre es bastante alto y yo creo que va a tener los ojos del padre. Verdes y no castaños como los míos. Y luego va a ser muy inquieta de carácter – ya lo es ahora – muy viva y despierta, traviesa quizás. Pero bueno, es bonito ¿no? porque ese tipo de gente es la que cuestiona las cosas, que mueve el mundo

entre lo que soy yo y lo que es su padre between what I am and what her father is. **Lo que** (literally, that which) what.
es decir that is to say (literally, 'is to say').
castaño use this word for dark-brown hair or eyes. It literally means chestnut. **Marrón** is the more usual word for brown.
Ya lo es ahora She already is (it) now.
quizá(s) perhaps. This word is variable: it sometimes has an **s** and sometimes not. There's no difference in meaning.
Ese tipo de gente es la que mueve el mundo That sort of person changes the world (literally, that type of people is that which moves the world). **Todo el mundo** everyone.

Taking Ana on holiday

LISTEN FOR...

los abuelos	the grandparents
los tíos	the uncles and aunts
los primos	the cousins
tener cuidado	to be careful

Guillermo	¿Vais a ir a Galicia?
María	Sí, vamos con la niña en avión; estaremos tres semanas
Guillermo	¿En Lugo vais a estar?
María	En Lugo vamos a estar una semana para que la conozca la familia, los abuelos, los tíos, mis primos ... Y después vamos a ir a Porto Novo, cerca de Pontevedra, una zona que tiene mucha vida, muchos bares ... Lo que a mí me apetece es tomar el sol, descansar y que Ana se lo pase bien en la playa
Guillermo	¿Cuánto tiempo tendrá en el verano?
María	Tendrá cinco meses, todavía muy pequeña, vamos a tener que tener mucho cuidado con el sol

▶ **los abuelos**   the grandparents

Note also ▶ **el abuelo** (grandfather) and **la abuela** (grandmother)

▶ **los tíos**   the uncles and aunts

Note also ▶ **el tío** (uncle) and **la tía** (aunt)

▶ **los primos**   the cousins

Note also ▶ **el primo** (male cousin) and **la prima** (female cousin)

▶ **después**   afterwards

▶ **la vida**   life

▶ **todavía**   still

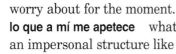

para que la conozca la familia   for the family to get to know her. **Conozca** is another example of the subjunctive, which you don't need to worry about for the moment.

lo que a mí me apetece   what I feel like doing (what appeals to me). **Me apetece** is an impersonal structure like **me gusta** and **me encanta**.

que Ana se lo pase bien   for Ana to have a good time. Again the subjunctive. Note **pasarlo bien** to have a good time. **Voy a pasarlo bien** I'm going to have a good time.

¿Cuánto tiempo tendrá?   How old will she be? Use **tiempo** rather than **años** for talking about the age of babies.

Vamos a tener que tener mucho cuidado con el sol   We are going to have to be very careful of the sun. **Tener mucho cuidado** to be very careful. **¡Ten cuidado!** Take care!

¿Qué te apetece hacer?	What do you feel like doing?
Me apetece …	I feel like …
¿Qué piensas/pensáis hacer mañana?	What are you thinking of doing tomorrow?
Pienso ir a (Marcelle)	I'm thinking of going to (Marcelle)
Iré a clase	I'll go to school
Pasaré por el mercado	I'll drop in at the market
Volveré a casa	I'll go back home
No sé si haré algo más	I don't know if I'll do anything else
Va a ser moreno/a	S/he will be dark
rubio/a	blond(e)
menudo/a	small
delgado/a	slim
alto/a	tall
muy alto/a	very tall
bastante alto/a	quite tall
bajo/a	short
inquieto/a	restless
vivo/a	lively
despierto/a	alert
travieso/a	naughty
bonito/a	nice/pretty
tranquilo/a	calm
nervioso/a	highly strung
con los ojos	with eyes
verdes	green
castaños	brown
azules	blue
la familia	the family
los abuelos	grandparents
el abuelo/la abuela	grandfather/grandmother
los tíos	aunts and uncles
el tío/la tía	uncle/aunt
los primos	cousins
el primo/la prima	male/female cousin
una zona que tiene mucha vida	an area with a lot of life
tomar el sol	to sunbathe
tomar unas copas	to have some drinks
descansar	to rest
pasarlo bien	to have a good time
tener mucho cuidado con el sol	to be very careful of the sun
en la playa	on the beach
en el campo	in the country

The Spanish political scene

THERE HAVE been enormous political changes in Spain since the death of General Franco in 1975. Although the **Generalísimo** tried to leave things in Spain **atado y bien atado** (well sewn up), after his death King Juan Carlos took up the reins of power, a new constitution was written, free trade unions were established and political parties were legitimized, within a few months of Franco's death. Elections were held for the first time in 1977 and were won by Adolfo Suárez of the **Unión del Centro Democrático** or UCD. In the next month, July 1977, Spain applied for membership of the European Economic Community. It had earlier been refused entry because of the Franco régime.

The writing of the new constitution was an extraordinary event. For the first time, people began to talk about **consenso** or consensus, a new concept for Spaniards who were more used to conflict than compromise. The writers of the new constitution included the right-winger Manuel Fraga from Galicia and both Catalan and Communist politicians. Only the Basques were missing – a serious omission in view of later events. In some quarters, it is also felt now that, in ensuring that the government was powerful (in order to prevent attempts to destabilize society), not enough attention was paid to keeping the judiciary, the military, the press and television truly independent from the ruling party.

It is important to know that the new Spain is divided into seventeen autonomous regions. Because they were historically independent, Galicia, Catalonia and the Basque country have greater powers than the others. Devolved powers include responsibility for education, the local police (in the Basque country), regional transport and health. Devolution is the root of much unrest in modern Spain. The Catalans and Basques demand even more powers and in the case of some Basques, try to extort them through violent means. Apart from the fact that devolved power is not always considered sufficient for all the autonomies, the major disadvantage of the system is expense. There are sometimes as many as five layers of bureaucracy in an autonomous region – Brussels, the Spanish state, the autonomous region, the province and the town.

Another problem is that different parties have different mandates at different levels and co-ordination and cohabitation can prove difficult.

In 1982, Spain entered NATO (**OTAN** in Spain) and from that time has played an increasingly important role in European affairs.

A coach trip to Spain

LISTEN FOR...

el año pasado fui a España	last year I went to Spain
paré allí un día	I spent a day there
muy descansadas	very relaxed

María de los Angeles El año pasado fui de vacaciones a España. Viajé en el autobús directamente desde Londres hasta Valencia. Paré allí un día y después fui a Cullera, un pueblecito cerca de Valencia. Paré con una amiga y sencillamente lo pasamos muy descansadas. Y todos los días fuimos a diferentes restaurantes, a probar diferentes platos típicos de la cocina valenciana

▶ **el año pasado**   last year
▶ **ir de vacaciones**   to go on holiday
▶ **parar**   to stay
▶ **sencillamente**   simply
▶ **probar**   to try, to taste

RESTAURANTE
Albacar

R a

Sorní, 35
Tel: 395 10 05
46004 Valencia

fui a ...   I went to ... **Fui** is the past tense of both **ir** and **ser**. **Fuiste** is the **tú** form. **¿Fuiste a México?** Did you go to Mexico? You will find the full verb on page 226.
viajé   I travelled. **Viajar** to travel.
paré   I stayed. **Parar** to stay.
Lo pasamos muy descansadas   We had a relaxing time (literally, we spent it very relaxed). **Descansar** is to relax or to rest.
Descansamos los fines de semana We rested during the weekends. **Lo pasamos muy bien** We had a good time. (The 'we' form of the past tense is the same as the present tense in regular verbs. **Pasamos** means 'we spend' or 'we spent' according to context.)
Todos los días fuimos a ...   Every day we went to ...

Reme talks about what she did yesterday

Reme   Ayer, como no tenía clase, por la mañana salí, hice unas compras, fui con mi hermana a tomar el vermut. Después de comer, salí a tomar café, luego hicimos unas compras por la tarde. Volvimos a casa a preparar algo para las clases del lunes y después a última hora, fuimos a un concierto

María   Y ¿te gustó el concierto?

Reme   Sí, estuvo muy bien

▶ **hacer las compras**   to do some shopping

▶ **algo**   something

▶ **el concierto**   concert

Salí   I went out. **¿Saliste?** Did you go out? You'll find the full forms of **-ir** verbs in the past on page 226.

Hice unas compras   I did some shopping. **Hice** is from **hacer** (to do) and is the **yo** form of the past tense. **Hiciste** is the **tú** form and **hicimos** the **nosotros** form. You'll find them all on page 227.

Fui a tomar el vermut   I went to have an aperitif. **Vermut** is a general term nowadays for an aperitif.

Volvimos a casa   We came back home. **¿A qué hora volviste?** What time did you come back? The full forms of the past tense of **-er** verbs are on page 226.

a última hora   very late (literally, at the last hour).

¿Te gustó el concierto?   Did you like the concert? **¿Te gustaron los conciertos?** Did you like the concerts?

Estuvo muy bien   It was very good. **Estuvo** is the past tense of **estar**. You will find it on page 227.

La SGAE cree que no hay barreras para la música. Ni distancia. Sólo hay ideas y esfuerzo. Por eso ayudamos.

LA MUSICA DEL PAIS VASCO

Teatro de MADRID
Avda. de la Ilustración, s/n-LA VAGUADA
Reservas Teatro de Madrid: 730 49 22
Reservas Caja de Cataluña: 538 33 33

OSKORRI
Jueves, 23 de Noviembre, 20:30 horas

BENITO LERTXUNDI
Viernes, 24 de Noviembre, 20:30 horas

MIKEL LABOA
Sábado, 25 de Noviembre, 20:30 horas

Sala REVOLVER
Calle Galileo, 26-ARGÜELLES
Reservas Sala Revólver: 594 26 79
Reservas Madrid Rock: Gran Via, 25/Mayor, 38/San Martin, 3/
Madrid, 80 (Getafe)/Avd. Dos de Mayo (Móstoles)

TAPIA & LETURIA BAND
SOROTAN BELE
Sábado, 25 de Noviembre, 24:00 horas

PRACTICE

1 Can you remember the verbs in the first conversation? Here are some key sentences with the verb missing. Complete each sentence: only look back if you have to!

a. _____ de vacaciones a España

b. _____ en el autobús

c. _____ allí un día

d. Lo _____ muy descansadas

ANSWERS P. 230 e. Todos los días _____ a diferentes restaurantes

2 Here is an account of how Reme spent yesterday – only things are in the wrong order. Rewrite each sentence, this time in the order in which the events happened.

a. por la mañana salí

b. fuimos a un concierto

c. salí a tomar café

d. hice unas compras

e. volvimos a casa

ANSWERS P. 230 f. fui con mi hermana a tomar el vermut

3 Match the questions with the replies. Notice how the **tú** form always ends in either '**-iste**' or '**-aste**'.

a. ¿Cuánto tiempo paraste allí?   i. Viajé en tren

b. ¿Dónde fuiste?   ii. Probé muchos platos catalanes

c. ¿Dónde comiste?   iii. Hice las compras con mi mujer

d. ¿Adónde saliste?   iv. Fui a Copacabana

e. ¿Cómo viajaste?   v. Paré con unos amigos

f. ¿Qué probaste?   vi. Comí en el Verruga

g. ¿Qué hiciste ayer?   vii. Paré una semana

ANSWERS P. 230 h. ¿Con quién paraste?   viii. Salí a un concierto

4 Marisa asks you about a recent holiday you had in Spain. Eliud will prompt with the replies. You'll need: **fui**, **viajé** and **paré**.

Claire asks Eme if he went on holiday last year

LISTEN FOR...

no recuerdo su nombre	I don't remember its name
no pudimos bañarnos	we couldn't bathe

Eme Pues sí, fuimos unos días a Portugal con mi familia. Fuimos a una ciudad del norte muy bonita, pero no recuerdo su nombre, y tiene una playa preciosa. Pero no pudimos bañarnos porque hacía mucho frío y mucho viento, así que lo que hicimos fue pasear por la ciudad y bueno, también visitamos algunos pueblos del interior

▶ **bonito/a**   pretty
▶ **así que**   so that
▶ **el interior**   inland

No recuerdo su nombre   I don't remember its name. **Recordar** to remember. As you see, **recordar** is a stem-changing verb.

No pudimos bañarnos   We couldn't bathe. **Pudimos** is the **nosotros** form of **poder** to be able.

Hacía mucho frío y mucho viento   It was very cold and windy. **Hacía** is a different past tense called the imperfect. It is used for descriptions rather than events in the past so you won't be learning it in this course.

así que lo que hicimos fue pasear ...   so what we did was to stroll. Here **fue** means 'it was' rather than 's/he went'. **Fue en Barcelona** It was in Barcelona. You can always tell the meaning from the context.

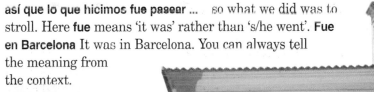

María asks Reme about her trip to England

LISTEN FOR...

me gustó mucho Londres	I liked London a lot
las dos me gustaron	I liked them both

María	¿Conoces Inglaterra?
Reme	Un poquito, nada más
María	Y ¿te gustó?
Reme	Sí, lo que conozco, sí, me gustó mucho
María	¿Qué te gustó más?
Reme	Como ciudad, me gustó mucho Londres y Manchester me gustó mucho
María	Ah ¿mucho? ¡qué bien! Y ¿qué te gustó menos?
Reme	Pues, no sabría decirlo, quizás el clima, pero las ciudades igual, las dos me gustaron

un poquito, nada más   only a little bit (literally, a little bit, nothing more).

Pues no sabría decirlo   Well, I couldn't say (literally, well, I would not know how to tell it).

Las dos me gustaron   I liked both (cities). Note how to say you liked two things in the past: **Los conciertos me gustaron** I liked the concerts (literally, the two concerts pleased me).

María asks Eme about a holiday in Scotland some years ago

LISTEN FOR...

hace muchos años	a long time ago
muy cambiado	very changed

María	¿Conoces Escocia?
Eme	Pues sí, desde hace muchos años
María	¿Cuándo fuiste?
Eme	Fui la primera vez hace veinticinco años, estuve en Edimburgo y también viajé por las Highlands
María	¿Qué más te gustó?
Eme	Pues lo que más me gustó, bueno, Edimburgo es una ciudad preciosa, y también el paisaje de las Highlands, pero, Edimburgo, creo que está muy cambiado desde entonces porque hace muchos años que no voy por allá

- **desde**   since
- **el paisaje**   countryside
- **cambiar**   to change (**cambiado** changed)
- **allá**   there

desde hace muchos años for a long time (literally, since many years).
hace veinticinco años twenty-five years ago. Use '**hace** + a time expression' for saying how long ago you did something. **Hace una semana** a week ago. **Hace un mes** a month ago.
Está muy cambiado It is very changed. **Cambiado** is used here as an adjective, so it agrees with its noun. **Está muy cambiada** she's changed a lot, she's very different.
Hace muchos años que no voy por allá I haven't been there for many years (literally, it's many years that I do not go around there). Notice how the verb (**voy**) is in the present tense. **Hace mucho tiempo que estudio españo** I've been learning Spanish for a long time. This type of phrase is used when describing events in the past that are still continuing.

PRACTICE

5 It's important to be able to describe or talk about when you did things. Write down a translation of the sentences that follow and then switch on your recording to see if you were right. You'll also find the written version on page 230.

a.   Last year I went to France _____

b.   Yesterday I did some shopping _____

c.   After eating, we went home _____

d.   Last of all (at the end of the day) _____

e.   Twenty-five years ago _____

f.   I haven't been for many years _____

6 Listen to Marisa telling you about her holiday last year in Barcelona. You may need to listen several times before answering the questions below.

a.   Who did Marisa go with to Barcelona?

b.   How does Marisa describe Las Ramblas?

c.   What was in the park that Marisa visited?

d.   What else did she visit in Barcelona?

e.   What did Marisa like most about Barcelona?

ANSWERS P. 230   f.   What did she like least?

7 These are the questions that María *could* have asked Eme in Conversations 2. Answer them for Eme, but this time, using your own words. Write down the answers *and* say them out loud. You'll find some possible replies on page 230.

i. ¿Cuándo fuiste a Escocia por primera vez?

ii. ¿Qué más te gustó?

iii. ¿Qué piensas de Edimburgo?

iv. ¿Crees que está todo muy cambiado?

v. ¿Hace cuánto tiempo que no vas a Escocia?

8 More about Italy. Marisa asks you about that holiday you had there last year and what you liked most. You'll hear the word '**el extranjero**' (abroad) and you'll need: **fuimos**, **visitamos**, **me gustó** and **me gustaron**.

Juana tells a friend about a recent car accident

LISTEN FOR...

¿qué te pasa?	what's wrong with you?
me choqué contra un árbol	I crashed into a tree
tuve que ir al hospital	I had to go to hospital
cuatro puntos	four stitches
me rompí la mano	I fractured my hand

Manolo	Hola, Juana, ¿qué te pasa en la ceja?
Juana	Es del accidente. El accidente de hace cuatro meses
Manolo	No me acuerdo. ¿Qué te pasó?
Juana	Sí, tuve un accidente con el coche, me choqué contra un árbol, iba un poco dormida por la noche, y me tuve que ir al hospital, me pusieron cuatro puntos y me rompí también la mano derecha. Pero ya estoy bien
Manolo	Fue un poco grave, ¿no?
Juana	Eh, sí, un poco por el hospital, pero ahora estoy bien. Se me ha olvidado ya

¿Qué te pasa en la ceja?   What's wrong with your (eye)brow? **¿Qué te pasa?** What's wrong? is a very useful phrase to know.
No me acuerdo   I don't remember. This is from **acordarse** to remember.
¿Qué te pasó?   This is the same phrase as we had earlier but in the past tense. It means 'what happened to you?'

Tuve un accidente   I had an accident. **Tuve** is the (irregular) past form of **tener** to have.
Me choqué contra un árbol   I crashed into a tree. **Contra** really means 'against'.
Iba un poco dormida   I was a bit sleepy. **Iba** is another example of the imperfect tense, describing how Juana was feeling at the time.
Me pusieron cuatro puntos   They gave me four stitches. Spanish says 'to put a stitch' from **poner** to put.
Me rompí la mano derecha   I fractured my right hand. **Romper** to break.
por el hospital   because of the hospital ...
Se me ha olvidado ya   I've already forgotten about it. **Olvidarse** to forget.

9 Link each phrase with the corresponding picture in the cartoon.

i. fui al hospital

ii. a las siete, estuve en el coche

iii. ¡ahora estoy bien!

iv. me rompí la mano

v. me pusieron cuatro puntos

vi. me choqué contra unos semáforos

vii. a las ocho, tuve un accidente

ANSWERS P. 230

10 Read the following short article about a man who died after being knocked down by a car in Palma.

Muere atropellado por un vehículo robado ...

José González Suárez de 33 años murió ayer, 14 de junio, cuando le atropelló un coche que se subió a la acera mientras hablaba con una amiga en un portal del barrio de San Isidro en Palma. Los tres ocupantes robaron el coche, un Fiat Uno, el día anterior, y lo abandonaron en mitad de la calle. González Suárez, casado y con dos hijos, fue trasladado rápidamente al hospital Nuestra Señora de la Merced, donde murió dos horas después.

New vocabulary

morir	to die
atropellar	to knock over
la acera	pavement
el portal	doorway
la mitad	middle

ANSWERS P. 230

Now fill in the grid, in Spanish, with the details suggested to you by the key words. You'll find that you have a summary of the article.

> ¿Quién? ....
>
> Edad (age) ....
>
> Estado Civil (marital status) ....
>
> ¿Qué pasó? ....
>
> ¿Cuándo? ....
>
> ¿Cómo? ....
>
> ¿Qué tipo de coche? ....
>
> ¿Cuándo murió? ....
>
> ¿Dónde murió? ....

Now try to re-create the story out loud. Base it on your notes. Then start your recording to hear our version of the events.

11 You've recently had a problem with your car. Marisa asks you all about it. You'll need: **tuvimos**, **fue** and **nos chocamos**.

GRAMMAR AND EXERCISES

In Spanish, there are several different ways of talking about things which have already happened. In this course, only the preterite tense is taught; it is the most useful past tense to know, because it relates past events and is almost directly equivalent to the English I went, I did, I saw and so on. There are two sets of endings:

Comprar to buy (*-ar* endings)

-é	compré
	I bought
-aste	compraste
	you bought (informal)
-ó	compró
	s/he bought
-ó	compró
	you bought (formal)
-amos	compramos
	we bought
-asteis	comprasteis
	you bought (informal plural)
-aron	compraron
	they bought
-aron	compraron
	you bought (formal plural)

-**er** and -**ir** verbs share the same endings:

Comer to eat

-í	comí
	I ate
-iste	comiste
	you ate (informal)
-ió	comió
	s/he ate
-ió	comió
	you ate (formal)

-imos	comimos
	we ate
-isteis	comisteis
	you ate (informal)
-ieron	comieron
	they ate
-ieron	comieron
	you ate (formal plural)

Comimos un buen filete   We ate a good fillet of steak

¿Escribiste a tu padre?   Did you write to your father?

Irregular forms in the preterite:

Fui I was/I went (from both *ser* to be and *ir* to go)

fui	I went, I was
fuiste	you went, you were (informal)
fue	s/he went, s/he was
fue	you went, you were (formal)
fuimos	we went, we were
fuisteis	you went, you were (informal plural)
fueron	they went, they were
fueron	you went, you were (formal plural)

Estuve I was (from *estar* to be)

estuv -e	I was
estuv -iste	you were (informal)
estuv -o	s/he was
estuv -o	you were (formal)
estuv -imos	we were
estuv -isteis	you were (informal plural)
estuv -ieron	they were
estuv -ieron	you were (formal plural)

Other useful irregular forms are:

puse I put (from **poner**)
tuve I had (from **tener**)
quise I wanted (from **querer**)
dije I said, (from **decir**) **dijeron** they said
hice (I did/made) (from **hacer**) **hizo** s/he, you did/made
Their endings (except where indicated) are like those of **estar**.

Talking about time

- Use **hace** to mean 'ago' in sentences like:
  Hace un mes, estuve en Puerto Rico
  A month ago I was in Puerto Rico
  Me casé hace dos años
  I got married two years ago
- Use **desde hace** to mean 'since' or 'for' in sentences like:
  Vivo en Madrid desde hace tres meses
  I've been living in Madrid for three months
  Trabajo para la empresa desde hace siete años
  I've been working for the company for seven years

Notice how the verb in Spanish is in the present tense.

12

Link up the pronoun with the correct form of each verb. (As the **él, ella, Vd.** forms are the same, there is more than one option for some sentences. Choose the one which makes most sense.)

a.	yo	i.	tomamos una cerveza
b.	él	ii.	no hicieron nada
c.	nosotros	iii.	no pude verlo
d.	tú	iv.	tuvo un problema
e.	las chicas	v.	hablaron con los chicos
f.	ustedes	vi.	no le dijiste nada
g.	usted	vii.	fue médico ¿no?

ANSWERS P. 230

13

Complete these sentences by using the correct form of the verb – in the preterite:

a. (We were) en España para las fiestas de San Fermín
b. (I went) a Edimburgo en octubre por primera vez
c. (We weren't able) ir de vacaciones este año
d. (They went back) a Australia en el verano
e. (They left) de Cuba para ir a Miami
f. (We got to know) el Perú hace treinta años
g. (I didn't remember) su nombre
h. (I wrote) a mis padres desde Bogotá
i. Mi mujer (had) una niña el treinta de agosto
j. (We travelled) en autobús por la sierra de Argentina

ANSWERS P. 230

14

Can you translate these sentences? They all contain a time expression.

a. Hace dos años fui a México por primera vez
b. Vivo en la ciudad de México desde hace seis meses
c. Hace tres meses, me casé con una mexicana
d. Desde hace dos meses vivimos en un piso en el centro de la ciudad
e. Trabajo para la empresa MEXITUR desde hace seis semanas
f. ¡Hace mucho tiempo que estoy muy contento con mi vida!

ANSWERS P. 230

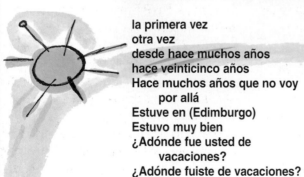

la primera vez	the first time
otra vez	again
desde hace muchos años	for a long time
hace veinticinco años	twenty-five years ago
Hace muchos años que no voy por allá	I haven't been there for many years
Estuve en (Edimburgo)	I was in (Edinburgh)
Estuvo muy bien	It was very good
¿Adónde fue usted de vacaciones?	Where did you go on holiday?
¿Adónde fuiste de vacaciones?	Where did you (informal) go on holiday?
Fui de vacaciones a España	I went on holiday to Spain
Fui a tomar el vermut	I went for an aperitif
Fuimos a Portugal	We went to Portugal
Viajé en autobús	I travelled by bus
Paré allí un día	I stopped there for a day
¿Qué hiciste ayer?	What did you do yesterday?
Hice unas compras	I did some shopping
Hicimos unas compras	We did some shopping
Salí	I went out
No recuerdo el nombre	I don't remember its name
No pudimos bañarnos	We couldn't bathe
Visitamos algunos pueblos	We visited some towns
Volvimos a casa	We went home
¿Qué te pasa?	What's wrong with you?
¿Qué te pasó?	What happened to you?
Tuve un accidente	I had an accident
Tuve que ir al hospital	I had to go to hospital
Me pusieron cuatro puntos	They gave me (put) four stitches
Me rompí la mano	I fractured my hand
Se me ha olvidado ya	I've already forgotten about it
Lo que conozco me gusta mucho	What I know I like a lot
Me gustó mucho Londres	I liked London a lot
Los/las dos me gustaron	I liked both

The new Spain

JUAN LUIS CEBRIÁN of the influential Spanish newspaper *El País* has remarked that when he was a child in the fifties, Spain was a poor country with a predominantly rural, Catholic population with family values paramount. Even in the early 1980s, the tourist industry promoted Spain as **diferente** and somehow exotic.

None of this is true any longer. Spain is a rich country: indeed it is the world's tenth largest industrial power. For several years after joining what is now the European Union, it enjoyed the prestige of having the fastest economic growth of all twelve member states. Spain is the world's largest producer of olive oil and, more glamorously, of sparkling wine. (Most of this is produced in Penedés and is known as **cava**.) It is also the third largest manufacturer of motor vehicles. In order to be in the Union's 'fast lane', Spain drew up a 'Convergence Plan' for the 1990s, which aimed, among other things, to reduce labour costs by a third, to raise its GNP by one per cent and to reduce imports also by a third.

According to one recent report, Spain has now the twentieth highest standard of living in the world (Britain is eleventh). Much of this wealth is due to foreign investment. At the beginning of the 1990s, thirty-two of Spain's leading companies were foreign controlled. Today the multinationals are present in almost every sector of the economy.

Tourism is of course big business in Spain. More than fifty million people visit the country each year and for the last thirty years, tourism has been Spain's biggest foreign exchange earner. But the tourist industry is presently bearing the brunt of the recession. Prices have risen – Spain is no longer a very cheap holiday destination. Many tourists have become more sophisticated. They no longer wish to go on package tours to the **costas**, which are as far away from the real Spain

as are Turkey and Greece. In response to these changing trends, Spain is developing a more upmarket kind of tourism into the hinterland and the Northern coast, with more ecological, historical, artistic and cultural holiday opportunities. One bright spot for the Spanish economy is the Andalusian coast, which has seen a boom in the construction of retirement developments for the European and Japanese markets.

The object pronouns are as follows:

me lleva	he takes me
te lleva	he takes you (informal)
le/lo lleva	he takes you (formal, m.)
la lleva	he takes you (formal, f.)
lo lleva	he takes it (m.)
la lleva	he takes it (f.)
le/lo lleva	he takes him
la lleva	he takes her

nos lleva	he takes us
os lleva	he takes you (informal pl.)
les/los lleva	he takes you (formal m. pl.)
las lleva	he takes you (formal f. pl.)
las lleva	he takes them (f.pl. objects)
los lleva	he takes them (m.pl. objects)
les/los lleva	he takes them (men)
las lleva	he takes them (women)

There is some controversy about the use of **le/lo** and **les/los**. Generally speaking, **lo/los** is used in Southern Spain and Latin America.

Some verbs take an INDIRECT OBJECT rather than a DIRECT OBJECT, e.g. 'He speaks *to* me' not 'he speaks *me*'.

The only difference between indirect and direct objects is in the third person form ('he', 'it'). Use **le** when saying 'to her, to him, to it' or 'to you' (**usted**) and **les** for 'to them' or 'to you' (**ustedes**):
le habla   he speaks to him/to her/to you (**usted**)
les habla   he speaks to them/to you (**ustedes**)

If you want to avoid ambiguity, add **a él, a ella, a Vd., a ellos, a ellas, a Vds.**:
Les doy el libro a ellos   I give them (m.pl.) the book
Les doy el libro a ellas   I give them (f.pl.) the book

POSSESSIVE ADJECTIVES are words such as *my, your* and *his*.

Possessive adjectives in Spanish are as follows:

mi casa	**mis casas**
my house	my houses
tu casa	**tus casas**
your house	your houses
su casa	**sus casas**
his/her/your house	his/her/your houses

nuestra casa	**nuestras casas**
our house	our houses
vuestra casa	**vuestras casas**
your house	your houses
su casa	**sus casas**

their/your house   their/your houses

When talking about parts of the body or clothes, Spaniards use the definite article rather than the possessive adjective:

Tengo el pelo moreno   I have dark hair

Numbers

0	**cero**	16	**dieciséis**	31	**treinta y uno(a)**	67	**sesenta y siete**
1	**uno/a**	17	**diecisiete**	32	**treinta y dos**	70	**setenta**
2	**dos**	18	**dieciocho**	33	**treinta y tres**	72	**setenta y dos**
3	**tres**	19	**diecinueve**	34	**treinta y cuatro**	80	**ochenta**
4	**cuatro**	20	**veinte**	35	**treinta y cinco**	90	**noventa**
5	**cinco**			36	**treinta y seis**	100	**cien(to)**
6	**seis**			37	**treinta y siete**	105	**ciento cinco**
7	**siete**	21	**veintiuno(a)**	38	**treinta y ocho**	200	**doscientos(as)**
8	**ocho**	22	**veintidós**	39	**treinta y nueve**	300	**trescientos(as)**
9	**nueve**	23	**veintitrés**	40	**cuarenta**	400	**cuatrocientos(as)**
10	**diez**	24	**veinticuatro**			500	**quinientos(as)**
11	**once**	25	**veinticinco**	41	**cuarenta y uno(a)**	600	**seiscientos(as)**
12	**doce**	26	**veintiséis**	48	**cuarenta y ocho**	700	**setecientos(as)**
13	**trece**	27	**veintisiete**	50	**cincuenta**	800	**ochocientos(as)**
14	**catorce**	28	**veintiocho**	51	**cincuenta y uno(a)**	900	**novecientos(as)**
15	**quince**	29	**veintinueve**	60	**sesenta**	1000	**mil**
		30	**treinta**	63	**sesenta y tres**		

1–100

Only those numbers ending in **-uno** have a masculine and feminine form; they do not have a plural form:

veintiún hombres
veintiuna mujeres

Note that, as in the case above, if **veintiuno** comes before a noun it is shortened to **veintiún**. However, if the number stands alone you should use the full form:

¿Cuántos hombres? Veintiuno.
¿Cuántas mujeres? Veintiuna.

100

Use either **cien** or **ciento** when using this number alone:

¿Cuántos hay? Cien/ciento.

Use **cien** with a noun that follows:

cien casas   one hundred houses
cien gramos   one hundred grams

Use **ciento** in combination with other numbers:

ciento cincuenta gramos   a hundred and fifty grams

Use **cien** with **cien mil**   a hundred thousand.

200–900

These numbers have masculine and feminine forms:

doscientos chicos two hundred boys
doscientas niñas two hundred girls

1000

Mil does not change its form:
mil novecientos noventa y seis   1996

GRAMMAR
IN THE COURSE

VOCABULARY

The feminine ending of adjectives is given in brackets, e.g. **abierto(a)** means that the masculine is **abierto** and the feminine **abierta**. Where there are no brackets, the feminine form is the same as the masculine, e.g. **canadiense**. Where **i**, **ie** or **ue** appear in brackets, this indicates a stem change in the verb.

The gender of nouns is given in brackets: m. – masculine; f. – feminine; m.pl. – masculine plural; f.pl. – feminine plural.

A

a to, at, on;
  a las ... at ... o'clock
abajo below
abierto(a) open
abogado(a) (m., f.) lawyer
abonado(a) (m., f.) subscriber
abonar to subscribe
abrazo (m.) hug
abril (m.) April
abrir to open
abuela (f.) grandmother
abuelo (m.) grandfather;
  abuelos (m.pl.) grandparents
acabar to finish;
  acabar de to have just finished
aceite (m.) oil
aceituna (f.) olive
aceptable acceptable
acera (f.) pavement
aconsejar to advise
acostarse (ue) to go to bed
actividad (f.) activity
acto (m.) function
acuerdo (m.) agreement;
  de acuerdo OK
adelantar to overtake
adelante forward;
  ¡adelante! come in
además besides
adiós goodbye
¿adónde? where (to)?
aeropuerto (m.) airport
África (f.) Africa
afuera outside;
  las afueras the outskirts
agosto (m.) August
agradable pleasant, agreeable

agua (f.) water;
  agua mineral mineral water;
  agua con gas fizzy water;
  agua sin gas still water
ahora now
aire (m.) air;
  aire libre open air
Alemania (f.) Germany
algo anything, something
algodón (m.) cotton
algún, alguno(a) any, some
alivio (m.) relief
almeja (f.) clam
almorzar to lunch
almuerzo (m.) lunch
alquilar to rent
alto(a) tall
alumno(a) (m.f.) pupil
allá over there
allí there;
  allí mismo right there
amarillo(a) yellow
Amazonas (m.) the Amazon
ambiente (m.) atmosphere
ambos(as) both
americano(a) Latin American
amigo(a) friend
andaluz(a) Andalusian
andar to walk
andén (m.) platform
angora (f.) angora wool
animal (m.) animal
antes de before
antigüedades (f.pl.) antiques
antipático(a) unpleasant
año (m.) year;
  ¿cuántos años tiene Vd.? how old are you?
aparcar to park

apartamento (m.) flat
apellido (m.) surname
apetecer to feel like
aprovechar to make (good) use of;
  ¡que aproveche! enjoy your meal!
aproximadamente approximately
aquí here;
  por aquí around here
ardor (m.) heat;
  ardor de estómago heartburn
aroma (m.) scent
arreglado(a) ready
arreglarse to get oneself ready
arriba above
arrogante arrogant
artículo (m.) article
asado(a) roast
ascensor (m.) lift, elevator
así like this;
  así que so that
aspirina (f.) aspirin
atender(ie) to look after
Atlántico (m.) the Atlantic
atraer to attract
atrás behind
atravesar (ie) to cross
atropellar to knock over
atún (m.) tuna fish
autobús (m.) bus
autocar (m.) coach
autopista (f.) motorway
avenida (f.) avenue
avión (m.) aeroplane
ayer yesterday
ayudar to help
ayuntamiento (m.) town hall
azafata (f.) air hostess
azul blue;
  azul marino navy blue

B

bacalao (m.) cod;
    bacalao a la vizcaína Biscay-style cod
bailar to dance
bajar to go down
bajo(a) short;
    planta baja (f.) ground floor
balón (m.) ball
banco (m.) bank;
    tarjeta de banco (f.) banker's card
baño (m.) bath
bar (m.) bar
barato(a) cheap
barco (m.) ship
barra (f.) loaf
barrio (m.) neighbourhood
bastante enough
beber to drink
bebida (f.) drink
beso (m.) kiss
bicicleta (f.) bicycle;
    montar en bicicleta to ride a bicycle
bien well;
    más bien rather;
    muy bien very good, very well
billete (m.) ticket
blanco(a) white
blazer (m.) blazer
blusa (f.) blouse
boca (f.) mouth
bocadillo (m.) sandwich
bolsa (f.) bag
bonito(a) pretty
bordo; a bordo on board
bota (f.) boot
bote (m.) can, (round) tin
botella (f.) bottle
botellín (m.) small bottle (of beer)
brisa (f.) breeze
británico(a) British
bronceador (m.) suntan lotion
bueno(a) good
bus (m.) bus
buscar to look for

C

caballero (m.) gentleman;
    caballeros gents (toilets)
cabeza (f.) head
cabo; al cabo de at the end of

cada each
caer to fall
café (m.) coffee;
    café solo black coffee
caja (f.) box, cash desk
calamares (m.pl.) squid;
    calamares fritos fried squid
calentar (ie) to heat
calidad (f.) quality
caliente hot
calle (f.) street
calor (m.) heat;
    hace calor it's hot
caluroso(a) hot
cama (f.) bed
camarero(a) (m., f.) waiter, steward, waitress
cambiado changed
cambiar to change
cambio (m.) change
camino (m.) way, path, road
camisa (f.) shirt
camiseta (f.) tee-shirt
camping (m.) campsite
campo (m.) countryside
canadiense Canadian
cansado(a) tired
cantidad (f.) quantity
caña (f.) glass (of draught beer)
capacidad (f.) capacity
cara (f.) face
caramelo (m.) sweet
caravana (f.) caravan
carne (f.) meat
caro(a) expensive;
    carísimo(a) very expensive
carretera (f.) main road
carro (m.) car, cart
carta (f.) letter
casa (f.) house;
    casa de huéspedes guest house
casado(a) married
castaño(a) brown (hair)
catedral (f.) cathedral
categoría (f.) category, class
catorce fourteen
cazuela (f.) saucepan
cebolla (f.) onion
cena (f.) dinner
cenar to dine
centro (m.) centre
cerca near
cerilla (f.) match

cero zero
cerrar (ie) to close
cerrarse (ie) to be closed
cerveza (f.) beer
champú (m.) shampoo
chandal (m.) tracksuit
chaqueta (f.) jacket
cheque (m.) **de viaje** traveller's cheque
cheviot (m.) type of woollen cloth
chica (f.) girl
chico (m.) boy
chocolate (m.) chocolate
chorizo (m.) spicy sausage
cierre (m.) lock
cigarrillo (m.) cigarette
cinco five
cincuenta fifty
cincuenta y cinco fifty-five
cine (m.) cinema
circular to travel
circular (adj.) circular
ciudad (f.) city
claro(a) clear;
    ¡claro! of course!
clase (f.) class, kind, sort
clásico(a) classic
cliente (m. or f.) customer
clima (m.) climate
cobrar to cover, charge
coche (m.) car
cochinillo (m.) sucking pig
cocina (f.) kitchen;
    cocina amueblada fitted kitchen
cocinar to cook
coger to get, to catch, to take
    (In Latin America use **tomar**.)
cole, colegio (m.) secondary school (private)
color (m.) colour
comedor (m.) dining-room
comenzar (ie) to begin;
    comenzar a to begin to
comida (f.) (main) meal, food
como as, like;
    como de costumbre as usual
¿cómo? how?, pardon?
cómodo(a) comfortable
compasivo(a) understanding
completo(a) complete
comprar to buy
comprender to understand, to include
comprimido (m.) pill, tablet

comprobar (ue) to check

con with;
    conmigo with me;
    contigo with you

concierto (m.) concert

condición (f.) condition;
    en buenas condiciones in good
    condition

conocer to know

conocido(a) known

conseguir to obtain

consomé (m.) clear soup

construir to build;
    construído(a) built

contentísimo(a) very happy

contrato (m.) contract

conveniente advisable, desirable

correos (m.) post office

correr to run

cortado (m.) coffee with a dash of
    milk

cortar to cut

cosa (f.) thing

coser to sew

costa (f.) coast

costar (ue) to cost

creer to believe, think

crema (f.) cream

cruce (m.) crossroads

cruzar to cross

¿cuál? which?, what?

cualquier any

cuando when

¿cuándo? when?

¿cuánto? how much?

cuarenta forty

cuarenta y cinco forty-five

cuarto (m.) a quarter;
    menos cuarto a quarter to;
    y cuarto quarter past

cuarto de baño (m.) bathroom

cuatro four

cubierto(a) covered

cuello (m.) neckline

cuenta (f.) bill

cuero (m.) leather

cuestión (f.) question

cuidado (m.) care

¡cuidado! careful! watch out!

cumpleaños (m.) birthday

curso (m.) school year

cuyo(a) whose, of whom, of which

D

dar to give;
    dar un paseo to go for a walk

de of, from

deber to have to, to owe

decir (i) to say

dejar to leave

delante (de) in front of

delgado(a) slim

demasiado too much

dentista (m. or f.) dentist

dentro (de) inside

depender (de) to depend on

dependiente(a) (m., f.) sales assistant

deporte (m.) sport

derecho(a) right;
    a la derecha on the right

desayunar to have breakfast

desayuno (m.) breakfast

descansar to rest

descanso (m.) rest

desde from, since

desear to wish for

despacio slowly

despejado(a) clear

despierto(a) alert

después (de) afterwards

desviarse to turn

detestar to hate

detrás (de) behind

día (m.) day;
    buenos días good morning, good
    day;
    el día del santo Saint's day

diario(a) daily

diarrea (f.) diarrhoea

dibujado(a) patterned

diciembre (m.) December

diecinueve nineteen

dieciocho eighteen

dieciséis sixteen

diecisiete seventeen

diez ten

diferencia (f.) difference

difícil difficult

digestivo (m.) product to aid
    digestion

dinero (m.) money

discoteca (f.) discotheque

disfrutar (de) to enjoy

distinto(a) different

divertirse (ie) to enjoy oneself

doblar to turn

doce twelve

docena (f.) dozen

documento (m.) document

dolor (m.) pain;
    dolor de estómago stomach-ache

domicilio (m.) home

domingo (m.) Sunday

don Mr

donde where

¿dónde? where?

doña Mrs

dormitorio (m.) bedroom

dos two

doscientos(as) two hundred

ducha (f.) shower

dulce sweet

dúplex (m.) two-storied
    flat/apartment

duración (f.) length of stay

durante during

durar to last

duro(a) hard

E

ecuatoriano(a) Ecuadorian

edad (f.) age;
    ¿qué edad tiene (Vd.)? how old are
    you?

edificio (m.) building

efectivamente precisely

eficaz effective

egoísta selfish

ejemplo (m.) example

el (m.) the

él he, him, it

ella she, her, it

ellos(as) they, them

empleado(a) (m., f.) employee

empresa (f.) firm

en in

encantado(a) delighted

encantar to delight

encima (de) on top of;
    por encima de over

encontrar (ue) to find, to meet

encontrarse (ue) to be found

enero (m.) January

enfrente (de) in front of, opposite

ensaladilla (f.) Russian salad

entero(a) whole

entonces so, then

entrar to enter, to go in
entregar to hand over
entremeses (m.pl.) hors d'oeuvres
entretener to amuse
enviar to send
época (f.) time
escaleras (f.pl.) stairs
escocés Scottish (man)
escocesa Scottish (woman)
escribir to write
ese(a) that
ése(a) that one
eso that
esos(as) those
ésos(as) those (ones)
España (f.) Spain
español(a) Spanish
espárrago (m.) asparagus
especialmente especially
esperar to wait (for)
esposa (f.) wife
esposo (m.) husband
establecimiento (m.) establishment
estación (f.) station, season
estanco (m.) tobacconist's
estar to be;
    ¿cómo estás? how are you?;
    está bien that's fine
este (m.) east
este(a) this
éste(a) this one
estilo (m.) style
esto this
estos(as) these
éstos(as) these (ones)
estrella (f.) star
estudiante (m. or f.) student
estupendo(a) marvellous
eterno(a) eternal
extenderse (ie) to extend, to spread
    out
extensión (f.) extension
extra 98 octane four star (petrol)
extranjero(a) foreign
extremo(a) extreme
extremo (m.) end

F

faena (f.) task
falda (f.) skirt
familia (f.) family
farmacéutico(a) (m., f.) chemist,
    pharmacist

farmacia (f.) chemist's shop
faro (m.) headlight
favorito(a) favourite
febrero (m.) February
fecha (f.) date
ferrocarril (m.) railway
festivo(a) festive;
    día festivo public holiday
fiebre (f.) fever
figura (f.) figure, figurine
fijo(a) fixed;
    precio fijo fixed price
final (m.) end;
    al final de at the end of
fino(a) fine
firma (f.) signature
flan (m.) caramel cream
fonda (f.) inn, pub
al fondo at the end
formar to form
francés French (man)
francesa French (woman)
frecuencia (f.) frequency;
    con frecuencia frequently
freír to fry
freno (m.) brake
fresa (f.) strawberry
frío(a) cold;
    hace frío it's cold
frito(a) fried;
    calamares fritos fried squid
fruta (f.) fruit
fuerte strong
fútbol (m.) football

G

Gales Wales
galés Welsh (man)
galesa Welsh (woman)
gallego (m.) language of Galicia
gallego(a) a person from
    Galicia
gamba (f.) prawn
ganar to win, to earn
garaje (m.) garage
gas (m.);
    con gas sparkling;
    sin gas still
gasolinera (f.) service station
gasolinero(a) (m., f.) service station
    attendant
gastar to spend
gazpacho (m.) spicy cold tomato
    soup

generoso(a) generous
gente (f.) people
girar to turn
girasol (m.) sunflower;
    aceite de girasol sunflower oil
gobierno (m.) government
gordo(a) fat
gracias (f.pl.) thanks;
    muchas gracias thanks very
    much
grado (m.) degree
gramo (m.) gram
gran, grande big, large
grave serious
grelos (m.pl.) turnip tops
gris grey
gritar to shout
grueso(a) thick
gustar to like;
    ¿te gusta? do you like (it)?;
    no me gusta I don't like (it)
gusto (m.) taste

H

habitación (f.) room, bedroom
hablar to talk
habrá there will be (future of **hay**)
hacer to do, to make;
    no me hace gracia I don't like (it);
    hacer la cama to make the bed;
    hacer las maletas to pack (the
    suitcases)
hacia towards
hasta up to, as far as
hay there is, there are;
    hay que you/one must
helado (m.) ice-cream
hermana (f.) sister
hermano (m.) brother
hija (f.) daughter
hijo (m.) son;
    hijos (m.pl.) children
histórico(a) historic
hoja (f.) de reclamaciones complaints
    form
¡hola! hello
hombre (m.) man;
    ¡hombre! good heavens!
hora (f.) hour;
    ¿qué hora es? what time is it?;
    a su hora on time
horario (m.) timetable
hostal (m.) hostel

hostilidad (f.) hostility, aggression
hotel (m.) hotel
hoy today
hueso (m.) bone; stone, pit (of fruit)
huevo (m.) egg

I

ida (f.) outward journey;
    ida y vuelta return journey
idioma (m.) language
igual the same
imitación (f.) imitation
importante important
impuestos (m.pl.) taxes
incomparable incomparable
indicador (m.) sign
ingeniero (m.) engineer
Inglaterra (f.) England
inglés English (man)
Inglesa English (woman)
inquieto(a) restless, anxious
insolación (f.) sunstroke
interior (m.) inland
intermitente (m.) indicator
invertir (ie) to invest
investigación (f.) research
invierno (m.) winter
ir to go;
    ir de tiendas to go shopping;
    ir de paseo to go for a walk
Isla (f.) island;
    Islas Baleares the Balearic Islands
itinerario (m.) journey, itinerary
izquierdo(a) left;
    a la izquierda on the left

J

jamón (m.) ham;
    jamón serrano smoked ham
jaquard (m.) jacquard weave
jarabe (m.) syrup
jardín (m.) garden
jefe(a) (m., f.) chief, boss;
    jefe de sección departmental manager
jubilado(a) retired
jueves (m.) Thursday
jugar (ue) to play
juguete (m.) toy
julio (m.) July

junio (m.) June
junto(a) together
justo(a) just, exactly;
    cien pesetas justas one hundred pesetas exactly

K

kilo (m.) kilo
kilómetro (m.) kilometre

L

la (f.) the, it, her
lacón (m.) shoulder of pork
lado (m.) side;
    al lado (de) by the side (of), next door (to)
lanzar to throw
lápiz (m.) pencil
largo(a) long
lata (f.) (flat) tin
lavabo (m.) washbasin
lavar to wash;
    lavarse to wash oneself
le (to) him, (to) her, (to) it, (to) you (sing.)
leche (f.) milk
lechuga (f.) lettuce
leer to read
lejos far away
lengua (f.) tongue, language
les (to) you (pl.), (to) them
levantarse to get up
libre free;
    ¿queda libre? are you free?
libro (m.) book
ligeramente lightly
limpiaparabrisas (m.) windscreen wiper
limpiar to clean
liquidar to liquidate, to get rid of
liso(a) plain
listo(a) ready
litro (m.) litre
llamada (f.) call
llamar to call, phone;
    llamarse to be called;
    ¿cómo se llama Vd.? what is your name?
llave (f.) key
llegada (f.) arrival
llegar to arrive

llevar to carry
llover (ue) to rain
lluvia (f.) rain
lluvioso(a) rainy
lo the, that which, it, him;
    lo que which, what
Londres London
luego then, later
lugar (m.) place
lujoso(a) luxury
lunes (m.) Monday

M

machista macho
maíz (m.) maize;
    aceite de maíz corn oil
mal badly;
    malo(a) bad;
    malas digestiones (f.pl.) indigestion
maleta (f.) suitcase;
    hacer la maleta to pack a suitcase
maletero (m.) car boot
manchego (m.) type of cheese
manchego(a) a person from La Mancha
mano (f.) hand
mañana tomorrow;
    pasado mañana the day after tomorrow;
    por la mañana in the morning
mar (m.) sea
marca (f.) brand
marcar to dial
marcharse to go
marisco (m.) shellfish
marrón brown
martes (m.) Tuesday
marzo (m.) March
más more, most, else, plus;
    ¿algo más? anything else?;
    más bien rather
matrimonio (m.) married couple;
    cama de matrimonio (f.) double bed;
    habitación de matrimonio double room
mayo (m.) May
mayor eldest, older, grown up;
    La Plaza Mayor Main Square
mayormente chiefly, especially
media see **medio**
medias (f.pl.) socks, stockings
medicina (f.) medicine

médico (m.) doctor
medida (f.) measurement, size
medio(a) half;
    media hora half an hour;
    las dos y media half past two
mediodía (m.) midday
mejor better, best
melocotón (m.) peach
menos less;
    las doce menos veinte twenty to twelve
mentira (f.) lie, false
menú (m.) menu
menudo(a) small, slight
mercado (m.) market
merendar (ie) to have an afternoon snack
merienda (f.) an afternoon snack
merluza (f.) hake;
    merluza a la romana hake fried in batter
mes (m.) month
mesa (f.) table
metro (m.) metre
metro (m.) underground railway
mi my
mí me
miércoles (m.) Wednesday
mil thousand
milla (f.) mile
minuto (m.) minute
mío(a) mine
mirar to look at
mismo(a) same, very
mitad (f.) middle
momento (m.) moment
moneda (f.) change
montaña (f.) mountain
montañoso(a) mountainous
montar en bicicleta to ride a bicycle
moreno(a) dark
morir (ue) to die
mortadela (f.) a kind of Italian sausage
mostrador (m.) **de facturación** check-in counter (at airport)
mostrar (ue) to show
mover (ue) to move
mujer (f.) woman, wife
mundial worldwide
mundo (m.) world
murallas (f.pl.) city walls
muy very

N

nacional national;
    la nacional uno name of a road, i.e. **N1**
nacionalidad (f.) nationality
nada nothing;
    de nada you're welcome
nadar to swim
naranja (f.) orange;
    color naranja orange coloured
natural, al natural plain
naturalmente of course
necesario(a) necessary
necesitar to need
negro(a) black
neumático (m.) tyre
nevar (ie) to snow
ni ... ni neither ... nor
nieto(a) (m. f.) grandson, granddaughter
nieve (f.) snow
niño(a) (m. f.) boy, girl
nivel (m.) level
no no, not
noche (f.) night
nombre (m.) name
normal normal
normalmente normally
norte (m.) north;
    al norte in the north, to the north
norteamericano(a) American
nos (to) us
nosotros(as) we, us
novecientos(as) nine hundred
novedad (f.) novelty
noventa ninety
noviembre (m.) November
novio(a) (m., f.) boyfriend, girlfriend, fiancé(e)
nube (f.) cloud;
    nubes alternas occasional clouds
nublado(a) cloudy
nubloso(a) cloudy
nueve nine
número (m.) number
nunca never

O

o or
octubre (m.) October
ochenta eighty
ocho eight

odiar to hate
oeste (m.) west
oferta (f.) offer
oficina (f.) office;
    oficina de turismo tourist office
¡oiga! excuse me
oír to hear
ojo (m.) eye;
    ¡ojo! look out!
oliva (f.) olive;
    aceite de oliva olive oil
oro (m.) gold
oscilar to oscillate, to vary
otoño (m.) autumn
otro(a) other

P

padre (m.) father
padres (m.pl.) parents
paella (f.) paella
pagar to pay
país (m.) country
paisaje (m.) countryside
pan (m.) bread
pandilla (f.) group, band
pantalones (m.pl.) trousers;
    pantalones cortos shorts
pañuelo (m.) handkerchief, scarf
paquete (m.) packet
par (m.) pair;
    par de zapatos pair of shoes
para for, to
parabrisas (m.) windscreen
parada (f.) stop;
    parada de autobuses bus stop
paraíso (m.) paradise
parar to stop, to stay
parecer to seem;
    me parece que ... I think that ...;
    ¿qué le parece? what do you think?
parque (m.) park;
    parque infantil playground
parte (f.) part
participar to participate
partido (m.) match;
    partido de fútbol football match
pasaporte (m.) passport
pasar to spend (time);
    pasadas dos horas after two hours
    pasarlo bien to have a good time
pasear to go for a walk

     Vocabulary

paseo (m.) walk;
    dar un paseo, **ir de paseo** to go for a walk
patata (f.) potato;
    patatas fritas crisps, chips
pedir (i) to ask for
peinarse to do one's hair
película (f.) film
pelota (f.) ball
peluquero(a) (m., f.) hairdresser
pensar (ie) to think
pensión (f.) guest house
peor worse, worst
pequeño(a) small
perderse (ie) to lose oneself/to get lost
perfecto(a) perfect;
    perfectamente exactly
perfumería (f.) perfumery
periódico (m.) newspaper
período (m.) period
pero but
perro (m.) dog
persona (f.) person
pesado(a) heavy
pescado (m.) fish
peseta (f.) peseta
peso (m.) weight
picante spicy
pie (m.) foot;
    a pie on foot
piel (f.) skin
pila (f.) battery
piscina (f.) swimming pool
pico (m.) floor, flat;
    el primer piso the first floor
planchar to iron
planta (f.) floor, story;
    primera planta first floor
plato (m.) plate, course;
    de primer plato as a first course;
    plato combinado one-course meal
playa (f.) beach
plaza (f.) square
plomo (m.) lead;
    sin plomo lead-free (petrol)
poco (m.) a bit
poder (ue) to be able to;
    se puede one can;
    no se puede one cannot
poliéster (m.) polyester
poner to put;
    ponerse de acuerdo to agree on

poquito (m.) a little bit
por along, by, for;
    por ahí over there;
    por aquí around here;
    por ciento per cent;
    por favor please;
    por encima de over, above
¿por qué? why?
porque because
portal (m.) doorway
posible possible
postre (m.) dessert;
    de postre for dessert
práctico(a) practical
precio (m.) price;
    a precio fijo at a fixed price
precioso(a) lovely
preferente 1st class
preferir (ie) to prefer
preguntar to ask (a question)
prensa (f.) press
preparado(a) prepared, ready
presidente (m.) president
presión (f.) pressure
prima (f.) female cousin
primavera (f.) spring
primero(a) first;
    de primer plato as a first course
primo (m.) male cousin
principio (m.) principle;
    en principio in principle
probar (ue) to try (on), to taste
procedencia (f.) point of departure
procedente de from;
    procedente de Madrid from Madrid
profesor(a) (m., f.) teacher
programa (m.) programme
programado(a) scheduled
propio(a) own, special
provincia (f.) province
pueblo (m.) village
puente (m.) bridge
puerto (m.) port
pues well
punto: en punto on time

Q

que that, which
¿qué? what? which?
quedar to be;
    quedarse to stay, to remain

querer (ie) to want, to wish;
    querer decir to mean;
    quisiera I would like
queso (m.) cheese
quien who
¿quién? who?
quince fifteen
quinientos(as) five hundred
quizá(s) perhaps

R

ración (f.) portion
rápido (m.) express train
rápido(a) fast
raqueta (f.) racquet
rato (m.) while;
    dentro de un rato in a while
realmente really
rebajado(a) reduced
recargo (m.) extra charge
recepción (f.) reception desk
recepcionista (m. or f.) receptionist
recibir to receive
recomendar (ie) to recommend
recto(a) straight;
    todo recto straight on
recuerdo (m.) souvenir
regalo (m.) present
región (f.) region
regional regional
regresar to return
regular regular;
    ¿cómo estás? regular. how are you? so-so.
reina (f.) queen
reír to laugh;
    echar a reír to burst out laughing
relajante relaxing
reloj (m.) watch
rellenar to fill in
reparar to repair
reservado(a) reserved
resultar to turn out
retraso (m.) delay
retrete (m.) lavatory
retrovisor (m.) rear-view mirror
reunión (f.) meeting
rey (m.) king
río (m.) river
rojo(a) red
romano(a) Roman

romper to smash, to tear
romperse to break
ropa (f.sing.) clothes
rosa pink
rubio(a) blond(e)
rueda (f.) wheel;
  rueda de repuesto spare wheel

S

sábado (m.) Saturday
saber to know;
  no sé I don't know
sacar to take out, to get out
sal (f.) salt
sala (f.) de estar sitting room
salida (f.) exit
salir to go out;
  salir de compras to go shopping
salón (m.) sitting-room
santo(a) (m. f.) saint;
  el día del santo saint's day
sardina (f.) sardine
se one, oneself
sea: o sea that is to say
sección (f.) department
seco(a) dry
secretario(a) (m. f.) secretary
seguida: en seguida at once, right
  away
seguido: todo seguido straight on
seguir (i) to continue, to follow
según according to
segundo(a) second;
  de segundo as a second course
seguro(a) sure, certain
seis six
selva (f.) forest
semana (f.) week
sencillamente simply
sencillo(a) simple;
  habitación sencilla single room
sentido (m.) direction
sentir (ie) to feel;
  lo siento I'm sorry
señal (f.) signal
señor (m.) Mr, gentleman
señora (f.) Mrs, lady, madam
señorita (f.) Miss, young lady
se(p)tiembre (m.) September
ser to be
servicio (m.) service;
  los servicios toilets

servir (i) to serve
sesenta sixty
setecientos(as) seven hundred
setenta seventy
sevillano(a) Sevillian
sexo (m.) sex;
  ambos sexos both sexes
si if
sí yes
siempre always
siesta (f.) siesta;
  dormir la siesta, echar una siesta to
  have a siesta
siete seven
siglo (m.) century
significar to mean
siguiente following;
  lo siguiente the following
simpático(a) nice
sin without
sitio (m.) place
sobre on;
  sobre todo above all
sol (m.) sun
solamente only
solo(a) alone;
  café solo black coffee
sólo only
soltero(a) (m., f.) bachelor, spinster
solucionar to resolve, solve
sombra (f.) shade, shadow
sombrero (m.) hat
sopa (f.) soup
sótano: la planta sótano basement
su, sus his, her, its, one's, their
suave soft
subterráneo (m.) underground
subterráneo(a) underground
sucio(a) dirty
suelto(a) separate, loose
suéter (m.) sweater
sumar to add
súper (m.) 96 octane (four star petrol)
suponer to suppose
supuesto: por supuesto of course
sur (m.) south
sus see su
suyo(a) his, her, theirs, yours

T

tabaco (m.) tobacco
tal: ¿qué tal? how are things?
talla (f.) size
tamaño (m.) size
también also
tampoco neither, nor
tanto as much, so much;
  tanta gente so many people
tapas (f.pl.) bar snacks
tardar en: ¿cuánto tiempo tarda en llegar?
  how long does it take to get there?
tarde late
tarde (f.) afternoon;
  buenas tardes good afternoon
tarjeta (f.) (credit) card
tarta helada (f.) ice-cream gateau
taxista (m. or f.) taxi driver
té (m.) (con limón) (lemon) tea
teatro (m.) theatre;
  obra (f.) de teatro play
Telefónica (f.) Spanish state-owned
  telephone company
teléfono (m.) telephone
televisar to televise
televisión (f.) television
temperatura (f.) temperature
templado(a) mild, lukewarm
temporada (f.) season;
  temporada alta high season
temprano early
tendero(a) (m., f.) shopkeeper
tenedor (m.) fork
tener to have;
  ¿cuántos años tiene Vd.? how old
  are you?;
  tener que to have to;
  tener cuidado to be careful
tenis (m.) tennis
tercero(a) third;
  tercera planta third floor
terminar to finish
ternera (f.) veal;
  ternera a la riojana veal Riojan style
terraza (f.) terrace
ti you
tía (f.) aunt
tío (m.) uncle
tiempo (m.) time, weather
tienda (f.) shop;
  ir de tiendas to go shopping
tinto red (wine)

típico(a) typical (Spanish)
tipo (m.) type, kind
todavía still
todo(a) all;
    sobre todo above all;
    todo seguido/todo recto straight on
tolerante tolerant
tomar to have, to take;
    tomar el sol to sunbathe;
    tomar unas copas to have some
    drinks
tomate (m.) tomato
tónica (f.) tonic water
tono (m.) tone, shade
tormenta (f.) storm
tortilla (f.) omelette;
    tortilla de patatas (f.) Spanish
    omelette
total (m.) total
turista 2nd class
trabajar to work
trabajo (m.) work, job;
    trabajo doméstico housework;
    trabajo de campo fieldwork
traer retraso to be late
traje (m.) outfit, suit
tranquilo(a) calm, quiet
traslado (m.) move, transfer
travieso(a) naughty
trece thirteen
treinta thirty
tren (m.) train
tres three
trescientos(as) three hundred
trucha (f.) trout
tu your
tú you
turismo (m.) tourism;
    oficina (f.) de turismo tourist office
turista (m. or f.) tourist
turrón (m.) type of nougat made of
    almonds
tuyo(a) yours

U

último(a) last
un(a) one, a, an
usted (Vd./Ud.) you
ustedes (Vds./Uds.) you (pl.)
útil useful

V

vacación (f.) holiday
vainilla (f.) vanilla
vale OK, all right
valenciano(a) Valencian
valer to cost;
    ¿cuánto vale? how much is it?
valle (m.) valley
variación (f.) variation
variados(as) various;
    tapas variadas selection of tapas
variedad (f.) variety
varios(as) various, several
vaso (m.) glass
¡vaya! really!
vecino(a) (m., f.) neighbour
vegetal vegetable;
    aceite vegetal vegetable oil
veinte twenty
veinticinco twenty-five
vender to sell
venir (ie) to come
ver to see;
    a ver let's see
verano (m.) summer
verdad (f.) truth;
    no es verdad it's not true
verde green
vergüenza (f.) shame
vermut (m.) aperitif
vestido (m.) dress
vestirse (i) to get dressed
vez (f.) time;
    a veces at times;
    algunas veces sometimes;
    en vez de instead of;
    más de una vez more than once;
    tal vez perhaps
viajar to travel
viaje (m.) journey
vida (f.) life
viejo(a) old
viento (m.) wind
viernes (m.) Friday
vino (m.) wine
visitante (m. or f.) visitor
visitar to visit
vivir to live
vivo(a) lively
volante (m.) steering wheel
volver (ue) to come back, to go back
vosotros(as) you
vuelo (m.) flight

W

wáter (m.) lavatory

Y

y and
ya now
yo I

Z

zapato (m.) shoe
zoológico (m.) zoo
zumo (m.) juice

INDEX

Have you enjoyed this course? Want to learn more?

Breakthrough Languages

Ideal for self-study . Practise and develop your skills . Learn a new language

Level 1 beginner's courses

Easy-to-use book and cassette or CD* courses.

Available in French, Spanish, German, Italian, Greek and Chinese.

* CDs for French and Spanish only.

Taking it further

Level 2 in Spanish, French and German
Level 3 in French

Increase your vocabulary, fluency and confidence with these higher level book and cassette courses.

Also available online for French and Spanish Level 1:

For students:

Multi-choice grammar exercises

For teachers:

Photocopiable exercise sheets, teacher's notes and tapescripts

For all courses:

A free site licence is available on request permitting duplication of audio material for classes (conditions apply)

Extra practice

Activity Books with imaginative and varied exercises

Available for Level 1 French, Spanish and German

Available from all good bookshops, or direct from Palgrave Macmillan.
Please call Macmillan Direct on 01256 302866
All course books are available on inspection to teaching staff where an adoption would result in the sale of 12 or more copies. Please email lecturerservices@palgrave.com
For further information log on to www.palgrave.com/breakthrough